S0-BBQ-966

The Road to Peace and Reconciliation

Muslim Perspective on the Mindanao Conflict

by: Amina Rasul

Amina Rasul
Editor

Felipe Parba
Ma Victoria Batac-Antonio
Publication Coordinators

MJ Rivera
Cover Design

GA Printing Inc.
Printer

Asian Institute of Management
Makati City, Philippines
ISBN 971-679-065-1

Table of Contents

Appendix

Preface

For decades now, the Philippine Government has been trying to either exploit or develop the island of Mindanao. Tracts of "public lands" have been given to settlers coming from Luzon and the Visayas to both develop agriculture in Mindanao, as well as to reduce the problem of peasant unrest elsewhere. Ethnic conflicts, fueled by issues of land ownership, then festered for decades especially with the Muslim tribes. The martial law years wrought havoc on the Mindanao communities when an armed solution was imposed on the so-called "Moro Problem".

Finding the military approach ineffective as a solution to conflict, President Corazon C. Aquino's administration prioritized peace negotiations with the Moro National Liberation Front (MNLF) and initiated the planning process to usher in economic development. The administration of President Fidel V. Ramos brought the peace negotiations with the MNLF to completion, and simultaneously pushed economic development. Multilaterals and aid agencies started pouring resources into rehabilitation and business development. Corporations, local and foreign, invested in joint ventures. Peace seemed to be at hand. Businesses flourished, even in the Muslim provinces.

How then could the ethnic conflict in Mindanao explode anew, attaining a level of international prominence or notoriety, and overshadowing the decades long MNLF armed struggle?

In theory, insurgency or rebellion should be on the decline at a time of economic growth. Why, then, did the Moro Islamic Liberation Front (MILF) revive its fight for secession at a time when government was trying to bring investments into Mindanao? Why did the Abu Sayyaf start sowing terror in Basilan and the rest of Western Mindanao as the MNLF was integrating into the body politic? Did the MILF resurface after rebuilding its organization during the peace negotiations between the Philippine Government and the MNLF? Or was it because the solutions emanating from Manila and Davao City did not focus sufficiently or effectively on the "trouble areas" and their real problems?

Manila-based political analysts have been quick to offer their own explanations. However, the Muslim perspective has been largely left out. Thus, critical errors are made such as the idea that armed conflict in the South can be stopped or that it can be resolved through economic development alone. Or the notion that Muslim Mindanao has always been a part of the Philippines, thus their clamor for independence has no basis.

The government of President Gloria Macapagal-Arroyo has begun its own initiatives in Mindanao. Negotiations are ongoing with the MILF, with the government even supporting the unification of the MNLF and the MILF. The Arroyo Administration started its own discussions for a comprehensive plan to address the unresolved issues in the island. But if legislation and development plans are to be effective and if these are to be acceptable to all sectors, there is a need to include Muslim and Mindanaoan perspectives into these discussions before and during the planning process. The bureaucracy has a tendency to prepare the plan then go on "road shows" to generate support in the guise of "consultations".

The research project, "The Road to Peace and Reconciliation: Muslim Perspective on the Mindanao Conflict," is our contribution to these discussions. The project started in November 2000. Respected Muslim political and religious leaders, former rebels and scholars wrote papers on topics pertinent to a greater understanding of the Mindanao situation.

These papers were discussed during conferences and workshops at the Asian Institute of Management on March 15 and 23. Muslim leaders dialogued with interested members of the Makati business community, academe, multilateral and aid agencies, among others, who attended the conferences. Perhaps for the first time, they became the foci of deliberations with representatives of the majority, instead of mere adjuncts in debates on issues that affect the lives of their communities. Proposals were formulated to help provide solutions to problems of inequity, underdevelopment, and poverty as well as the political instability of Southern Philippines.

Subsequently, workshops were conducted in the cities of Marawi and Zamboanga to validate recommendations made during the conferences. The Mindanao State University, Southern Philippines Development Authority, Office on Muslim Affairs, and Ateneo De Zamboanga supported the regional workshops.

The papers are intended to assist policy makers and program implementers in formulating appropriate strategies to resolve the conflict in Mindanao. The target audience encompasses all sectors of Philippine society whose actions and decisions impact on and are affected by the present situation in Mindanao, particularly Congress, government agencies involved in policy formulation and program implementation, local government units in Mindanao, the business sector, academe, peace advocates and religious institutions, multilateral and aid agencies. Hopefully, the project would educate the general public as well, to bridge the widening gulf of misunderstanding and suspicion between the majority and the Muslim tribes.

The papers and recommendations cover a wide range of topics chosen to shed light on the many facets of the Mindanao Conflict. Diverse Muslim perspectives weave a tapestry with a unifying theme: whether the subject is governance, education, justice, or women's rights, Muslims must be allowed to live according to their beliefs and principles. The impact of this concern leads to the controversial proposal that has been gaining more support: self-rule through true autonomy. If an independent Islamic State is unattainable, then perhaps the road to peace and reconciliation is through federalism. However, this book does not attempt to enter into the deliberations on a federal form of government. That would require substantive research and exhaustive local and national debates beyond the parameters of this project.

This book is a compilation of the papers and speeches prepared for the conferences and the recommendations made by the participants. As Project Director, I have included papers that were not circulated during the conferences, which could enrich discussions on the situation of the Muslims of the Philippines. For instance, the workshops on women and poverty were conducted without the benefit of papers to guide the discussions due to unanticipated changes in speakers. The research papers included could provide the reader with the necessary background to understand the issues and recommendations given by the participants.

It must be stated, for the record, that the views and opinions expressed are those of the individual writers, not necessarily of the institutions that have supported the project.

AMINA RASUL
Research Fellow
Washington Sycip Policy Center
Asian Institute of Management

Acknowledgments

The summer of 2000, I read a best selling book analyzing the conflict in Mindanao. I was dismayed by some of the conclusions the authors made, worried that these would be accepted as truth. Why did the authors not talk to more Muslim scholars and leaders, I wondered. I decided to respond, thanks to Romy Bernardo who posed the challenge, "Why not do something about it?"

I am greatly indebted to friends and family who believe in the principle of mutual understanding as the basis for real solutions and who supported the idea that led to this book.

Maraming salamat to forward looking institutions who support efforts to bring Muslim voices–no matter how strident to the ears of the majority: Ford Foundation and United States Agency for International Development for funding the research project and the conferences, and Friedrich Ebert Stiftung for providing a grant to publish the book as well as the Konrad Adenauer Stiftung. *Daghang salamat* to Nene Guevarra who has found a more pleasant (less confrontational) way to help her country; Gary Hawes who hears the stifled voices of minority groups; Patty Buckles and Charlie Feibel who have allowed Mindanao into their blood; Rudy Traub-Merz who, though relatively new to the Philippines, understands our ethnic issues; and Willy Frehner who has been adopted by Mindanaoans.

Magsukol to the Asian Institute of Management's (AIM) Washington Sycip Policy Center, Kennedy School of Government Alumni Association, Magbassa Kita Foundation, Foundation for Economic Freedom, Mindanao State University, University of the Philippines and the University of the Philippines (UP) Institute of Islamic Studies for lending institutional support.

- Heartfelt gratitude to Bobby de Ocampo and Poch Macaranas who opened the doors of AIM to the "Muslim outsiders"
- To Chato Calderon and Wykes Wycoco, who share the truism that governance of the country is good only if all its parts are involved

• My thanks also to UP President Dodong Nemenzo who went out of his way to enrich our discussions

• For advice and support in steering the project, special mention must be made of Prof. Samuel K. Tan, Dr. Camar Umpa and Dean Carmen Abubakar and

• The Muslim members of the 11th Congress especially Congressmen Simeon Datumanong, Gerry Salapuddin, Nur Jaafar and Jun Macarambon.

The contributing authors are a distinguished group of writers, scholars, leaders and fellow Mindanaoans who unselfishly and courageously shared their thoughts with us in the eternal quest for peace and reconciliation. **Sukran.**

The road to peace and reconciliation would have been long and without end if not for the members of an excellent team: Philip Parba who cracked the whip, Carmi LaoGuico who slaved without complaints, Laly Usero who stayed calm, Mir Tillah and Rey Trillana who have a way with words, my sisters Fatima who obtained unobtainable information, and Salma who was my "sounding board." Thanks also to Ima Verzosa who encouraged me via the Internet.

AMINA RASUL
Manila, 2001

This book is dedicated to my parents,
Ambassador Abraham Rasul and Senator Santanina T. Rasul,
who made me believe in public service
and gave me pride in being a Tausug.
And to my children, Ibba, Mini and Peppy,
who give me reason to strive.

Foreword

The problems in Mindanao have been with us for centuries, and they continue to be with us today. Indeed, they have become increasingly complex. For as long as can be remembered too, is the endless description of Mindanao as a Land of Promise, which sad to say, has seemed to be more a case of unfulfilled promises.

We have not heeded the calls of history—the recurring Mindanao conflict dates back to ancient colonial eras. There have been long years of violent struggle in the case of ethnic groups unified by an Islamic ideology. More recently as well, a significant, though less violent struggle to recover rights to ancestral domain has arisen from the indigenous Lumads. Refusal to recognize Mindanao not as a mere appendage of Luzon and Visayas, but a land that historically had a thriving civilization with distinct political, social, and religious structures is the root of the perennial so-called "Mindanao Problem."

The time for action is not just now but yesterday. Because of procrastination and neglect, problems in the region have been aggravated. The incidence of poverty in Mindanao is higher than in any other region of the Philippines, and has alarmingly increased over the past decades. This can only further exacerbate the unrest that seethes in the peoples of this region. We have to take action urgently and move beyond the empty promises that several administrations mouth at every turn. We must today make sure that in this century, at least, the dormant seed of a unified nation will finally take root—perhaps not in our generation, but hopefully, in the next.

The Asian Institute of Management (AIM) is proud to have sponsored the seminar-workshop, "The Road to Peace and Reconciliation: Muslim Perspectives on the Mindanao Crisis," which was envisioned by former Secretary Amina Rasul, an AIM alumna and at present, a research fellow of the Washington Sycip Policy Center. Under her stewardship, the speakers and the participants were steered to focus on and grasp the urgent need of the Muslims for lasting peace.

AIM stands for excellence in education and management of knowledge. It strives to be at the cutting edge not only of analysis in business applications, but in the broader context of improving national governance. Indeed, a great chunk of the problem that is attendant to Mindanao may be traced to poor national governance.

While there may be no assurance that the coverage of this book will lead to immediate action, the energetic discussions of the issues that surround the Mindanao problem indicates that this is one resource that provides new approaches from a wider range than the standard paradigms that are touted up each time a crisis rears its head. This book tackles Mindanao from the viewpoint of people who know Mindanao and care about Mindanao - and view it from the social, cultural, historical, and other aspects that define Mindanao and its people. We, at AIM, are honored to have been part of this undertaking.

ROBERTO F. DE OCAMPO
President, Asian Institute of Management and
Former Philippine Finance Secretary

Message

The road to peace and development, once again, appears to be back on track in Mindanao. I stand firm in my belief that the holistic approach adopted by President Gloria Macapagal-Arroyo and her Administration paves the way for renewed hope in the quest for genuine and lasting peace in "The Land of Promise." The policy framework and agenda of the Arroyo government puts peace and development in Mindanao at the forefront. This stems from our basic belief that without peace, there will be no effective and sustainable development. These principled views on Mindanao were earlier embodied in my own book on our peace process with the MNLF and other rebel groups called ,"Break Not The Peace."

I welcome the publication of "The Road to Peace and Reconciliation: Muslim Perspective on the Mindanao Conflict," a brainchild of Amina Rasul who was the former Chair of the National Youth Commission, and a member of the Cabinet in the Ramos administration. This book comes at on opportune time – when peace must be given a second chance through the continuing negotiations with the MILF, and the ongoing quest for a comprehensive solution to the root causes of conflict in Mindanao. It is imperative to involve the National Government, Christians, Muslims, Indigenous Peoples, Local Government Units, the private business sector and other actors of civil society in addressing the totality of social cultural, economic, political and security problems in Mindano.

The growth benefits generated by peace will become its own assurance that never again must Filipinos be so desperate as to take up arms against each other.

Let me recall a message I frequently conveyed to various audience as a tribute to democratic peace-building," ...that a people exercising their free will, under a Government that listens to their collective voice and leads them in accord with their authentic aspirations–such a people will consistently forge an honorable peace among themselves."

Mabuhay ang Mindanao at ang nagkakaisang Pilipino!!!

FIDEL V. RAMOS

Introduction

Since the advent of colonialism over four centuries ago, the dichotomy of war and peace has marked the face of Mindanao and its people. This seems to be the concern of Dr. Parouk Hussin in his paper, "Challenge of War and Search For Peace." Today, demographic and political changes have skewed the dichotomy towards war rather than peace. The struggle of the marginalized sectors for freedom and well being has become more difficult, pathetic and, often, tragic. The case of the Bangsamoro people captures the dilemma and ambiguity of the Mindanao problem. And the serious threat the problem poses to peace and security is no longer confined to Filipino interests. It is also dragging more and more of Southeast Asia into its vortex, as Julkipli Wadi posits in "Southeast Asian Regional Security and the Mindanao Conflict."

On September 11, 2001, the world-shattering attacks by Muslim terrorists of Osama Bin Laden's Al Quaeda network on the New York Twin Towers and the Pentagon brings to mind the prospects and implications to human destiny of Samuel Huntington's "clash of civilizations." The prognostication of the eventual confrontation between Islamic and Christian civilization poses the horrifying consequences of apocalyptic dimension that humanity must anticipate, given the tremendous progress in the techonologies and strategies of war. It is this inconceivable yet possible fall of humanity into the ultimate pit of a global religious war that has rekindled the flickering fire of the peace process to prevent the transformation of the war in Mindanao into a fanatical, violent struggle between Islam and Christiantiy.

The two-day conference at the Asian Institute of Management–bringing together noted Muslim personalities of different tempers and persuasions, but sharing the common passion for Mindanao peace and progress–was designed to discuss the timely topic of "the road to peace and reconciliation" in their homeland of Mindanao. Obviously, the lofty aim was to shape a consensus on what may be the "Muslim perspective" of the Bangsamoro struggle and its relation to national, regional and global interests. The various papers and remarks presented, including the spontaneous intellectual exchanges, give reason for some kind of optimism to those who believe in the ultimate triumph of social justice in Mindanao. This hopeful outlook is also suggested by Alma Evangelista in "Government Negotiations and Modes of Conflict Resolution" and by Abraham Iribani in "The GRP-MNLF Peace Talks and the 1996 Peace Agreement."

In more recent times, the search for enduring peace in Mindanao has never been so imperative with the return of MNLF Chairman Nur Misuari and his forces in the direction of a separatist path. The violent outbreaks between MNLF rebels and government forces in Zamboanga and Sulu only underlined the virtual abrogation of the 1996 Peace Accord between the MNLF and the government. It also revived the centuries-old Muslim grievances and aspirations and their ultimate resolution, from Muslim perspective, in the rise of an independent Islamic State for the Bangsamoro people in the Southern Philippines where their ancient heritage and tradition can be retrieved, preserved, and developed; where their identity as a people can rest, free from all threats, and secured as part of Darul Islam (World Ummah).

The perspective derived from the Muslim understanding and studies of their own struggle for freedom and social justice begins rightly from the belief in a historical imperative and determinism that makes the recovery of ancestral lands and rights the meaning of their search for peace, identity, justice and progress. This is what was underlined by Samuel K. Tan in "History of the Mindanao Problem" and by Nasser Marohomsalic in "Road Map to the Bangsamoro Islamic State."

In a sense, what the Muslims were, constitute inseparably the ever-present source of motivation for their continuing conflict with the State, as well as the avenue for peace by negotiations and compromise. It is this idea of historical rights and justice that is clearly obvious in the premises, and figures of the conference papers. And yet, interlaced or con-substantially integrated into the historical niche is the imperative of cultural identity and integrity, which derives meaning from religion, education, and social equality.

This is the burden of Santanina T. Rasul in "Muslims in the Philippines or Filipino Muslims?" She draws from the historical inertia of colonial injustice, oppression, and subjugation as the rationale behind the continuing Bangsamoro armed struggle, and the need for urgent restitution of rights and justice the Muslim people deserve from the State. The same is true for Saaduddin A. Alauya's "The Impact of Religion on the Negotiations by and Between the Government and the MILF," which underlines the absolute and sacred role of Islam in Muslim life and affairs, including the negotiations for the resolution of the conflict with government. Camar A. Umpa and Salipada S. Tamano in "The Status and Impact of Education and the Madaris Among Muslims in Mindanao" reveal the problems of Muslim education, and the need to integrate the Madrasah system into mainstream Philippine education as a fundamental approach to peace.

Added to the historic co-cultural search for social justice is the equally important pursuit of liberation from the bondage of poverty and marginalization due to the underdevelopment of Muslim potentials for progress, unabated graft and corruption in the government, particularly in the Muslim South, and the inequitable distribution of political and economic benefits. This aspect of the Muslim perspective of their problems and struggle is apparent in several discourses.

In "The Moro Woman: Herstory and Role," Amina Rasul notes the local and global concerns for the struggle of women for their rights beyond the traditional limit of their domestic role. She clarifies that in Islam, the Qur'an guarantees the high regard society must give to women, including their right to political participation and leadership. In "The Poverty Situation in Muslim Mindanao," she presents the worsening index of poverty that is aggravated by persisting conflict. By comparative statistical tables and figures, she laments the present deplorable situation of Muslim Mindanao as she looks back at their higher quality of life before Martial Law. Contributing to the Muslim lack of social progress and well being is the endemic corruption affecting leadership in Muslim society as illustrated in "A Culture of Corruption? A Look at Corruption in the ARMM."

As a result of the continuing underdevelopment of Muslim Mindanao, Michael Mastura poses the crucial issue of Muslims' socio-political survival in "Political Islam in the 21st Century: Can it Survive?" Alunan Glang deplores the lack of adequate government response to nagging problems of the Mindanao conflict in his "Assessment of Government Negotiations and Modes of Conflict Resolution."

But obvious from the range and thrust of the conference output is the absence or lack of significant reference to, or discussion of the role of external interests, influences, or entities, particularly the Organization of Islamic Conference (OIC), in the Muslim perspective on peace and reconciliation. Only in a few papers, such as those of Wadi, Hussin, and Iribani is a general reference made or implied to it, but this is largely confined to the Southeast Asian context of the Bangsamoro struggle, or to OIC participation in past agreements on Muslim autonomy — not independence. However, it is premature to suggest that this unintended omission in the conference framework reflects a Muslim consensus to domesticize or de-internationalize the search for peace and the resolution of the conflict. In this regard, it may be relevant to mention that this theoretical premise of conflict resolution has been the basic stand of government since the Marcos presidency. In short, is it accurate to assume that the Muslim perspective of their long struggle has finally converged on a common ground with that of the government: that, in reality, the Mindanao conflict is a domestic Filipino problem between two brothers alienated by religious differences, but sharing a common, ancient heritage?

In a sense, the nexus of socio-economic problems, aggravated by the horrors and aftermath of continuing violence and bloodshed, has refocused Muslim attention to what immediate satisfaction or relief can be derived from a government already under tremendous pressure to give the indigenous and marginalized sectors what they deserve as Filipinos. In effect, whatever the theoretical thrust of the struggle is, at least a consensus–a perspective –has been drawn by Muslim minds in the conference to take the practical and passable road to peace and reconciliation.

DR. SAMUEL K. TAN

List of Abbreviations

AFP	Armed Forces of the Philippines
ARMM	Autonomous Region in Muslim Mindanao
ASEAN	Association of Southeast Asian Nations
BIMP-EAGA	Brunei, Indonesia, Malaysia, Philippines - East Asia Growth Area
BUF	Bishops-Ulama Foundation
CA	Consultative Assembly
GRP	Government of the Republic of the Philippines
MILF	Moro Islamic Liberation Front
MINCAARD	Mindanao Support and Communication Center for Agrarian Reform and Rural Development
MNLF	Moro National Liberation Front
MSU	Mindanao State University
NDF	National Democratic Front
NEDA	National Economic Development Authority
NPA	New People's Army
NUC	National Unification Commission
OIC	Organization of Islamic Conference
RCC	Regional Consultative Commission
SEA	South East Asia
SOCSARGEN	South Cotabato, Sultan Kudarat, Saranggani, General Santos
SPCPD	Southern Philippines Council for Peace and Development
SUC	State Universities and Colleges
SZOPAD	Special Zone of Peace and Development
USAID	United States Agency for International Development
UN	United Nations
WB	World Bank
ZNCSD	Zamboanga Norte Center for Social Concerns and Development

History of the Mindanao Problem

DR. SAMUEL K. TAN

DR. SAMUEL K. TAN
Director, Mindanao Studies Program (UP-CIDS)
Consultant, Southern Philippines Development Authority

Dr. Samuel K. Tan is currently the convenor of the Mindanao Studies Program of the Philippines, and the history and culture consultant of the Southern Philippines Development Authority. He holds a Bachelor's Degree in History from Zamboanga A. E. Colleges, Masters in History at the University of the Philippines, and Doctorate in Social Science Interdisciplinary at the Syracuse University in New York.

Dr. Samuel Tan has gained prominence in the field of the history, as he has previously chaired institutions such as the National Historical Institute, National Committee on Historical Research, and U.P.'s Department of History. He has likewise done extensive work as Director of the Mindanao Studies Program at the U.P. Center for Integrative and Development Studies, Member of the UNESCO Advisory Committee for the Study of Southeast Asian Cultures, and Research Fellow and Consultant of the Office of the President.

ABOUT THE PHOTO : Taken during the coronation of the Sultan of Sulu. Seated on the right is Sultan Mahakuta Kiram. To his left is his son, Crown Prince Muedzul-Lail Kiram.

Today, the Mindanao problem has become increasingly complex. It has created not only difficulties in finding, at least, a more enduring and sustainable solution, but also dilemmas in implementation. It has, in a sense, contributed to the rise and fall of administrations. Consequently, to understand Mindanao, we must begin with the history of its problem and look back to as far as we wish and can. It is no enough to state the issues and problems as we see them today. To do so is to create more ambiguity in the quest for answers. How far back we should look to history in order to meaningfully assess Mindanao today and its prospects for progress depends on whether or not we subscribe to the "historical imperative" or to the "contemporary realities" as fundamental to the solutions of nagging political, economic, social, and cultural problems of the region.

Those who tend to follow the "contemporary" approach generally come from sectors or groups whose interests in Mindanao are strongly secured by existing laws and the previsions of the Constitution pertaining to (1) individual or corporate ownership of vast tracts of land in Mindanao, (2) security of business establishments and their vast activities, and (3) access to state power and resources. To them, going back to past eras to redress grievances or to recover lost glories is to make the future of Mindanao hostage to the past that has inevitably been altered through centuries of change and demographic transformation. In effect, this contemporary approach justifies the transformation of tribal and Muslim Mindanao to predominantly Christian Mindanao today with the exception of only four or five provinces of Mindanao (Tawi-Tawi, Sulu, Maguindanao, and Lanao del Sur with Basilan almost equally divided). To them, the recovery of ancestral land or ancient political power and rights is at best and academic or theoretical issue. Any change in the status quo is out of the question and will be resisted.

But those who follow the "historical imperative" are represented collectively by the three social movements in Mindanao that have beginnings in ancient, colonial, or neo-colonial eras. First is the *Lumad* struggle, which has taken a significant turn in contemporary times through active demonstration and protest action to recover rights to ancestral domain. It is the weakest of the social movements, being devoid of an organized armed group or a unifying ideology to bring together the twenty or more ethnolinguistic groups in various parts of Mindanao.

The second is the *Bangsamoro* struggle, which is the longest and strongest movement in the region covering almost 400 years of violent struggle against Spanish, American, Japanese and Filipino rule. Today, the movement has become more determined to recover the losses of political, economic, and social power and resources to the colonial powers and, subsequently, to their Filipino heirs. Although they represent only 25 per cent of Mindanao's population (a reverse of the situation a century ago), the Bangsamoro people have openly expressed the will to ultimately establish their own independent Islamic state through the MNLF, MILF, the Abu Sayyaf and other emerging groups more radically organized along the rigid lines of Islamic fundamentalist movements, also known as "political Islam" in intellectual and academic circles. Unlike the Lumad, the Bangsamoro struggle, although still distinguished by ethnic leadership, is unified by an Islamic ideology with local essence and character. It is a social movement that draws powerful emotional energy from an ancient historical "Moro Nation" ruled by the Sultanate and the Datuship.

The third social movement is the NDF-NPA struggle in Mindanao whose rational is the radical restructuring of Filipino society by the overthrow of the status quo in Mindanao following a Marxian model for Philippine society. Like the Bangsamoro struggle, it has a unifying ideology based on the Marxist-Leninist line although different from the Bangsamoro Islamic paradigm. It also subscribes to a historical root of struggle in the colonial and feudal exploitation of the Filipino masses, including the Muslims and Lumads. It therefore shares with the Lumad and Muslims the primary use of armed struggle to achieve the "liberation" of the masses from those who dominate and control Mindanao society and resources through a neocolonial capitalist system. It is not surprising that the three social movements in Mindanao can tactically and temporarily unite against what they perceive as a "common enemy."

How has the government responded to the persistent problem of conflict and the lack of development and progress for the Mindanao masses? Specifically, how has the state reacted to the three social movements in the southern Philippines? In Spanish times, the colonial state pursued the twin method of conquest-pacification and Christianization, while at the same time systematically depriving the native inhabitants, through legal means, of rights to their lands and controlling their political, economic, and social-cultural life. By the end of Spanish rule, the State has succeeded in establishing a strong and dominant Christian community, which even the Philippine Revolution did not negate except to create a Filipino version of Catholicism in the Aglipayan Church to satisfy nationalist, not spiritual, aspirations. Only the Muslim and Lumads, remained unconquered against the onslaught of colonialism.

The establishment of American rule after a brief interregnum of the Filipino-American War saw the continuation of the Spanish twin thrust of military conquest, but with a new element added: democratization. The latest allowed the non-Christian sector to have a limited participation in their own local government and allowed outside groups and entities to participate in Mindano's political, economic, social and cultural development. Before long, American laws and programs had changed Mindanao demographically from a non-Christian to a Christian majority by the time of the Commonwealth in 1935 and had also enabled the colonial and Christian majority to legally alienate as homestate or corporate estates vas tracts of ancestral lands in the region.

The withdrawal of American sovereignty in 1946 bequeathed to the newly restored Filipino rule, after a traumatic experience under Japanese imperial domination and oppression, the colonical prejudice and exploitation of Mindanao. Unfortunately for non-Christian Mindanao, Filipino rule has not fundamentally and radically changed the system and process that have made Mindanao for the Lumads and Muslims still a "land of unfulfilled promises" and for the poor and landless Christian migrants a "land of broken dreams." This to me, is what Mindanao is today in nutshell. This, also explains logically the emergence of the three social movements that regard the State of a common enemy dominated by foreign and Filipino interests rightly or wrongly perceived as callous to the centuries old plight of Muslim, Lumad, and Christian masses seeking social justice and rights as Filipinos.

The present administration is not unaware and oblivious to the realities in Mindanao. It is obvious from policy changes and implementation of failed projects and unfulfilled promises in the pursuit of a pro-poor objective in Contrary to persisting impressions, Mindanao has not been lagging in growth and development. Statistical data shows how much the development of Mindanao's potential and resources has contributed to the country's exports. What has been lamented by Mindanaoans is the small share, percentage wise, of Mindanao from incomes and benefits derived by individuals and companies who own the various businesses in the region. On the part of the non-Christian sector, its share from the meager benefits is nil compared to the Christian majority who are in a better position to rally national and international pressures to bear upon the consciences of those who have successfully exploited the wealth of Mindanao.

Although the administration is trying its best to correct the imbalance, it is handicapped by at least three perceived roadblocks:

1. The colonial heritage and bias against non-Christians have not been reduced or meaningfully altered but on the contrary have increased in importance.

   This fact was revealed by a social-scientific survey of prejudice level by a Filipinas Foundation-funded team in 1977 supervised by two prominent UP professors, Dr. Alfredo Lagmay, and Dr. Ruben Santos-Cuyugan. After thirty years, I repeated the survey but in a comparatively smaller scale and limited to just a seminar group.

   The random survey indicated an alarming increase, not decrease, in mutual levels of prejudice between Christians and non-Christians. The implication becomes quite pronounced against the background of numerous peace process initiated by the government and the private sectors in the local, national, and international levels.

2. The increasing level of frustrations of the marginalized sectors regardless of differences, on account of the State's inability to full redress their grievances and satisfy their needs. The frustration has been ideologically transformed into Islamic fundamentalism in the case of the Muslim community and into Marxist-Leninism in the case of the poor masses. Lamentably, the State does not have as yet an ideological answer to either the Islamic or Marxist-Leninist paradigm beyond palliatives for hungry mouths and homeless families and rhetorics and propaganda for the tri-media.
3. The unwillingness of the individual and corporate sectors that control the economic resources and potentials of the region from within or without, to equitably share the greater part of their profits and incomes with the masses. In short, there is an absence of true altruism which should be the controlling principle in our capitalist system–if such system were to truly serve the ends of social justice and the universal principles of Christian, Islamic and animistic ideology.

Lastly, it is imperative to conclude that the search for a lasting breakthrough in the Mindanao peace process might ultimately be found in what genuine federalism can offer to a highly pluralistic society as the Philippines, a society marked by increasingly irreconcilable religious ideologies and by diverse ethnic traditions that refuse to die. The merits of federalism as an approach to the nagging Mindanao problem had been recognized as far back as the Malolos Republic. No less than Gen. Emilio Aguinaldo advocated this system to integrate the various sectors that Aguinaldo advocated this system to integrate the various sectors that constituted the national community. Surprisingly, even, James Blount in his *The American Occupation of the Philippines, 1898-1913* supported this model and even suggested the structural justification for federalizing the whole archipelago. In short, the government must seriously consider federalism if it wants to pre-empt the inevitable implications of social movements that advocate either independence or radical reform of society.

Challenge of War and Search for Peace

DR. PAROUK S. HUSSIN

DR. PAROUK S. HUSSIN
Governor, ARMM

Dr. Hussin is currently the Governor of the Autonomous Region of Muslim Mindanao (ARMM). Prior to his election, Dr. Hussin was the Presidential Adviser on Muslim Affairs Office. Elected as chairperson of the MNLF Council of 15, Dr. Hussin is now viewed by many as the head of the MNLF. He was the Foreign Minister of the Moro National Liberation Front (MNLF) and the chairman of the MNLF Panel that negotiated the 1976 Tripoli Agreement in Manila. As Chairman, he represented the MNLF in various meetings of United Nations' (UN) agencies in Europe, Latin America, UN headquarters in New York, USA; meetings of the Organizations of African Unity; Arab League; Non-Aligned Movement; and Organization of Socialist International.

Since 1974, Dr. Hussin has been an active delegate of annual and special meetings of Foreign Ministers of Islamic Countries, the Islamic Summit Meeting under the auspices of the Organization of Islamic Conference and the World Muslim League.

Introduction

The challenge of war and the search for peace are persistent themes in the history of the Moro people in southern Philippines.

Scholars, policymakers, politicians, and experts have listed a long litany of the causes of this war. And yet, only one thing is clear: the continuing struggle of the Muslims in southern Philippines cannot be merely explained in simplistic and myopic terms. Religion, while significant, is not the sole reason for the conflict. And while the conflict is more glaring in military terms, over two decades of military operations have failed to end the conflict. Indeed since the last quarter of the 16th century up to the present, there is no Moro generation that has not fought or witnessed war in their homeland.

Historically, it was only during the American colonial regime that Moroland became gradually incorporated into the Philippine body politic either by force or persuasion by the American colonizers and their native allies.

This paper proposes that the problem in the South is primarily political. It will further argue that a combination of discontinuities in history and diametrically opposed routes in nation-building has led to a seemingly unending conflict that has cost the lives of many people and has made the prospect of peace dim.

Islam in Philippines (Moros)

Moros, in history, refer to the thirteen (13) Islamized ethno-linguistic groups in the Philippines. They share a distinct culture, speak different languages, and are varied in their social formation but share a common belief in Islam. This is a uniting factor among the different groups. This religious unity will also serve as the basis of the struggle for Moro independence. Spanish and American colonial propaganda had infused derogatory connotations to the word Moro. Hence, some Muslims in the Philippines would prefer not to be called Moros prior to the rise of the MNLF in the early 70's.

Islam and indigenous traditions as embodied in *adat* (customary laws) constitute the basic foundations of the socio-cultural heritage of the Muslims in the Philippines. This heritage is one of the bases of their sense of nationality, that is, the feeling of belonging to a national community distinct from the other segments of Philippine society.

The demands for independence of the people of Mindanao cannot be properly understood without an understanding of the Islamic era that began in the year 1310 AD, two centuries before Spanish colonization, through the efforts of Arab traders, travelers, *sufis* (saintly Muslims) and Muslim missionaries. Islam became the unifying element of politics, economic systems, justice system, and culture in these areas. It soon spread and, later, Islamic principalities in Sulu and Maguindanao were established.

In the 15th century and early 16th century, four Moro states had emerged: the Sultanates of Sulu and Maguindanao, the Buayan Sultanate, and the Apat na Pangampong. Each sultanate was independent, had sovereign power and had diplomatic and trade relations with other countries in the region. And although the sultanates were politically independent and exercised sovereignty over a particular territory, they were linked by a common religion, shared customs and tradition, and through inter-marriages among the royal families. Other Muslim principalities known as emirates, like those of Rajah Sulayman in Manila and the emirates of Panay and Mindoro, were also born. These emirates represent 500 years of political history, so far the longest political experience compared to other groups in the whole Philippines. These also provide proof of early attempts at state-formation and nation- building by the Muslims. The early development of Islam stands on record as the first political institution, the first institutional religion, the first educational system and the first civilization in the Philippines, and that its economy was far advanced than those of the other indigenous communities. This historical path, however, was to be thwarted by foreign invasions and a conflict with the Christianized Filipinos' attempt at their own nation- building.

While Filipino nationalism was essentially anti-Spanish, the nation that was created after the 1896 Revolution remained Catholic. This paradox contributed to the alienation of the Moro people from the nation that rose from the ashes of Filipinos' struggle against Spain and, later, the United States. This is exemplified by the sultan of Sulu's refusal to heed the request of Emilio Aguinaldo to join forces against the new colonizer.

The inauguration of the Filipino nation, therefore, presented a paradox. On one hand, it was able to establish a state and a semblance of an identity. On the other hand, while the new nation tried to consolidate its newly found sovereignty, the Moros, reeling from decades of animosity with the Christianized Filipinos, have tilted towards autonomy, federalism or secession instead of integration. This historically parallel development of the Filipino nation and the Muslims gave the rebellion its ideological character in calling for the realization of a separate Moro nation in contradistinction with that of the Filipino nation.

This paradox is not exclusive to Filipinos. The point of Asian history when most nations were liberated from their colonizers not only resulted in the establishment of new states but also the emergence of ethnic and cultural communities challenging their incorporation into the new state, hence disrupting its ability to form a cohesive nation.

War

Struggles to defend their freedom, homeland, and way of life were dominant themes in the mainly successful resistance of the Moro people led by their sultans and datus against Spanish colonialism. The more than three centuries of armed conflicts between the Spaniards, who enlisted the support of Christianized natives in the North, and the Moros is recorded in history as the Moro Wars. Among the most disastrous consequences of the Moro wars were the heavy casualties suffered by the Moro people and the destruction of their communities.

When the Americans arrived in Moroland at the turn of the century they started from where the Spaniards had left. The Americans succeeded in taking away the freedom and political independence of the Moro people. Thousands of Moros, including women and children, died during decades of American "pacification campaigns."

The MNLF-led struggle in southern Philippines since the early 1970s is a continuation of the old struggles and represents the emergence of a radical articulation of Moro interests. The MNLF's original goal was an independent Bangsamoro homeland. However, it accepted autonomy within the Philippine state as envisioned in the 1976 Tripoli Agreement and the 1996 GRP-MNLF Agreement.

Peace Process

Historically, the Moros' persistent search for peace over centuries was best demonstrated by their treaty relations with Spain, as well as with the British, the French, the Dutch, and the Americans. For example, the Sulu Sultanate had peace and commercial treaties with Spain in 1578, 1646, 1725, 1737, 1805, 1837, 1851, and 1878; with the British in 1761, 1764, 1769, 1849, and 1978; with the French in 1843 and 1845; and with the Americans in 1842, 1899, and 1915.

The almost three decades of war in southern Philippines since the declaration of Martial Law in 1972 has led to terrible losses on the part of the Moro people in terms of lives and properties. Thousands of Moros were, and still are, displaced particularly those in Sabah. The decision to work for peace on the part of the MNLF leadership is one of its efforts to heal the wounds of war, particularly in the southern Philippines.

Marcos Regime

The escalation of violence in Mindanao was one reason cited by the late President Ferdinand E. Marcos when he declared martial law on September 21, 1972. Military response to the MNLF-led Moro struggle for self-determination dominated the early years of the martial law regime. Marcos opted for peace talks with the MNLF under the auspices of the OIC when the indiscriminate use of military force failed to intimidate the Moro people and to neutralize the growing popularity and strength of the MNLF in the mid-1970s.

Negotiations between the GRP and the MNLF began in 1995 in Jeddah, Saudi Arabia, and led eventually to the signing of the Tripoli Agreement on December 23, 1976. Subsequent negotiations failed to resolve their differences on how to implement the agreement. The Marcos administration decided to grant its own version of autonomy for the Muslims in the southern Philippines without the participation of the MNLF.

Aquino Administration

President Corazon C. Aquino also embarked on peace negotiations with the MNLF. President Aquino herself went to Jolo, Sulu, in September 1986 to meet MNLF leaders, particularly Chairman Nur Misuari. The Aquino government insisted on keeping all discussions during the peace talks within the framework of the 1987 Constitution, which the MNLF refused to accept. Thus talks with the MNLF broke down in 1987. In spite of this development, the Aquino administration inaugurated in 1990 the four-province Autonomous Region in Muslim Mindanao (ARMM) in accordance with the constitutional mandate and without the participation of the MNLF.

Ramos Administration

The MNLF, together with the GRP during the Ramos administration, hoped to remove from the southern Philippines the roots of dissidence, injustice, and inequality that gave rise to the Moro rebellion and the almost three decades of instability. With the peace agreement, the MNLF envisioned the south as a progressive social, economic, and political component of the Philippines that has advantages in terms of its rich resources and proximity to the Asean countries, particularly Indonesia, Malaysia and Brunei.

The first Exploratory Talks between the GRP and the MNLF was held in Tripoli Libya on October 3-5, 1992 under the auspices of the Libyan government. This meeting established contact lost after the 1987 peace negotiations and came out with a "Statement of Understanding" to hold another round of talks to be hosted by the government of Indonesia on April 14-16, 1993 at Cipanas, West Java. The second round of Exploratory Talks produced the second "Statement of Understanding" with both parties agreeing to hold formal peace negotiations with the participation of the Organization of Islamic Conference (OIC). The guidelines for the formal negotiations focused on the modalities for the full implementation of the 1976 Tripoli Agreement in letter and spirit.

Between October 27 – November 7, 1993, the first round of formal negotiations hosted by Indonesia was held in Jakarta. Two documents were signed: the 1993 Interim Ceasefire Agreement and the Memorandum of Agreement. The Ceasefire Agreement created the Joint Ceasefire Committee (JCC) tasked to formulate a ceasefire agreement conducive for the duration of the formal talks while the Memorandum of Agreement reactivated the Mixed Committee that will study in detail the points stated in the Tripoli Agreement. The second round of formal negotiations was also held in Jakarta, Indonesia on September 1-5, 1994. The talks focused on the recommendations of the Mixed Committee. With optimism and confidence, most of the agreements reached by the Mixed Committee were accepted by both panels. The deployment of the OIC Monitoring/Observer team composed of Indonesian military officers was also agreed upon. Thus, the second round of formal negotiations ended with the signing of the 1994 Interim Agreement by both parties.

Two crucial issues–the establishment of the Provisional Government and the integration of the MNLF fighters in to the Armed Forces of the Philippines –remained unresolved following the third round of formal talks held in Jakarta, Indonesia on November 27 - December 1, 1995. The parties decided that these issues will have to be decided by the Mixed Committee meetings to be held in the Philippines. The third formal talks ended with the signing of the 1996 Interim Agreement which consolidated all points of consensus reached since 1993.

The final and fourth round of formal negotiations were successfully held in Jakarta on August 28-30, 1996 and led to the initialing ceremony of the GRP-MNLF peace agreement in Merdeka Palace, Jakarta on August 31, 1996 with the presence of former President Suharto. The historic ceremony followed on September 2, 1996 at Malacañang Palace, Manila witnessed by then President Fidel V. Ramos and officials of the OIC.

The Peace Agreement settled the more than two decades of armed conflict involving the MNLF in the South and ushered new hopes for peace and harmony. The next three years from 1996-1999 covered Phase One of the Transition Period. It is mandated through Executive Order No. 371 issued on October 2, 1996 which formally established a Special Zone of Peace and Development in the Southern Philippines (SZOPAD) with its primary implementing mechanism, the Southern Philippines Council for Peace and Development (SPCPD) and its Consultative Assembly (CA). Both bodies operate under the Office of the President. The SPCPD shall serve as the lead agency in promoting, coordinating, and monitoring development efforts in the SZOPAD while the CA shall act as an advisory body to the SPCPD.

The SZOPAD is composed of 14 provinces and 10 cities, representing around 23 percent of the Philippines' total land area. It has a total population of 9,808,000 as of 1995 or around 14.3 percent of the Philippine population. Fifty percent of the mineral production in the South is located in the areas of SZOPAD. The SZOPAD also generates about 25 percent of the Philippines' aquatic and marine production. The Sulu Sea, located in this zone, is the largest land-locked body of water in the Philippines.

Summary

The road to peace in the South has been a difficult one, marked by ceasefire agreements and the subsequent outbreak of hostilities. Between the Tripoli Agreement of 1976 and the Manila Agreement of 1996 is twenty years, three administrations, three ceasefire agreements, and three versions of "implementation" of the Tripoli Agreement. The MNLF does not look forward to any fourth version.

The GRP during the Ramos administration and the MNLF pursued the peace negotiations for four years with considerable patience. Where its two predecessors failed, the Ramos administration, with the help of the OIC, succeeded in convincing the MNLF to go along with the Philippine constitutional framework in determining the modalities of the interpretation and implementation of the Tripoli agreement.

So far, the GRP and the MNLF have religiously kept their commitment to enhance peace and development in southern Philippines. No hostility has occurred between the two parties since the signing of the 1996 agreement. There is also some relative success in the integration of MNLF Forces into the Armed Forces of the Philippines (AFP) and the Philippine National Police (PNP), except for the occasional and mutual complaints and the fatal shooting in Basilan involving MNLF Integrees and AFP regulars.

The economic components of the peace process however, have not been generally felt by the intended beneficiaries, particularly by the poor MNLF members and their families. So far, only the new foreign-assisted multi-donor programs of SPCPD-NEDA-UNDP remain to help some former MNLF combatants. Once again, the MNLF feels that it is being left out in the cold, particularly on matters related to the pursuit of peace and development in the southern Philippines. The socio-cultural (including religious) components of the peace process have also been neglected. Aside from the economic and political reasons for waging war, these overlooked socio-cultural factors would help explain the emerging popularity of the Moro Islamic Liberation Front (MILF), Abu Sayyaf, and other movements that are advocating the Islamic cause.

The problem we face today, and the same is true for the generations before us, is how Moro aspirations, particularly their sense of nationality can be accommodated within the framework of the Philippine national community with less tension or conflict. Some Moros believe that autonomy is enough to safeguard and enhance their way of life. Considering, however, the prevailing realities in the southern Philippines as a world of claims and counterclaims among the various forces at play, other Moros still believe that secession is the only alternative. The MNLF believes that the search for peace and unity among the various segments of Philippine society will have a fair chance to succeed if the Filipino people (including the Moros), particularly their leaders, are imbued with a more refined and sensitive attitude towards various cultural elements in a pluralistic Philippine society.

It is recommended that the national leadership enhance the full participation of the MNLF in governmental affairs, particularly in the formulation and implementation of policies and programs related to the pursuit of peace and development in the southern Philippines. This gesture will demonstrate greater sensitivity to MNLF conditions and aspirations on the part of the national leadership. It must be noted here that the GRP-MNLF peace agreement provides an excellent opportunity for both parties to undertake joint efforts aimed at advancing the cause of genuine reconciliation and national unity. We should take full advantage of the agreement to build a new system of peace, stability and growth in the Muslim Philippines.

Conclusion: Conflicting Histories

The history of the Philippine Muslims is part of the backbone of the historical development of the whole country. Filipino historians like Renato

Constantino asserted that no Philippine history would be complete without a study of Muslim development. But it is the victors, a popular adage reminds us, who write history. And as such, even in history, the Moros have been marginalized. The problem here lies in the diverse and numerous historical developments, and, consequently, the different identities that were formed by these events. So different, in fact, that to Christian Filipinos, Moro history and identity is but marginally noted in the history of their nation. Similarly, Moros never considered themselves as integral to the Philippine nation-state.

The Philippine has, in fact, two lines of political and historical developments. The first line, which is the older, came to develop in Mindanao and Sulu. And this refers to the Muslim line of historical development. Had not this line been disturbed by western colonialism, Islam might have charted the entire destiny of the Philippine nationhood. On the other hand, external factors swept into the country to bring the second line. This is the product of the great historical experiences of the Filipino people under western rule. It is this diverse historical trajectory that inflames the animosity between the Philippine government and the Moro people. Obliterating one historical line or the other cannot achieve genuine peace. Somehow, the contesting parties would have to find a way to respect each other's identities and history, to agree to compromise and meet each other half-way in the true spirit of brotherhood and fraternity.

Reference

Abinales, P.N. (1998) An American Colonial State: Authority and Structure in Southern Mindnao. In P.N. Abinales (Ed.), **Images of State Power: Essays on Philippine Politics from the Margins** (p. 1-62). Quezon City: University of the Philippine Press.

Asani, A. (1985, July) The Bangsamoro People: A Nation in Travail. **Journal Institute of Muslim Minority Affairs,** pp. 295-314.

Buendia, R.G. (193, 2nd Quarter) Ethnic Identity, Self - Determination, and Human Rights: Majoritarian Democracy Re-Examined. In **KASARINLAN: A Quarterly of Third World Studies,** pp. 81-99.

Che Man, W.K. (1990) **Muslim Separatism: The Moros of Southern Philippines and the Malays of Southern Thailand.** New York: Oxford University Press.

Goodnow, J.B. (1991) **The Philippines: Land of Broken Promises.** London: Zed Books Ltd.

Kessler, R.J. (1989) **Rebellion and Repression in the Philippines.** New Have: Yale University Press.

Majul, C.A. (1973) **Muslims in the Philippines.** Quezon City: University of the Philippines Press.

McKenna, T.M. (1998) **Muslims Rulers and Rebels.** Berkeley: University of California Press.

Paderanga, C., Jr. (1995) **Mindanao Studies Reports: A Review of Land Settlements in the Philippines.** Quezon City: UP Center for Integrative and Development Studies.

Muslims in the Philippines or Filipino Muslims?

SENATOR SANTANINA RASUL

HON. SANTANINA T. RASUL
Former Senator

Hon. Santanina T. Rasul is the first Muslim woman to be elected Senator and the first Muslim senator to be re-elected. Currently, she is the Chairperson of the Magbassa Kita Foundation and Bantay Dagat, Inc. as well as the President Emeritus of the Muslim Professional and Business Women's Association of the Philippines,Inc. Senator Rasul was a member of the Philippine Government Panel in 1996, which successfully forged the Peace Agreement with the Moro National Liberation Front while at the Senate, she authored major laws pertaining to the civil service, indigenous peoples, women's and civil service rights issues, including the promotion of literacy.

Senator Rasul earned her doctoral units in Public Administration from the University of the Philippines. She has received various awards during her distinguished career in service, notably the Golden Heart Presidential Award in recognition of her work as a Member of the Government of the Republic of the Philippines-Southern Philippine Autonomous Group (GRP-SPAG) negotiating panel.

ABOUT THE PHOTO: Sultan Mahakuta Kiram with his Wazir[1], Abraham Rasul and the Ruma Bichara[2].

1. Prime Minister
2. Literally "House of Speech," it means council of advisers.

To be truly understood, any social problem such as the search for the place of Muslims in the making of the Filipino nation must be situated in its proper historical perspective. I would like to begin by quoting one of our esteemed historians, Renato Constantino, from his work entitled, "Identity and Consciousness: The Philippine Experience."

> *"Had the Spaniards not arrived, the rest of the islands would surely have been Islamized and thoroughly exposed to the great Asian traditions."*

Then he continues in another paragraph:

> *"Because it was the Christianized natives rather than the Muslims who eventually became the dominant force in the country, it is the shaping of their developing consciousness that must be our principal concern."*

Very interesting statements indeed. In one sentence, he affirms what is a known historical fact but has seen little light of day in our history classes - that prior to our colonization, there was a thriving Islamic civilization in our islands, with distinct political, economic and religious structures such as those found in the Sultanate of Sulu in Mindanao, slowly expanding, with established outposts in Luzon and Visayas.

And in the succeeding statement, all of these are brushed aside, even though they constitute the elements in what was to become, as he labels it, the "aborted civilization" of the Philippines. The rationale is that the Muslims were not successful anyway. History is, indeed, written by the victors.

The moro-moro plays. The huramentado. "A good Moro is a dead moro." The headlines that scream "5 Muslim Bandits Captured." "Gulo na naman sa Mindanao" as intoned by the newscaster. As we continue to write the history of our grandchildren, it is becoming more apparent that history will be reflective of the dominant people's ideals, values, and aspirations.

What then is to become of the non-dominant peoples like the Muslims? Will they be relegated to the dustbins, or serve as a footnote in history books? Or will they be conjured up in tales told to children to scare them to bed. Whatever the result, it shall always mean one thing - injustice. This is what the Muslims have been resenting. The gross injustice of being neglected, being set aside, being overlooked. That they have remained outside the mainstream of Philippine society, and must eke out an existence in the periphery. All human development factors such as literacy and economic productivity are, as a rule, lowest in the Muslim-dominated areas. Coincidence or accident of history? The net result is the same–marginalization and alienation of the Muslims.

And when the Muslims rise up in arms to decry their neglect, the entire might of the military is brought to bear upon them. Not only secessionist forces, but THEM, the women, the children, the aged people living in the villages. Bullets, after all, do not discriminate. Neither do mortars, that have bombed out mosques and schools in Mindanao. And when a camp is taken, and the Philippine flag is hoisted with much fanfare over the ruins of a mosque, the pictures speak for themselves. Put yourself in the shoes of someone who uses that same mosque to commune with God, and think about how he or she feels.

I am not saying that I am for war. Having experienced the horrors of war, I abhor it. But I cannot say that I disagree with what all these groups, from the Mindanao Independence Movement to the Moro Islamic Liberation Front, aspire for. I disagree with the means (sometimes), but I vigorously support the ends. Justice for the Muslims, justice for Mindanao.

From the Spanish wars of the reconquista imported to Philippine shores sowed the first seeds of distrust when Christianized "indios" were used to quell the Moro, to the present anger at the acts of a few terrorist brigands. This historical thread weaves the blanket of hatred that the majority bears towards the Moro people. And when there is no voice in government that can legitimately represent us, there will be no lifting this cover of hatred. And this is what our children, and their children will learn–to distrust, fear, and hate the Moro.

We do not want to admit it but these emotions have already seeped into our consciousness. This is evidenced by people's support for the all-out war policy in Mindanao, as gathered in a nationwide survey. Of course they support it. They will not witness firsthand the blood and tears. Their innocent relatives will not be buried alongside the very few outlaws who seem to think that a religion that espouses brotherhood and peace is a convenient excuse to commit crimes.

Speeches have been delivered full of words like "our Muslim brothers and sisters." But this is merely rhetoric that is so artificial and hypocritical because it is only in this context that we ever use these words. We do not say our Cebuano brothers and sisters, do we? This cleavage manifests itself in simple terms like these, although I might be accused of making a meal out of it.

How can we mold a country that will make Muslims an integral part of that vision? How can we achieve unity as one nation that includes the aspirations and dreams of the Moro people? More importantly, is it acceptable and truly reflective of what is it that the Moro people truly need and want? Does the answer lie in autonomy? Or federalism?

My answer is yes, with reservations. We need autonomy, but backed by a genuine and real effort, with the aim of federating this multicultural and diverse archipelago. Let us reject a watered-down version that only corrupts and co-opts well-meaning leaders. Let us reject a mere structural solution to what is a multi-faceted problem. The social issues run deep, deeper than the questions of economics or politics.

Thus, the national agenda of the administration should include a clear enunciation of its Mindanao policy, to include the concerns of all sectors. The members of the cultural communities, however, have had few opportunities to become part of the collective minds that decide what determines the national agenda. We welcome the initiative by Amina and the Washington Sycip Policy Center of the Asian Institute of Management to provide a forum where the leaders of the Muslim tribes can discuss their concerns with those who help determine the national agenda.

We must begin with education. We must educate people on ethnicity, its functions, its potential dangers, and the nation that we are striving to build. We must highlight the contributions of people other than those from the dominant group — all being Filipinos. The discussion should not be limited to the superficial, 3-minutes worth of glossy footage of cultural minorities portrayed during the playing of the national anthem on television or movie houses.

We must teach our people that history and the making of our nation did not begin when Magellan landed in Limasawa island. We must try to make them unlearn the distrust, and anger, and hatred of the past. We must tame the power of the media to mold opinions and minds of our people, and channel it to a more useful purpose. The media use of "Muslim bandits" is such an unfair label that it reeks of ethnocentrism. An NPA attack somewhere in Quezon is not branded as "conflict in Luzon," is it?

And as any genuine social or NGO worker will tell you, any development intervention must necessarily involve the beneficiaries for it to be meaningful. Hence, for efforts in Mindanao to make any headway, it is crucial for the Muslims to have adequate representation in government, and genuine participation in development efforts. There should be abundant representation in ALL branches of government - the judiciary, the executive and both Houses of Congress. The latter institution is the most crucial because it is where the law is made, and you do not serve at anyone's pleasure except the sovereign people's.

As we now face homogenizing forces from globalization, it is crucial to have a firm anchor on who we are, collectively - not just as Bicolanos, or Ilonggos, or Kapampangans, or as Muslims. Because if we don't, we shall be consumed by the burning cauldron of prejudice and distrust and miss the goals of nation building.

Our problems may not be solved in our lifetime. But everyday we continue to write history. This is more important than the material world because we are dealing with the very soul of our nation. If history is written by the victors, the Filipino could become a mere footnote in history collectively, because we failed in our struggle to find peace within and amongst ourselves.

Roadmap to the Bangsamoro Islamic State

COMMISSIONER NASSER A. MAROHOMSALIC

COMMISSIONER NASSER A. MAROHOMSALIC

Commission on Human Rights

Commissioner Marohomsalic of the Human Rights Commission is a lawyer, writer, human rights activist, and diplomat. He finished his law degree at the University of the Philippines and is an honorary alumnus of the Mindanao State University.

Under a research project of the Mindanao State University and the Ramos Peace and Development Foundation, Commissioner Marohomsalic recently completed a book entitled, "Aristocrats of the Malay Race: A History of the Bangsamoro Muslims in the Philippines." The Foreign Service Institute recognized him in a book entitled, "Muslim Leaders of the Philippines" (as one of the regional leaders of Muslim Mindanao.)

In the first phase of the conference, a political analyst of note situated the so-called Moro Problem within the context of public administration and accused local Moro bureaucrats as its progenitors calling them corrupt and incompetent.

Of course, that is just a part of the story. The central plot is a bigger story that tells why Moro bureaucrats or anybody for that matter becomes corrupt and incompetent and lives an immoral public life.

Flawed Social Order

As fish is cradled in a body of water, so is man by his social environment or under a social order. When that social order affords man every opportunity to develop his potentials according to his needs and aspirations, he becomes an asset rather than a liability. Sadly, in the Philippines, what exists is a social system ordained by majority rule which prescribed uniformity and centralism in most parts of public and private life, disinheriting the *Bangsamoro* of their past and depriving them of the future they aspire for. So we have a society dichotomized into two hostile camps, the dominant majority and the belligerent minority. Under such a state of affairs, failure of governance is an ordinance of fate especially at the local level of government in the hands of the minority who may find public service as a matter of convenience rather than a function of citizenship. *Maranao* oral traditions refer to the Philippine government as a *Beberno a Saroang-a-tao* or "a foreign government."

Autonomy in the Qur'an

A non-Muslim may wonder why in every country its Muslim minority is difficult to govern and why they invariably seek independence or autonomy.

The reasons may be as complex as the kind of government that Muslims pay allegiance to. Nevertheless, as in all liberation movements, in the pursuit of self-determination by Muslim minorities may be found a common motivation and pervasive character—religion. Islam is not only a system of religious rites but a way of life, a form of government. Thus, even under a most liberal non-Muslim government, Muslims will always demand autonomy that will give them complete opportunity for full expression. Islam, in fact, consecrates in the Qur'an the right to self-determination of peoples, to govern their own affairs freely and determine their own destiny through a social system of their own choice and consensus. The Qur'an counsels, thus:

> *Let there be no compulsion in religion (Al Baqora or the Cow, Surah 2: Verse 256)*

And the reasons therefore exalt man's place in God's creation, thus:

> *If God had so willed, men would not have fought each other (and have one faith) (Al Baqara, Surah 2: Verse 253)*
>
> *And if your Lord willed, all who are on earth would have believed together. Would you compel people to become believers? (Yunus, Surah 10: Verse 99)*
>
> *If thy Lord had so willed, He could have made mankind one nation, yet they will not cease to dispute . . . (Hud, Surah 11: Verse 118-119)*

The Qur'an concludes that even when one persists winning others to his religion or system of life, there will always be a section of humanity who will remain unmoved. Thus:

> *In spite of your zeal, most people still will not become believers (Yusuf, Surah 12: Verse 103)*

However, in order to keep man's brotherhood and humanity, God ordains the rule in the Qur'an, thus:

What is yours is yours and what is mine is mine. (Al Kafirun or The Unbelievers, Surah 59: Verse 6).

On these divine instructions, Prophet Muhammad (May peace be upon him) granted local autonomy to the non-Muslim Jews of Khaybar at Madinah and they were allowed to live their life to their content as long as they do not disturb or subvert the peace, stability and security of the Islamic State and the general populace.

Muslims, therefore, regard it as a matter of religious obligation to govern themselves by their own social system or to grant autonomy to sectoral minorities in their society. They believe that autonomy, as a system of political governance, is a natural order of political development in society. It does not only come along with the growing needs of an expanding society and the corresponding widening differences or divergence in ways and modes of living and outlook in life between and among various sectors of the community, but a political formula to keep the bond of unity among heterogeneous peoples.

A Call for Federal System of Government

And what will genuine autonomy for the *Bangsamoro* be like?

The Mindanao Independence Movement headed by Reuben Canoy, which counts Bangsamoro of note for its membership, like the late Chairman of the Regional Consultative Commission for Muslim Mindanao, Dr. Tocod D. Macaraya, Sr., endorsed the idea of a federal republic for Mindanao's 24 provinces and cities. In this setup, political power was proposed to be shared between the Bangsamoro and the Christian population in Mindanao, with the office of the elected President and the Vice President alternately occupied by a Muslim and a Christian.

The idea of a federal system of government for the whole country with every region thereof, a constituent state is bannered as a priority or political platform by two national parties, the Partido Demokratiko ng Pilipinas-Laban (PDP-LABAN) and the National Union of Christian Democrats-United Muslim Democrats of the Philippines (NUCD-UMDP).

A multi-sectoral, non-political, non-partisan National Movement for Economic Reconstruction and Survival (Nation Movers) was founded by noted Christian leaders in 1988 to advocate a transition towards a federalized form of government to suit the culturally diverse nature of the country. Among its members are former Assemblyman Homobono Adaza of Misamis in Northern Mindanao, Former Vice President Salvador H. Laurel, former Senator Rene Espina, former Minister of Labor and Assemblyman and now Senator Blas Ople, and the leading businessmen in the country including Enrique Zobel.

The grand old guards of Muslim politics founded the Muslim Federal Party in 1984 as a political vehicle to launch the establishment of a Federal Republic for the Bangsamoro within the territorial integrity of the Philippines. Among the founders were the late Senator Mamintal A. J. Tamano of Lanao, former Senator Salipada Pendatun of the Cotabato provinces, and Ambassador Abraham Rasul of Sulu together with then young Muslim professionals and leaders like Abul Khayr Alonto (former Vice Mayor of Marawi City and Speaker of the defunct Autonomous Government of Region 12 in Southern Phillppines), Professor Ibrahim Mama-o (former Moro rebel and now Economic Adviser to the Embassy of the Royal Kingdom of Saudi Arabia in the Philippines), Almarim Tillah (former Governor of Tawi-Tawi) and Saidamen Pangarungan (former Assemblyman of the defunct Autonomous Government and Governor of Lanao del Sur, 1987-1992)

Former Vice President Salvador Laurel observed that decentralization of government throughout the Philippines would be the key to attaining peace in the country, particularly in Muslim Mindanao. He explained that the nation began as a collection of distinct tribes that had their specific needs and problems.

Social Landscape

Generally, there is a unity of opinion among *Bangsamoro* and Filipino Christian leaders in Mindanao and in the country that the federal system of government is best for the country. Indeed, its advantages are easily discernible. To emphasize, the country is composed of more than 80 tribes scattered all over the 7,000 islands separated by bodies of water and natural barriers. Each tribe speaks a dialect different from the other, possesses different character traits, and owes regional or tribal loyalty while having a sense of nationhood and with peculiar cultures, customs and traditions.

Social Friction

In the distant past, the Muslim and Christian populations of the country fought each other for religion and supremacy. Echoing a provision of the 1987 Constitution, Congressman Hilario de Pedro III of South Cotabato observed in an interview in 1989 that there is no commonality between Muslims and Christians in the Philippines.

History and the social landscape of the country, indeed, provide a host of reasons for the Bangsamoro to struggle for genuine and Islamic autonomy and enlist the support of their Muslim brethren from foreign lands for the purpose.

But these currents to the secessionist tendencies of the Bangsamoro are allowed to flourish by sufferance or deliberate act of government and by the neglect and iniquitous treatment of the *Bangsamoro* by the Filipino majority. And this situation may remain the order of relations for a long time to come.

To emphasize, it is not only the differing historical experiences between the majority Filipinos and the minority *Bangsamoro* that set them apart or that determines their attitude towards each other. It can be attributed too, to their opposing socio-cultural backgrounds and religious affiliations or professions. Mutual respect for each other's beliefs, which is the teaching of every religion, may not carry the relation far enough as to erase any tinge of ill-will that may be obtained especially when they are contending against each other during elections.

In Lebanon, Muslim and Christian Arabs went to war against each other many times in the past, and they are still at it though in a more subdued level, over disagreements in policies and power sharing.

In Russia, where the Orthodox Christians are the majority, the Muslim ethnic minority felt the need for secession, as they eventually did in 1991, from the Soviet Union because the government controlled by the majority was hostile to their faith and ways of life which are requirements of their religion. It was only in 1988 that the Government of the Soviet Union returned a 14th century Qur'an to its Muslim population. The Muslim Turkish Cypriots felt the same rejection from their brother Christian Cypriots. And so do the Muslim Thai Patanis vis-a-vis their brother Buddhist Thais, and the Muslim Indians vis-a-vis their brother Hindu Indians, and so on.

This 'social friction' is not only true among peoples of different ideological or religious persuasion. Although it may not be as pronounced as it is among heterogeneous communities, antagonism may even be an order of relations among more or less homogenous people especially when they have been kept apart by difference of language or dialect or natural barriers. And this is reflected in our electoral experience. An Ilocano Filipino who is a Christian from the North will prefer a fellow Ilocano to a Cebuano Filipino who is also a Christian from the South as president of the country and vice versa. The same situation exists the world over. Christian Catholic Ireland has been agitating for independence from Christian Anglican England. Muslim Kurds in the North of Iraq have been battling for secession from the country whose government is controlled by Iraqi Arabs who are their brothers in Islam. In Spain, the Catholic Basques enjoy autonomy from the majority Catholic Spaniards. In Muslim Indonesia, Muslim Aceh is a special province.

It is a truth with nary a doubt that as a system of political governance, federalism will keep the differing regions of the country intact and its tribes or nations united.

Contradictions

Apprehensions were raised in the first phase of the conference against devolution of government to the *Bangsamoro* adverting to three contradictions obtaining in Moro society which stand in the way of good government and the development of good political relations between the Moro tribes, and the majority Filipinos and the minority *Bangsamoro*. These contradictions are: Tribalism vs. Nationhood, Feudalism vs. Assertive Citizenry, and Secularism vs. Islamic Fundamentalism.

Tribalism

Divided into 13 major ethnic groups, some of whom are as socially disparate as their geographic distance from one another, the *Bangsamoro* have indeed individually developed among themselves a pattern of hostile behavior when faced against each other as competing interest groups especially in political contests.

I remember in the 1980s, some Maguindanoan leaders expressed revulsion over the ascendancy of the *Maranaos* in the field offices of the national government in Cotabato City. Most recently, some sectors of *Maranao* society made public their displeasure over the non-appointment of a *Marnao* in national government while one Moro tribe was offered two plum posts.

Tribalism will persist as a recurring influenza in the relationships among the Moro tribes. The current experiment in autonomy that placed them under one structure of power, like the autonomous government in Muslim Mindanao, only fans its flame. Since its inception in 1987, the regional government has been reduced into a tribal redoubt of every regional governor, its bureaucracy a political tilth for his tribe.

One would miss the point though, if he were to adduce this political experience as an argument against the devolution of government power to the *Bangsamoro*. In the first place, the design of the autonomous government does not consider the stresses brought to bear upon it by history. Congress overlooked the recommendations of the 1988 Regional Consultative Commission (RCC) for Muslim Mindanao whose members hail from the region and who made extensive studies and conducted multi-sectoral consultations on the so-called Moro Problem.

The RCC prescribed a collegial executive-council type of government for the *Bangsamoro* composed of elective representatives of their respective tribal aggrupations, who will elect among themselves the chairman of the autonomous government and the secretaries of its various line agencies. By this arrangement, it was hoped that tribalism would, in due time, recede into insignificance. But Congress chose for the *Bangsamoro* a unitary regional government whose control is placed in whoever garners a plurality of votes in a region-wide election that pits the candidates from the different tribes. As it engenders social frictions among the tribes, this electoral exercise only reinforces their sense of tribal loyalty.

Nevertheless, the Moro experience in self-government during olden times provides inspiration that under a conducive social environment they could exorcise themselves of the evil of tribalism.

Dean C. Worcester, an American Secretary of Interior during the American occupation wrote that among the Malay race, it is the *Bangsaaoro* that has attained unaided the highest stage of civilization in their sultanic system. (Vic Hurley, *Swish of the Kris*. 1936: E.P. Hulton & Co. Inc. New York, p, 10)

The four earliest Moro sultanates—Sulu, Maguindanao, Buayan, and Butig—founded in the 15th century by half-caste descendants of Arab traders and missionaries, thrived as a polity individually and separately of each other inspite of Spanish divide-and-rule warfare against them. They had military alliances. They maintained inter-state relations including trade and commerce. Diadic alliances were forged between their ruling families particularly between the Maguindanao and Iranun-Maranao royalties. The Maguindanao and Lanao sultanates got closest to forging a commonwealth during the reign of Sultan Kudarat in 1605. His sister named Goyang was married to a leading *Maranao* nobility at the time, Amatunding-a-Nuni of Butig. In the latter part of the 19th century, the Parliament or *Ruma Bichara* of Maguindanao invested the title of *Rajah Laut* or Admiral of the Navy to a M'ranao member of the Maguindanao royalty, Datu Ilian, who was later made Datu Amirol or Amirol Omrah or Prince of Princes of the realm in 1879. (Reynaldo C. Ileto, Maguindanao 1860-1888; The Career of Datu Otto of Buayan, Mindanao State University Research Center, Marawi City, p 21) When the Maguindanao Sultanate was reduced to penury in the closing years of the 19th century and the Spanish colonial government subsidized its upkeep in exchange for their barrack-presence in the seat of the Sultanate, the people along the Illana Bay looked up to their *Maranao* kin in Ganassi whose ruling nobility is the sanguinary relation of Datu Ilian. (Cesar Adib Majul, Muslims in the Philippines. 1973: UP Press, Quezon City, p.288; Reynaldo C. Ileto, ibid., p. 21). The M'ranao branch of the Sultanate of Maguindanao has two from among its members who have individually sported the title of Sultan and Rajah Muddah of Maguindanao.

The Sultanate of Sulu also carried on a military alliance with the Lanao and Maguindanao sultanates. In 1704, in the dynastic rivalry over the throne of Brunei between two cousins, Muaddin and Mubbin, the Sulu Sultanate intervened in favor of Muaddin. With the assistance of an army of Iranuns, M'ranaos and Maguindanaoans, the Sulu Sultan established Muaddin to the throne of Brunei. (James Francis Warren, The Sulu Zone, 1768-1898. 1985: New Day Publishers, Quezon City p. 157: Nasser Marohomsalic, Aristocrats of the Malay Race, 2001: V.J. Graphic Arts, Inc., Quezon City).

The royalties of Maguindanao and Lanao claim common ancestry through Sharif Kabungsuan.

The point is, had Spain not engaged the *Bangsamoro* into a war of attrition that lasted for more than 300 years, the individual Moro sultanates could have flourished into modern city-states or constitutional or democratic monarchies like its Malaysian likeness. Or they could have gone the way of the Malay kingdoms and formed a federation among themselves.

Feudalism

This brings me to the second tension that will provide the dysfunctional value that will prevent the development of Moro society from becoming a modern progressive and democratic state.

It must be clarified, at the outset, that our feudal political culture is one big hurdle in our quest for good government. The democrats among the *Bangsamoro* may be disheartened with its implications in their aspirations for greater autonomy. It is no excuse, however, for detractors in government to look the other way and suggest that the *Bangsamoro* doehs not deserve greater autonomy. The decadent ways of the *Bangsamoro* leadership and its throttlehood on the socio-economic and political life of the Moro society only mirror the national scene. As we all know, the political dynamics of our national society reacts to the tempo of our flawed electoral democracy which thrives on manipulation by the few elite of the formal and informal apparati of power.

It must be mentioned at this juncture that in its early beginnings, the Moro society was not a picture of social, political and economic dwarfism. Its structure of power was not a closed enclave of feudal lords and its general public were not a whole lot of galley-rowers and kris-wielding warriors bonded to sultans and datus. In brief, Moro society was not a closed society.

During colonial times, Lanao evolved from one sultanate into a bastion of 15 grand sultanates. The Maguindanao Sultanate spun into another sultanate, Kabuntalan, and the Sulu Sultanate acquired Sabah from the Sultanate of Brunei. Support datus to the Sulu Sultan like the Panglimas asserted their independence on issues that concerned the cultural and political integrity of their realm. In the domain of the Maguindanao Sultanate grew an Iranun Sultanate of Linek in the 20th century.

As in the early pre-Islamic baranganic society, ordinary people who acquired wealth, reknown and prestige could earn royal titles, climb to positions of power and enjoy eminence in the sultanates.

In a well-researched book, *The Sulu Zone*: 1768-1898, American scholar Warren notes that it was not unusual in relations with Jolo to see individuals of the lowest class participating in serious affairs (of State). (Montero y Vidal, Historic de Filipinos. Cited in James Francis Warren, The SuluZone: 1968-1898, 1985).

In fact, many of those of *banyaga* origin (or those Christianized Filipinos from Visayas and Luzon whom the Moros captured), had climbed to royalty by wealth and marriage, and others earned manumission and accorded a place in the royal hierarchy in Moro society by their education, intelligence, and piety as Muslim converts and by decrees of their Moro masters.

It is well known that the Spanish Moro half-caste, Datu Mandi, became a Rajah Muddah (Crown Prince) of the Maguindanao Sultanate (John Foreman, "The Philippine Islands, 1906).

Datu Piang, a Chinese adopted by Maguindanaoan Chieftain Datu Uto of the Sultanate of Buayan, was integrated into the Moro society upon his conversion to Islam and became one of the most influential datus during the American period. (According to Reynaldo C. Ileto in Maguindanao: 1860-1888, Datu Piang was Minister of Lands of Datu Uto).

Princess Tarhata Kiram of the Sulu Sultanate has Spanish blood on her maternal side. (W. Cameron Forbes, The Philippine Islands, 1945). Panglima Tadema, a Christianized Indio in Zamboanga, who commanded an army of Indios against the Moro Samals of Basilan, became the undisputed leader of the Samals upon his conversion to Islam.

Panglima Hassan, who defied American rule in 1903 and met a heroic death with about 500 of his followers at the crater of Mount Bagsak in Jolo was, according to American Governor-General Leonard Wood, originally a slave born on Pata Island who rose to leadership in the island of Jolo next to the Sultan and Datu Jokanlen. (Leonard Wood Papers, 18 August 1903. Cited in Warren's The Sulu Zone: 1768-1898).

As a social and political institution, the sultanates, however, were not allowed to flourish to their natural synthesis by accident of history. The Spaniards who had just then overthrown the Muslim Moors of Africa from southern Spain in 1492 came to the Philippines in 1521 and waged war against the sultanates for more than 300 years.

Secularism

Lastly, it is posited that Moro society is "fractured" into the secularist Moro and the Islamist Moro.

True, as in some Muslim countries reduced into colonies by foreign power, the intellectual elite among the *Bangsamoro* became converted votaries of alien, especially American, ideals but these are not foreign to Islam, except the principle of separation of church and state.

American tutelage of the Moro for 50 years did not subvert his cultural and religious make-up. Neither did the Filipino educational system. Steeled with sediments of the Islamic faith for 400 years, he has remained in the homeland of Islam. Indeed, except for the arts and sciences of his American and Filipino benefactors and teachers, he has not imbibed their secularist orientations. I have had no encounter with any local Muslim who claims a secularist worldview of government and confines religion to personal and family affairs. Otherwise, one ceases to be a Muslim.

Wave of Islam

Islam is a pervasive influence in the life of a Moro Muslim. Quoting an academic study, Moro historian Samuel K. Tan said at the first phase of the conference that a Moro, when asked about his identity, will first refer to his ethnic origin to identify himself, then his identity as a Muslim, and lastly to his Filipino nationality.

Invariably, the social and political organizations of the *Bangsamoro* or not banner their aspirations for an Islamic State, or an autonomy where the *Shari'ah* is, or some Islamic objectives are enforced.

In 1996, the Moro National Liberation Front forged an agreement with the government. With heavy Islamic slant, the Moro Islamic Liberation Front is fighting for an Islamic State where Islamic laws, including its criminal jurisdiction, are observed. Two of the most powerful and the biggest non-government organizations of the *Bangsamoro*—the Tableegh and the Sabbab-propagate Islam. The Islamic resurgence in Muslim Mindanao, which began in the latter part of the 1950s, has created among the *Bangsamoro* self-styled guardians or keepers of the faith who live a life of simplicity and piety, not a few of whom have turned to extremism to pursue their aspirations for self-determination.

Moro political leaders have not escaped from the heat of the Islamic intensification in Moroland. To keep their peace and secure their interests, not a few have temporized in one way or another with their undertakers especially during elections.

Indeed, if I may bring home the point, Islam will be, as it is now, the dominant determinant in the social and political transformation of Moro society. Tribalism, feudalism and secularism cannot stop the wave of Islam in Muslim Mindanao.

Political Islam in 21st Century Philippines: Can It Survive?

CONGRESSMAN MICHAEL MASTURA

HON. MICHAEL O. MASTURA
Former Congressman, LD Maguindanao

A lawyer, professor, and political figure, Atty. Michael Mastura was elected Delegate to the 1971 Constitutional Convention representing the lone district of Cohabite. He was then appointed Deputy Commissioner for Region XII, Central Mindanao (1976-1979) and Deputy Minister for the Ministry of Muslim Affairs, which is now the Office on Muslim Affairs (1979-1982). Professor Mastura obtained his Bachelor of Laws degree from Notre Dame University, Cotabato City, and his Master of Laws from the University of the Philippines. He taught at the UP Law Center, and the UP Institute of Islamic Studies. He has also written numerous articles on Islamic issues, the most recent of which are "Reflections on the Philippine National Awakening: The Moro Problematics as a Factor" (1998); and "The Colonial State and the Sultanate: Between Republicanism and Patrimonialism," (1998). At present Atty. Mastura is a Member of the Board of Directors of the Philippine Communication Society, Philippine Political Science Association, and the World/Asian Conference on Religion and Peace at the house of Representatives. Atty. Mastura served as the Congressman of Maguindanao District 1 for 2 terms.

Contemporary Muslim societies in Southeast Asia range from being bound up in a monarchy in Brunei and Thailand to being parliamentary subjects in Malaysia, republican citizens in the Philippines, Indonesia, and Singapore or indigenous peoples in Burma and Cambodia. Their geographic dispersion and ethnic distribution in the rapid pace of the decolonization process have made them separate species as either a majority or minority public. That is why early on, between them, the great colonial powers redesigned the Muslim polities and principalities into zones of influence. Analysts saw the struggle over ideological hegemony at an end after the Cold War but for the new race to control mundane economic and technical resources.

My concern in this essay is political Islam and its justificatory framework: institutional Islam. The concern for an Islamic vision is not so much directed at the organization of the state, whether monarchy or republic, as the formation of the community. There have been no intra-Islamic games of life with implications for economies and polities in our part of the globe. For all common grounds, the great games of people and government, market and community are played up to spur overall political development of the region's nations without consideration for the context of the Islamic discourse.

Statement on *Bangsamoro* Themes

Can political Islam survive the 21st century in the Philippines with the political sea of change underway? Those who theorize about the civilizational clash identify the Philippines as among the *cleft country* on the fault lines between Muslims and Christians. Just the same, it is seemingly a disguised variant of the ideologizing of politics. If so, is today's Islamist adversary yesterday's Communist enemy? As always, we now reflect on Southeast Asia, and in our propensity to be *au courant* can one predict the implications of the latest creation of the White House Office of Faith-Based and Community Initiatives? There is a perception that the U.S. as a sole superpower plays a vital role in determining the areas of conflict and defining the terms of the conflict. Does the U.S. policy towards political Islam remain as enunciated in the Meridian House doctrine of constructive interaction at all levels—government-to-government, group-to-group, person-to-person, and faith-to-faith?

As we see it, in several conferences and forums, one proclaims above all an ideal Islam. One is asked in this workshop at least to make a statement of Muslim themes that correspond to the reality (situation) in which we live. I read through current materials in a series of sessions only to absorb the consequences (foreseen or unforeseen) in the history of the structures of power and social order. This is our summary statement:

- An ample awareness of the *Bangsamoro* people problem (or crisis sans post-colonial self-importance) calls into question the transformation of power relations without their plebiscitory consent and justness of the original position.
- A simple desire on the part of politically aware *Bangsamoro* people to mobilize Mindanao's economy puts at issue the legitimacy of complacency (or complicity in corruption) of incumbent elites and fairness of the current situation.
- An integral paradigm shift from *jihadic* resistance in favor of the *ummatic* movement (which is politically correct Islamic thinking) empowers the *Bangsamoro* people with a degree of organizational solidarity and pragmatic orientation.

Continuing the State Formation

If we go back a bit in history, there was a unified body politic outside the Spanish colonial hegemony from which the Philippine modern state emerged. A prefiguration of a wider organizing idea was contained in General Emilio Aguinaldo's attempt to negotiate with the sultans of Sulu and Maguindanao to establish "national solidarity on the basis of a true federation." Certainly, it has never been anachronistic, as the *Bangsamoro* political activists assert, that their dynastic realms are more fundamental than the unitary state itself. The provision that distinguishes the head of the state from the head of government in the federal system is a key formula to resolve collateral issues.

Part of the political structure of the sultanates was based on Islamic models that certainly included legitimacy to rule. Juxtaposing the Islamic bases of government as laid down in Islamic *shari'ah* norms and the modern state structures has not ceased to agitate the *Bangsamoro* people. For over a century the mosaic of towns (*pueblos*) and friar estates (*encomiendas*) inherited from Catholic Spain's colonial state was consolidated into the political map of the Philippines that we know today. Needless to say, it was the unhappy fate of the Muslim communities in Mindanao and Sulu to be annexed under an easy and less than desirable relationship in the course of the political changeover. The common themes, I think, too easily assumed how political influence through their sultanate system of governance has ceased to be relevant in our own time since it has not found constitutional anchor. The need to rectify this political injustice is particularly compelling today.

The Changing Political Structure

Legal writer and lawyer Soliman M. Santos, Jr. is right in posing the constitutional problem:

> "What is the best possible *structure* for the *political* relationship between the central Philippine government and for that matter the Filipino people, on the one hand, and the Bangsamoro people in the Southern Philippines, on the other hand? Or, is there space, can *space* be created, in the Philippine republican polity and constitutional system to accommodate a Moro Islamic system of life and governance (the main aspiration represented by the MILF)?"

No one can oppose the argument that the possibilities of non-independence solutions should be explored and exhausted first before resorting to independence solutions. A series of commitments on the part of the national government are being worked out both in charter amendment and peace agreement. There are a number of dimensions to this: opposing constitutional paradigms, helpful Filipino charter provisions and Islamic devises, and initial common grounds.

Three sets of fundamental arguments about the constitutional structure are often debated in Muslim scholarship and advocated in public policy forums:

1. The sovereignty movement for referendum as the only alternative to the current structure of the Philippine republic, whether it evolves as a non-constitutional adaptation or constitutional adjustment.
2. The movement for a constitutional shift from the present unitary system to the federal structure, whether the Philippine republic is organized on the presidential or parliamentary form of government.
3. The constitutional change from the present presidential system to the parliamentary form, whether the Philippine republic is reformed to recognized variations in autonomy via constitutional asymmetry.

From our present perspective, the choice is not necessarily limited to sovereignty (no. 1) or federation (no. 2). Not enough had been said about no.1 so we will discuss it in a separate section. But federation (no.2) and autonomy (no. 3) can be taken up together under our present elaboration.

The notable feature of granting Autonomous Communities its own statute, as in the Spanish approach, situates the structure between the unitary nature of Britain and the federal system of Germany, Norway, and Sweden. Its characterization is practically the expanded power devolution model. Agreements with the central government are set within a framework of constitutional asymmetry—specifically to differences in the status or legislative and executive powers assigned by the charter to the regional units. The current set up of the Autonomous Region in Muslim Mindanao (ARMM) resembles it in some aspects. The arrangements for "opt in" and "opt out" (possibly as addition to coverage) under the amendatory changes to the Organic Act of ARMM is an example of limited asymmetry. In other aspects, it is questionable that a provision would cover relations between Muslims, Christians, Lumads, and Jews. It tinkers with Islamic *shari'ah* law and this has ominous implications.

Moves Toward Federalism

The noted academic Jose V. Abueva views as crucial the urgency, readiness and timing of constitutional change. Thus our political experience in democratic governance is a hallmark of the readiness of crucial leaders and sectors of society in responding to them. Amid chronic problems of mass poverty, injustice, inequity and high population growth, the consolidation of democracy will be sustained. Talk about intense competition and other pressures from globalization conditioning our sense of urgency for structural adjustments. Briefly, Abueva proposes to consolidate the 78 provinces into ten federated states in order to make them more economic in size and resources as well as politically viable. Metro Manila, the national capital, will have the status of a federal territory. We are conscious, of course, about the dismissive treatment of the proposal by those who harbor presidential ambitions.

Some remarks here may be made about the LPM (Lihok-Pideral Mindanao) initiative. The pioneering efforts of some individuals and organizations were aligned to the mainstream agenda for Federal System of Government. It has kept that movement alive since 1991. On my suggestion at the Kusog Mindanao forum, Rey Magno Teves and Lito Monico Lorenzana convened in Davao City a group of experts to prepare the broad outlines of a draft constitution of the Federal Republic in early May 2001 in Davao City. To broaden the core group, it was decided to link up with Dean Carmen Abubakar of the UP Institute of Islamic Studies in convening the Zamboanga City round table discussion this month. To dovetail the federal structure with the form of government, Dr. Pablo Tangco's group whose project has given serious efforts to complete a draft constitution that adopts the Parliamentary System of Government, was contacted. It is highly important that Gaudioso C. Sosmena of the LOGODEF (Local Government Development Foundation) would provide the network for ready transitional mechanisms.

Because the term *federalism* is not descriptive but normative, it conceptually refers to an advocacy of multi-tiered government. Structurally, it combines the elements of shared-rule and regional self-rule. Its premise is the value and validity of combining unity *and* diversity: to accommodate, preserve and promote distinct identities within "a perfect political union." The entrenched individual rights and judicial review that encourages political technique in the unity system needs to be balanced by normative justificatory concepts of "third generation rights" built into the federal system.

Moves for Referendum

There is a variety of views on the question of referendum that leads to the status quo *ante bellum*. Whether one takes a political view focusing on self-determination as a human right, or a legal view tracing the de facto existence and de jure treaty relations of the sultanates, it is a cause recognized internationally. There are other instruments and documents that do not fit into these categories but the historical antecedents are of long duration. This is something I already discussed elsewhere in relation to our historic Muslim community as a community of obligation. It is the nature of political realism to be given dynamic constructs so I try to provide a critique of the quest for micro-theory across paradigms rather than a grand theory of ethnicity and politics.

The swing between desire for a broader autonomy and secession of the MNLF (Moro National Liberation Front) under Chair Nur Misuari does not render the movement for sovereignty moot. The fact is that the MILF (Moro Islamic Liberation Front) Chair Salamat Hashim has openly espoused the use of, and possibly need for referendum to test the will of the *Bangsamoro* people. A related but often overlooked point is that membership in the OIC (Organization of Islamic Conference) is an *ummatic* (read community-based) means of broadening representation for the *Bangsamoro* people. As an improvisation, some such discourse travels under the rubric democratization of the consultation process. But a common understanding of represent is "personated" to "act for" as a legal agent. Clearly, it was the *Bangsamoro* People as an entity which was given Observer Status, with the MNLF as its "sole representative." It was determined at the onset of MNLF relationship with the OIC member-states to give controlling weights to Muslim protection as a community.

The central point remains: Can one expect a referendum underway? How might a provisional government be set up after the failed implementation of the 1996 Peace Accord?

The boundaries for this type of inquiry are amorphous but it provides useful insights into actual politics and situations. Some Muslim lawyers and professionals ask very different kinds of question to explore non-constitutional political adaptation. Lawyers such as Musib Buat have done working constitutional drafts culled from the various Moro documents with updated suitable provisions. Finding the political process similar to the U.N. sponsored "Popular Consultation," for instance, Buat recommends that only the bona fide native inhabitants falling under the concept and definition of Bangsamoro People will qualify to participate or vote in the referendum. How might we Muslims put a claim to test? More than once, lawyer Macapanton Abbas, Jr. found himself moving from the rhetorical to the paradoxical end of the argument. Comes, again, the question of the constitutionality of the ARMM amendatory act.

Visualizing the Political Community

As we know it, the dominant statist experiments (strong or soft) are the product of the grand *siecle* of the European political thought along with the reawakening of curiosity of the varieties of human conditions we live in. Christianity, too, in its *Episcopal* form is a result of European religious experience. What is so significant about "modern state" as an umbrella framework for the diversity of politics? Simply put: that society was born out of the *state* as an association detached by powerful abstraction.

The idea of political community is now lost on our current understanding of cultural unity (albeit sentimental) when the focus is *only* on state as paradigm entity, *because*, there are also cantons, provinces, protectorates and trustee territories or federated states. Just as there is spurious historical unity in lumping together city-states, feudal-states, nation-states, and the empires, our aggregation is unified *rather* in part by being governed by the same government (presidential or parliamentary in form). This is a sampling of the diversity found in various political communities.

The growth of European commerce, even with its eclipse of the seaborne trade in the hands of Middle Eastern or south and southeast Asian merchants, created other roles and associative relationship in the political economy. Strikingly, market was different from social and political life. The modern economy was likewise called "political" to distinguish the prosperity achieved through "free" labor (in the process of production) from ancient servitude. And thus, mechanization sets in for repetitive performance and economic efficiency. Once this "genie of limitless human possibilities" was released, the minds of those who think about politics were reconstructed: a metaphor for the dominant drive of *homo politicus* and *homo economicus* and the role they played in enterprise. So it is that some modernization enthusiasts would mislead us even into believing that Middle East and Muslim societies face a stark choice : "Mecca or mechanization."

Let us remind ourselves that modern capitalism encourages the individualist society to be self-moving at the expense of the community. This has still to be compared in the context of Muslim culture: an individual is subordinate to the *ummah*—a community of common faith. And the identification with it clearly conveys the idea of solidarity. Strongly emphasizing the highest value placed in equality in the sight of God, the egalitarian concept of Islam favors collective values over individual ones.

Security of Political Life

Today the popular usage of "political development" implies collective identity. (If, at the outset, I sound academic we must clear the way for our preliminary organizing framework in the social and political aspect of religion —Islam in this case—within the theories of development). Beginning in the 1970s, understanding the whole field of "non-Western nations" has built on Area Studies, for which reason "identity theory" entered into political research. Geographical areas, however, provide an unrealistic basis of analysis in a world that is increasingly interdependent, so a limited problem set was focused on theories of political development and theories of economic growth.

Despite its own sponsors, and with its principal preoccupations on "what is trendy," Development Studies has not much answered the lack of local knowledge offered by Area Studies. It fails to disentangle the intellectual history of *colonisibility* (specific to direct or indirect rule) from the image of the modern state as a body politic in "crisis" or problematic-an imperfect analogy to a "sick man." Lucien Pye specified six crises to overcome for the nation-state: *identity*, *legitimacy*, *penetration*, *participation*, and *integration* (which later lost appeal). Yet each stands for a theory but hardly unified and with its own classification. Nor have its progressive critiques come up with credible alternatives. A case in point, the economic and political backside of Sudan began not with the introduction of *shari'ah* law but with the "breadbasket" theory that called for the expansion of agricultural production and supplies for exports that proved untenable.

A crucial formulation of "modernization" theories in the 1950s and 1960s assumed that religious belief and practice would become privatized and recede from public political life. (Throughout this period and into early 1970s religion in America was quiescent). Indeed, the very idea that separates religion from politics—we know it as secularist, capitalist or socialist answer—to be a positive factor in the development process of Third World nations has not been a very successful project. For example, in Iran, nationalism has always been perceived as "a toward-the-west" leaning political movement. The question is: why was it that the religious nature of the Iranian revolution enabled it to have the confidence of so many people? The movement itself provided an indigenous identity and religiosity: an Islamic one comprehensible and acceptable.

Choose from a political philosophy that has propelled statism for the Marxian materialistic faith in progress on one hand, and corporation for nothing other than the Weberian orientation toward "a desire to have ever more and go ever further;" on the other hand, it can been seen as a single episode of political incoherence. In such a world event, man's security has to be sought in economic success that, I believe, leads to a dead end. Here the question of "what is due" (hence of human responsibility) is not asked: it is about the role and potentiality of the religious task. When one adds intellectual pursuit, as constitutive of the psychosocial, then (in state, society, economy, and culture) we have current public policy alternatives compatible with the Islamic view of the proper role of government in relation to the economy. Do we find this in the echoes of the old framework of modernization? Or merely the language of postmodern times essential in the Qur'anic message itself?

Without a new political paradigm, state borders can become quite porous and the central government does not penetrate deep and far enough. The Sipadan episode, as pointed out by some analysts, severely tested the rigid statism of ASEAN. The hostage crisis was a spin-off from mainland Mindanao where the "all-out-war" policy was pursued to its fullest in July 2000. And so, if the resurgence of piracy continues due to chronic deprivation, it would be a mistake to find predominant security solutions. If the neighbours fail to pro-actively address the problems of political and economic disintegration in Mindanao, these countries will be fighting entire communities at war in which neither country can prevail.

Constructing the Islamic Republic

Quite contrary to the Islamic Caliphs who were elected from a system of consensus the Malay culture permitted a model of hereditary succession. The *Diwan* Sulu, *Luwaran* Magindanaw, *Hikayat Melayu* and other law digests have been the source of indigenous rules on governance. The starting point of Muslim political doctrine is the concept of *walaya*, or vested authority, if we follow diachronically Mawardi's classical treatise, *al-Ahkam as-Sultaniyya* (Ordinances of Government). Synchronically, we can juxtapose Imam Khomeini's *Vilayat-I-Faqih* (Guardianship by the Legists) in our own time in discussing comparative models:

1. Consider the powerful juristic tradition with its root in philosophy that man, in the 'original' state, has control over himself-*al-walaya ala'n-nafs*. This originality in control, Mawardi's view, can become *mut'addiya* (transitive); that is, extended over others. Only is it possible as when a difference in capacity for freedom (liberty) exist. For instance, guardianship over a minor or control is freely delegated contractually. Thus, Mawardi concludes, the *walaya* may or may not be inherent in the relationship.

   Now contrast the ideal that one may call "liberty" (after the Roman god Liber) or "freedom" (after the Greek god Dionysus) meaning those held dear to the head of the household. In western tradition of democracy, freedom functions as a term of self-identification: sometimes for republican constitution without monarchical authority such as the Aquino Freedom Constitution.
2. Consider further a contemporary work on the justification of the Islamic polity. Muhammad Baqer as Sadr: "The Islamic state is sometimes studied as a legal necessity because it institutes God's rule on earth and incorporates the role of man in the succession of God." But in the corpus of his work one reads that the 'Quranic State' is premised on an intrinsic dynamic Islamic principle: "Original sovereignty (*al-wilaya bil-asl*) rests only with God.

There is no bifurcation of the spiritual and the temporal in Islam and so its organizing structure is *not* a theocratic state. Where both parliamentary and Islamic republican models differ, it is found in the argument over *ulil amr* (those in authority) that was merged with the discussion over the formula *vilayat-I-faqih*. It was Khomeini's purpose to extend the meaning to the political guardianship in hands of the *mulla*. Sayyid Qutb, the theoretician Egyptian Muslim Brotherhood, dwelt more on the system of the governance and life in Islam rather than the position of the *ulama* in it.

3. Consider finally contemporary work on the principles of the Islamic polity. Popular sovereignty is embodied in the social contract of the *bay'a*, the duty of consultation or *shura*. In Abul Ala Mawdudi's view, the first principle of the Islamic state is its recognition of the sovereignty of God. And the Qur'an vests vicegerency in the entire Muslim citizenry of the Islamic state. A commonality of sovereign purpose of the Islamic Republic of Pakistan and Islamic Republic of Iran exists.

   It is my own understanding that enforcement of shar'ia law demands a Muslim state for the firm establishment of the faith (*tamkin*). The political force of Islam derives from the Quranic precept: Muslims are they who, when given power, establish *salah* (prayer) and enjoin *zakat* (poor-dues). The mosque is a locus of authority and so is the whole world a mosque. Gaining legitimacy (and winning the hearts and minds of the people) is one of the most crucial ways for a government to cope with its crisis.

Re-evaluation: Moves for Reconciliation

This, I have read from a book on politics subtitled "A Very Short Introduction." Political moralism "takes the independence of the citizen not as a guarantee of freedom" but (this is the paradox) "as a barrier to the project of moralizing the world." Such is the paradox of the reconciliation policy that our new President Gloria Macapagal Arroyo has set to reconstruct. A discursive recollection of that "all-out-war" policy provides vivid pictures of "otherness" of the Mindanao victims from that of the architects of the policy. What is their political significance? Media hypes and story-telling fights. Military might and human rights. Distortions and anomalies.

And so on. And yet, knowing ourselves as a nation, we have to be reminded: short sightedness comes from short memories. This policy to be reconstructed was worked out to shore up the sagging image of the national leadership using people in Mindanao as pawns in the political game. However, in our Islamic discourse, there was a paradoxical realism in that it provided images of the hostility of heavy-handed men in government toward the Muslim community. Call it *Islamphobia*. The defilement of mosques particularly has left indelible imprints. The feasting on lechon and liquor - all of them abominable *naguish* items—at Camp Abubakar where the *salah* (prayer) is regularly performed by the *ummah* (community) was an act of *najasa* (defilement) on the part of the head of the state, together with his military officers and men (women too). This precipitated declaration of a *jihad* and *hijra*. Surely, one of the most fundamental points communicated by international law, I recall to mind, is this: A state that protects human rights is a more secure state than otherwise—at least from internal threats.

Our overall re-evaluation indicates that over a few decades, as the early 1970s to 1980s and 1990s, the religious movements as a collective human agency of political and social change have revitalized in the Muslim world. The formation of an Islamic-based national state in Indonesia after independence was truncated, but recent economic stagnation and political crisis revived the political drive to transform the roles of Islamist-intellectuals in public life. The debate lies here: By what signs can the possibility of Islamic governance arise in the region? Transitional impacts such as the electoral victory of leaders of Muhammadiyah and Nadhlatul Ulama in Indonesia; the strong electoral showing of Partai Agama Islam in Malaysia; or even the demand for establishment of an Islamic state in Mindanao, not to mention Acheh, empower Islamic conceptions of politics and social life.

Peace-Building in Mindanao: A Partnership Between Government and Civil Society

ALMA R. EVANGELISTA

ALMA R. EVANGELISTA

Executive Director
Office of the Presidential Adviser on the Peace Process

Ms. Evangelista previously served as Undersecretary at the Office of the Presidential Adviser on the Peace Process. In this capacity, she supervised technical assistance for the implementation of the national comprehensive peace process. She is the Chairperson of the Technical Committee assisting the Government Peace Panel engaged in formal peace negotiations with the Moro Islamic Liberation Front (MILF). She also chaired the Inter-agency Committee tasked with the development and implementation of a comprehensive program for children involved in armed conflict.

Ms. Evangelista has extensive experience in government policy formulation, particularly in the planning and implementation of the national comprehensive peace process that includes peace negotiations with rebel groups, peace education and advocacy, and area-based peace and development programs. She has addressed various social development concerns by focusing on peace and conflict-resolution, which include programs that promote the culture of peace in the Philippines.

It is a privilege to speak before this group of peace builders and peace advocates this afternoon. It is always heartwarming to be among men and women who are interested in peace-building and the peaceful resolution of armed conflict, and all the more so at this time of renewal and opportunity for building peace in Mindanao as well as the entire nation.

Amina Rasul approached me some weeks ago and asked me to participate in this worthy undertaking by speaking on government's peace negotiation efforts in Mindanao. I told her however that I would like to depart from the usual expectations from government at a time like this, which is to brief the audience on how it is faring along the peace negotiation arena. I will instead focus on citizens' participation in peace-building in Mindanao, the role of the peace constituency in promoting peace, and government's efforts to support and complement civil society peace initiatives.

When the peace process is mentioned, it is usually associated with peace talks with rebel groups, and the public watches for the conclusion—or collapse of the talks—measuring possibilities for peace against the pace and outcomes of the negotiations. Yet there is a need to build awareness of the larger context within which peace negotiations are conducted, and to appreciate the role of various sectors in the overall peace effort for Mindanao. The task of building peace must not be perceived solely in the light of discussions between two parties across a negotiating table, but as a collective effort involving a multiplicity of actors from the grassroots communities all the way up to the policy-making level. There is a remarkably strong and active peace constituency in Mindanao, which has been at the forefront of peace advocacy, peace education and the promotion of inter-cultural, inter-ethnic tolerance and dialogue. This same constituency can strongly influence the course of the peace negotiations, and has the potential for a direct facilitative role in the talks.

Allow me first to share some basic thoughts on conflict and peace, which shall provide the context within which I shall discuss citizens' peace-building in Mindanao.

The noted peace researcher Johan Gating holds that peace may be manifested on two levels: "negative peace" and "positive peace." Negative peace is the condition where the violent, physical manifestations of conflict —such as war—are removed. It is a fragile, uncertain peace anchored on a cessation of hostilities or a ceasefire. Positive peace, on the other hand, refers to a condition where the roots of conflict—its structural causes such as social inequity, injustice and poverty—are addressed, towards establishing a just and enduring peace. Peace, therefore, does not simply mean the absence of conflict. It means that various interests are adequately represented in the overall scheme of governance and development, and that grievances and differences are resolved through means that are commonly defined and accepted. Peace is not a matter of military action or law enforcement simply intended to achieve stability or public safety. Beyond this, it means the establishment of stable democratic institutions and an enabling environment for the people to participate in governance and to interact under conditions of fairness, mutual respect and social justice. Peace requires a transformation process that involves not just a settlement across the negotiating table, but a deliberate effort to address the roots of conflict and unrest. It is thus a continuing holistic process that requires the participation of all sectors. This perspective is clearly articulated in the three guiding principles which have governed the government's comprehensive peace process, which was formulated based on nationwide public consultations held by the National Unification Commission (NUC) in 1993. These three principles are:

One, the peace process should be community-based and should reflect the sentiments, values and principles important to all Filipinos. All Filipinos should define it not by the government or the different rebel groups alone, but as one community;

Two, the peace process must consistently strive to forge a just, equitable, humane and pluralistic society, where all individuals and groups are free to engage in peaceful competition for predominance of their political programs without fear, through the exercise of constitutional rights and liberties;

Three, the peace process must aim for the principled and peaceful resolution of armed conflict, with neither blame nor surrender, but with dignity for all concerned.

These three principles guide the implementation of the national comprehensive peace process, which is being pursued along "six paths to peace:"

First, the pursuit of social, economic and political reform to address the root causes of conflict;

Second, consensus-building and empowerment of the people for peace through various consultation processes and their participation in decision-making on issues that directly affect them;

Third, the negotiated settlement of armed conflict, or peace talks with armed rebel groups;

Fourth, programs for reconciliation, reintegration and rehabilitation of former combatants;

Fifth, conflict management and the protection of civilians caught in armed conflict; and

Sixth, building and nurturing a climate for a lasting peace.

These six paths are mutually reinforcing processes that must be pursued simultaneously. They constitute a holistic, comprehensive effort to achieve a durable, equitable and comprehensive stability for our nation.

Within the context of the three principles and the six paths to peace, therefore, our negotiations with rebel groups is not an independent process by itself, but part of a larger peace-building effort. The other five paths serve to reinforce and support the negotiation process, in the same manner that the negotiations provide support and enhancement to the other paths to peace.

This peace-building framework has been reaffirmed by the Arroyo administration through the issuance of Executive Order No. 3 shortly after the President's assumption to office. As you may all know, the reconstruction of the peace process is a top priority of the President. She has formed an all-civilian, all-Mindanao peace panel, and she has undertaken various confidence-building measures towards the resumption of the talks with the Moro Islamic Liberation Front (MILF). The MILF has shown some very encouraging responses towards this end, and we are optimistic that the talks will resume soon. As we prepare for the talks, however, it is imperative to involve the people and actively seek their inputs in the overall Mindanao peace agenda. The essence of peace-building, after all, lies in the citizens' active and continuing participation in defining and implementing this agenda. While the resumption of the peace negotiations are high on the government's priority peace concerns at this time, we must not lose sight of the role that civil society has played and will continue to play in the achievement of a just and enduring peace for Mindanao. Citizens' peace-building has been clearly manifested in bringing about peaceful change through EDSA I in 1986 and, again, through EDSA Dos just recently. On a more deliberate peace-building level, people participation was also clearly demonstrated in the formulation of the government's comprehensive peace process, through the nationwide consultations held in 1993 to examine the roots of conflict and to recommend ways to address them, resulting in the "six paths to peace" that today continue to provide the framework for the government's peace process.

Philippine social science and peace researchers led by Ed Garcia and Miriam Coronel-Ferrer have offered several categories of peace-building in the Philippines, which range from peace constituency-building, peace advocacy, networking, conflict reduction efforts, mediation and facilitation of negotiated settlements and peace research. Nowhere else in the country, except probably in the Cordilleras, has this range of civil society-initiated peace efforts been more clearly manifested than in Mindanao.

Allow me at this point to mention some of the Mindanao constituency's peace-building initiatives, some of which government has had the privilege to support or participate in.

Government, through our office, has actively engaged Mindanao's peace-building constituency in a partnership consisting of various non-governmental organizations, people's organizations, religious groups, schools, and local government units, aimed at building and nurturing a culture of peace among all the sectors in the region.

Kalinaw-Mindanaw

The partnership for the promotion of peace in Mindanao has been pursued to a significant degree within a loose organization known as "Kalinaw

Mindanaw." Historically, the idea of consolidating our peace partners into one network evolved from a series of meetings held in the early months of 1996, parallel with our efforts in finalizing the peace agreement between the Philippine government and the Moro National Liberation Front (MNLF). At that time, we wanted to address the imperative of establishing a more relevant and culturally sensitive educational system through the integration of peace education in the curriculum, and through networking with local government units and NGOs in advancing peace education. In July of the same year, our office co-convened a peace education workshop in Cagayan de Oro City, participated in by our peace partners. Out of this workshop was born the "Kalinaw Mindanaw."

Today, Kalinaw Mindanao consists of organizations and agencies that are extensively involved in peace building, peace education and advocacy, especially in areas heavily affected by armed conflict. This includes the Notre Dame University in Cotabato city, which is acknowledged to be the pioneer in peace education in the Philippines, the Mindanao State University Iligan Institute of Technology (MSU-IIT), and Notre Dame of Jolo College in Jolo, Sulu, all of which have established peace centers actively engaged in peace education and advocacy. Other schools include MSU Marawi and MSU Maguindanao, St. Therese College in Tandag, Surigao del Sur, and St. Vincent's Academy in Kauswagan, Lanao del Norte, among others.

The NGO members of Kalinaw Mindanaw include the Zamboanga Norte Center for Social Concerns and Development (ZNCSCD), an organization in Dipolog City which is active in community development work and in dealing with development aggression issues; the Silsilah Dialogue Movement, an institution in Zamboanga City which promotes inter-religious dialogue; and the Mindanao Support and Communication Center for Agrarian Reform and Rural Development (MINCARRD) based in Cagayan de Oro City, which pursues initiatives in line with peace and development, environmental protection and agrarian reform and cooperative promotion for Mindanao civil society groups. MINCARRD also serves as the secretariat of the Kalinaw Mindanaw.

Church workers and lay persons from various dioceses, vicariates and social action centers, as well as indigenous people's organizations, are also heavily represented in Kalinaw Mindanaw.

Over the past four years, the network has conducted several culture-of-peace seminar-workshops and trainors' training using the "Panagtagbo sa Kalinaw," a basic orientation manual designed specifically for the promotion of a tri-people culture of peace in Mindanao communities. Kalinaw Mindanaw encourages citizens to face the conflict situation in the region with a clear understanding of its historical roots, to see conflict as an opportunity for growth and transformation and to actively participate as agents of peace in their communities.

Promoting a culture of peace through dialogue: the Bishops-Ulama Forum

Civil society's participation in peace-building in Mindanao is also manifested in the Bishops-Ulama Forum (BUF), a unique partnership of Christian and Muslim religious leaders, with the participation of indigenous people's leaders, for the promotion of peace and tolerance through dialogue. The forum, through its continuing dialogue process since 1996, has provided input and advice to both government and rebel groups towards collectively building peace in Mindanao, towards building citizens' awareness and involvement in peace-building. The Bishops-Ulama Forum spearheads the annual celebration of the Mindanao Week of Peace in the last week of November. As an interfaith organization, it also has the potential to assume a facilitative role in the conduct of the GRP-MILF peace negotiations.

Community-initiated peace zones

I must also mention grassroots-based efforts to build peace in Mindanao by citing the community-initiated peace zones in Tulunan, North Cotabato. These are communities caught in the crossfire in the conflict between the Armed Forces of the Philippines and the New People's Army (AFP-NPA) in the late 1980s and early 1990s that took the bold step of declaring themselves armed conflict-free zones, and negotiated their own peaceful environment through dialogues with the AFP and the NPA. Although the true character of the zones has been questioned, the experience of the communities have largely demonstrated the power of grassroots peace constituency-building in bringing about peaceful change.

Conclusion

This is a time of great opportunity for peace-building in Mindanao. The reconstruction of the peace process remains paramount in the agenda of the Arroyo administration. As we anticipate the resumption of talks with the MILF, we must also undertake parallel efforts to strengthen and enhance civil society's participation in the comprehensive peace process. Even as we support and promote people's peace-building initiatives, we must also ensure that their voices are heard and that they input significantly to the peace negotiations.

Peace negotiations are basically creative processes. Parties start out with defined objectives and their own views as to the outcomes they want, but as the talks move forward, it often becomes clearer that both sides do not always get one hundred percent of what they want. This underscores the need to seek out the participation of civil society in the negotiations.

Intrinsic to the negotiation process must be an effective mechanism of consultation with the people. The items of negotiation must be constantly validated by the political will, and broad consultations from the top echelons to the grassroots must be held so that all are participants in any resulting agreements. Consultation is an effective tool for strengthening the political perimeters of the negotiations. Connected with this must be an effective communication flow. Good channels of communication—even the small and informal—with counterparts, facilitators, participants, external publics and constituencies are pivotal to the success of any negotiation.

There are crucial challenges to peace-building in Mindanao today. The question of expanding the area of autonomy in Muslim Mindanao must be decided upon in a plebiscite. We are also set to decide on a new set of local leaders. We are about to embark on renewed negotiations with the MILF. We must see these challenges as opportunities to build peace, to constructively transform conditions of conflict to a just and enduring peace. The government and civil society must work hand in hand to strengthen people's participation in the peace process, involving them in dialogue, consensus-building, peace education and advocacy and conflict management and resolution in their own communities, as well as helping to promote understanding of the common peace values and bases that make a culture of peace possible among the tri-people of Mindanao.

Assessment of Government Negotiations and Modes of Conflict Resolution

AMBASSADOR ALUNAN GLANG

Ambassador Alunan Glang

Consultant, MILF Peace Panel

Ambassador Glang graduated with a Doctorate Degree in History and Journalism at the Cairo University in Cairo, Egypt. He also obtained his Masteral Degree in History and Journalism at the same university. From 1989 to 1992 Amb. Glang was the Chief of Mission, Class 1, Ambassador Extraordinary and Plenipotentiary of the State of Kuwait.

He was the recipient of the "Awards of Recognition" presented by the Commission on National Integration (CNI) for his contribution to the advancement of the cultural communities in the field of historical writings.

What in a nutshell is the Moro Problem? Dr. Najeed M. Saleeby in a book published in 1905 entitled, "Studies in Moro History, Law, and Religion" defined for us this problem, thus:

> "By Moro problem is meant that method or form of administration by which the Moro and other non-Christians who are living among them can be governed to their best interest and welfare in the most peaceful way possible, and can at the same time be provided with appropriate measures for their gradual achievement in culture and civilization, so that in the course of reasonable time they can be admitted into the general government of the Philippines Islands as a member of a republican organization."
>
> "The Moros are a law-abiding people, provided, however, they feel that the government that rules them is their own. They do not regard the present government as their own. They look upon it as something that has been imposed upon them. They have the feeling of being conquered, and proud and resentful, they struggle for freedom. They have never felt themselves a part of the Philippine Islands or of the Philippine Government and until they are made to feel this, resentment and resistance will continue."

In the book, "Muslim Secession Or Integration," Prof. Alunan C. Glang, a Muslim contemporary writer on the problem earlier defined by Dr. Saleeby, points out that whatever ways and means the government may institute to win over the Muslims will not succeed unless the religious leaders and Muslim masses lend their support through their traditional leaders, namely the datus. This fact is partly due to the pervasive influence that the datus had for centuries exercised on the Muslim thinking and social pattern. "Like all other cultural societies," Delegate Michael O. Mastura points, out "the Muslim Filipinos have a mechanism for compelling the behavior of its members. In one sense, the datuship is a form of social control, which, if properly utilized as a mechanism to arrest antipathy towards the government, can be a crucial factor in the take-off process. The datu, as it were, still holds the authority to bind and influence to direct action. Since it takes much longer to change many minds than to change a few and the datus who, though fewer in number, make up for the many, we might as well work on the datus."

There are those who argue that the datuship is antiquated and feudalistic, and, therefore, must be abolished. There is here a need to make a distinction between the datuship as an institution and the datu who exercises the binding authority in feudalistic terms. The datuship, as a system, is founded on the rule of Islam. What is meant here in effect is that the Moro masses should obey the rule of a datu only as long as it does not contravene the Holy Koran and the Sunna of the Prophet Muhammad. The Holy Qur'an is the guiding principle in the exercise, not independence of opinion: "O you who believe! Obey Allah and obey the Messenger and those in authority from among you; then if you quarrel about anything, refer it to Allah and the Messenger."

Unfortunately, however, in recent years the great majority of Moro datus not only have misled their "sacup" (traditional area of influence) but have even exploited them. In a weekly column entitled, "IMAMAN KANO!" (Bewarel in Maguindanao), this writer wrote on December 19, 1970, "The Muslims could repel this idea of national unity by liberating themselves from the corrupt, incompetent, dynastic, oppressive, opprobrious, and myopic leadership foisted upon them by their so called datus. And above all, the Muslims could also effect national unity by developing their potentials as a people through the faith that has given their identity—in Islam. This unity, too, may start, on the other hand, with our Christian brothers and all men of goodwill if they open their hearts wide to the message of justice and charity which Jesus Christ, the Prince of Peace, brought to the world."

The socio-economic progress of Moro society leaves much to be desired. The Moro datu owes it to himself and to the Moros to be more responsive to change. The Moros should not content themselves with living on the glory of the past alone. This is an age of change and the Moros should aim to achieve a sense of identity. Feudalism must go if the Muslim sector of this country is to move forward to take their place side by side with their Christian brothers. The vacuum created by the crisis in Muslim leadership must be filled by selfless and dedicated young Muslim men and women who are atuned to the changing times and conditions in the world around us today, particularly in the islands of Mindanao and Sulu.

We have at length extrapolated from the original position of Dr. Saleeby that "modernizing reforms could and should be instituted through the traditional leaders and structure of Muslim society, principally the datuship," in order to determine the realities and illusions in the present Moro conflict. The past of the Moro conflict has no nutshell definition. This is one of the realities in the conflict.

Dr. Jerome D. Frank, Professor of Psychiatry at the John Hopkins has written that psychologically, the crucial part of the "reality world" of any group is its belief about the meaning of existence. Human beings, he says, shield themselves from the unendurable realization that individual life is fleeting and insignificant by embracing an ideology or religion which links their lives to some larger and more enduring purpose. This ideology is vital to their existence; it gives meaning to their lives. Any threat to this ideology, any demand that it be surrendered, is intolerable. "It would represent a kind of psychological death harder to contemplate than biological death."

The main thesis of this paper is that in the Moro conflict in the South of the Philippines, the Moros (as Muslim Filipinos are popularly called) have been, and still are, threatened with psychological death. This is another reality, which is the main cause of the present conflict. A series of events, both gloomy and dark, have conspired to convince the Moro mind that there is a government program designed "to kill him alive" (in Maguindanao, this would be something like this: "*bpag-imatayan sa di pabpulogon*"). This is one form or a manifestation of this psychological death process. What are these events that the Moros interpret as part of an overall scheme intended to eliminate his Moro identity or, to put it correctly, his identity in Islam?

The conflict in Muslim Mindanao and Sulu should be understood not in terms either of elimination or duality but in terms of a synthesis. Thus, this movement towards Moro irredentism and the renaissance in Muslim society should be reconciled as the expression of the Muslim's unending search for national identity.

In the words of a noted Muslim scholar, Dr. Cesar Adib Majul, "national community is believed to be conducive to individual happiness and what is conceived to constitute order in society or social well-being". Thus, the elements of national identity might include expectations that transcend goals pertaining to mere security and modernization. They may include values properly classifiable under the category of "spiritual culture." Clearly, commitment to a national community is equivalent to identification with its values. It is the determination of such values that may bring about a contest between different institutions or cultural groups in society.

One can easily see that the ferment beneath the conflict in Muslim Mindanao and Sulu is rooted deeply in this search for national identity. Like the racial monitory in William Harvard's *The New Minds of the South,* the Muslim today moves between the extremes of a quest for identity in Islam and a sense of belonging to the national community. Clearly, the insurgents in Mindanao and Sulu can no longer reconcile the two extremes, as repeatedly indicated in their published documents called *TANTAWAN.* The rebels of Muslim Mindanao have already said in no uncertain terms what they want, a crusade to "ASSERT" their identity as a people in the family of nations. With a keen perception of the trend of events during the last few months in the Muslim areas in the country and with a deep insight into the social forces that make modern history, it is now possible to discern the movement of Muslim thinking as they seek to establish or rather to "assert" this national identity, their right to respect, freedom, and national self-development. The first tangible manifestation of this extreme quest for identity in Islam is strong affinity to the Muslim world, even transcending the barriers of the national loyalty. In recent months, considerable attention has been drawn to the Muslim conflict in the South by the leaders of the Muslim world (e.g. Saudi Arabia, Kuwait, Libya, Senegal, Somalia, and others). What could have accounted for this show of concern with the plight of the Moros? It is not difficult to find out why this must be so. The brotherhood of the Muslim peoples the world over, is a Koranic injunction. A Muslim reads in the Holy Koran (Books of books of the Muslims) this verse: "All Muslims are as one body. If a man complaineth of pain in his head, his whole body feeleth the pain, and if his eye pains his whole body feeleth the pain." The difficulties, the sufferings and tribulations of the Tausogs and Maguindanaon are pains in the whole body of the Muslim faithful from the "shores of the Atlantic even into the walls of China".

Fight, even unto death, for the honor and dignity of the Muslims. Something must be done to stop these abuses; otherwise, there will be no end to the tragedy. In the words of Moslimen Sema, a ranking rebel leader, "without respect and dignity given to the Muslim as a people, this promise of socio-economic development is useless." Elaborating on this, Mr. Sema pointed out that the government may build golden bridges to span to rivers of Mindanao and Sulu, cement roads to criss-cross their forest and plains, but what good are these roads and bridges freely because of their being Muslims.

The ultimate reality would be that the problem is far from being solved and that the backbone of the insurgency has not been broken, in fact, it has not even been scratched. The application of solutions, other than those that will emerge out of goodwill and understanding of the recognition of the fact that the Muslim intends to preserve his identity in Islam, will never solve this conflict.

The GRP-MNLF Peace Talks and the 1996 Peace Agreement

ASST. SECRETARY ABRAHAM S. IRIBANI

ABRAHAM S. IRIBANI
Asst. Secretary, DILG

Asec. Abraham S. Iribani, holds a Masters Degree in National Security Administration from the National Defense College of the Philippines (NDCP), and a Master's Degree in Business Administration from the Ateneo de Zamboanga University. He also received his undergraduate degree in Economics from the Ateneo de Zamboanga.

He is currently Assistant Secretary at the Department of Interior and Local Government. Prior to joining DILG, Asec. Iribani was a a consultant and Project Director of the Mindanao Challenge Research Program at the NDCP and served for twenty years at the Philippine Amanah Bank. Lt. Col Iribani received his AFP appointment from the Philippine Army Reserve Force in December of 2000.

Introduction

The purpose of writing this paper is to present a first-hand account and an analysis of the 1992-1996 GRP-MNLF Peace Talks from this writer's perspective as an active participant. This is an account of how the GRP and the MNLF with the active participation of the Organization of Islamic Conference (OIC) successfully negotiated a peace formula for the final resolution of the Mindanao conflict. This formula is now officially known as the GRP-MNLF Final Peace Agreement. It is considered "in many ways, a milestone" as "all previous attempts to negotiate an end to the 24 years of civil war - in which over 120,000 people died - had failed to define a sustainable settlement."[1]

Indeed, this episode of peacemaking in the country's contemporary history is believed to have produced "valuable lessons with possibly some applicability elsewhere,"[2] said then President Suharto of Indonesia. No less than former President Ramos came up with a book[3] about it (with emphasis on 'Lessons Learned') but "there is still so much that remains to be drawn to get the whole story of the GRP-MNLF peace process."[4] Ramos cautioned though that "the root causes of the problems that led to these decades of conflict in Mindanao will not go away with this Agreement. Left unattended, they can worsen and undo much of the confidence and optimism created by the goodwill between us."[5]

This is precisely the objective of writing this paper: not to leave the peace document unattended, but to study it, review the events surrounding it, draw important lessons from it, encourage a review of its implementation and the attendant problems encountered, and seek answers to important questions which if left unanswered may put serious doubts to the integrity of the agreement. But the opinions and views expressed in this paper, however, are solely that of this writer and do not necessarily represent the official views of the MNLF, the OIC and the GRP whose top officials were the principal characters in the negotiations.

The various questions now being raised on the Peace Agreement "cannot just be answered by a dry account of positions taken and agreements reached."[6] The four years of negotiations were filled with occasions of hard bargaining across the negotiating table. On several instances, the negotiations were affected and influenced by the occurrence of certain events or the involvement of certain people that have special or personal relations with key members of the negotiating party.

Historical Background

The 1992-1996 GRP-MNLF Negotiation was the last of a series of negotiations initiated by the Philippine Government following the 1974 Kuala Lumpur OIC Resolution that called for a negotiated political settlement to the Mindanao conflict "within the framework of the national sovereignty and territorial integrity of the Philippines."[7] The conflict that erupted into a full scale war a couple of months after the declaration of Martial Law in September 1972 posed as the most serious threat to national security since the country's independence in 1946. In the words of now Retired General Fortunato Abat (Commander of AFP's Central Mindanao Command, 1973-1976), "the continued escalation of unrest in Central Mindanao reached national security proportions that required the... AFP to react with a massive response to check the full grown threat to the nation's sovereignty and territorial integrity."[8] But the conflict escalated despite government's massive military response and reached its peak when the town of Jolo became the scene of bloody fighting between government and MNLF forces in February 1974.

The OIC Meeting (June 1974) that issued the so-called Kuala Lumpur resolution[9] paved the way for the start of the negotiations under the auspices of the OIC which resulted in the signing of what is now known as the Tripoli Agreement in Tripoli, Libya on December 23, 1976 . This agreement called for the establishment of autonomy in the 13 provinces in Southern Philippines. A Ceasefire Agreement was also signed in Zamboanga City on January 20, 1977. But further meetings and contacts including direct exchange of cables between the Heads of States of Libya and the Philippine Government to complete the provisions for the implementation of the agreement bogged down in April 1977.

Nevertheless, then President Marcos proceeded with what he believed was the correct implementation of the Tripoli Agreement.[10] Using his Martial Law powers, he declared Autonomy in southern Philippines".[11] He conducted a plebiscite in the 13 Provinces covered by the Tripoli Agreement on April 17, 1977 and with the results of the plebiscite on hand, he created the Autonomous Regions IX and XII.[12] Regional elections were held in 1979. Muslim leaders including former MNLF commanders who "surrendered" to the government were elected and appointed to several key positions in the Regional Governments.

Expectedly, the MNLF rejected Marcos' 'unilateral' implementation of the Tripoli Agreement and so did the OIC. To them it was a violation of the 'letter and spirit' of the Agreement because it divided the Muslims. The Agreement called for ONE REGION AUTONOMY and not two regions. The MNLF leadership then wanted to preserve what they believed was the political unity of the Muslim leadership.

The 1977 Peace Talks finally collapsed following the fatal ambush of Brig. Gen. Bautista and over 30 of his men in Sulu. Accordingly, "the Marcos government used this incident to repudiate the ceasefire altogether and announced the resumption of full-scale war as air, naval, and ground units of the AFP launched three major assaults against the MNLF near Zamboanga City."[13]

The collapse of the talks led to what many called the crisis in the MNLF leadership.[14] Accordingly, then MNLF Vice Chairman, Ustadz Salamat Hashim, "acquiescing to the popular clamor of the leaders in the field, executed the 'Instrument of Takeover' in December 1977." That was an attempt to take over the chairmanship of the MNLF from Misuari. Ustadz Salamat sent his "Instrument" to the OIC to declare the existence of the New MNLF Leadership.[15] But the OIC continued to recognize the leadership of Misuari in the MNLF. In fact, "following the 1977 fiasco, the MNLF (under Misuari) was accepted in Tripoli, Libya during the 8th ICFM, as an observer. After the persistent refusal of the Philippine government to comply with the OIC's repeated calls for peace talks and for full implementation of the Tripoli

Agreement, the MNLF status was enhanced from a mere "legitimate representative" to that of a "sole legitimate representative" of the Bangsamoro people. This occurred in Sana'a, the capital of the Republic of Yemen, on the occasion of the 15th ICFM in 1984.[16] In the same year, "the Central Committee of the New MNLF Leadership... officially declared itself a separate organization called the Moro Islamic Liberation Front... with Islam as its official ideology."[17]

In 1986, the newly installed Aquino Government resumed contacts with the MNLF. President Aquino even met with Chairman Misuari in a Carmelite Convent in Jolo, Sulu on September 5, 1986. That historic meeting was followed by the GRP-MNLF Talks witnessed by the OIC Secretary General in Jeddah, Saudi Arabia in January 1987 which produced the so-called Jeddah Accord. But the 90-day Technical Committee Meetings that followed in the country between the GRP and MNLF representatives without the participation of the OIC ended in an impasse in May. The talks collapsed in July 1987 but the two parties made commitments to honor the agreement on the Cessation of Hostilities signed in September 1986.

The Ramos Peace Initiatives

The Ramos Administration that assumed office in June 1992 again initiated the resumption of peace talks with the MNLF. But it was not an easy job for the then newly installed Ramos Government. In fact, not many people believed that the Ramos peace initiatives would succeed. Ramos would admit later that "in the beginning and up to the final days of the negotiations, the quest seemed like a 'Mission Impossible'..."[18] Even the MNLF leadership was initially doubtful. "When we embarked on our lonely road to peace", the MNLF Chairman said, "we had no illusions about the difficulties that lay ahead... owing to our tragic experiences during the previous administrations."[19] Ramos could not be any different, the MNLF thought, because of his past involvement in the conflict. But Ramos would declare later that "as events unfolded, however, skepticism turned to hope and later, hope turned to confidence."[20]

The initial contacts developed into what became the 1992-1996 GRP-MNLF Peace Talks. And unlike the failed 1986-1987 Talks of President Aquino, the Ramos peace process was conducted with the active participation of the Secretary General of the OIC and the OIC Ministerial Committee of the Six headed by Indonesia with the active participation of Libya.

Stages of the Peace Talks

The Exploratory Period and the First Round of Formal Talks. After establishing contacts through the good offices of the OIC and the Libyan Embassy in Manila,[21] the First Exploratory Talks was held in Tripoli Libya from October 2-4, 1992. The parties signed the "Tripoli Statement of Understanding," where they agreed to "pursue formal talks towards a peaceful, honorable and dignified resolution of the conflict..."[22] With the formal assumption of Indonesia as Chairman of the OIC Ministerial Committee of Six,[23] the Second Exploratory Talks followed in Cipanas, West Java from 14 to 16 April, 1993. Among others, the parties agreed that "the agenda for the talks will focus on the modalities for the full implementation of the Tripoli Agreement in letter and spirit..."[24]

Then the **First Round of Formal Talks** followed in Jakarta, Indonesia from October 25 to November 7, 1993. The parties signed the 1993 Memorandum of Agreement, which among others contained the following:

1. Creation of the Joint Secretariat
2. Reactivation of the Mixed Committee
3. Creation of five (5) Support Committee and the Ad Hoc Working Group

The Committees were to hold meetings in the Philippines. In addition, the 1993 Interim Ceasefire Agreement was also signed and the Joint Ceasefire Committee to be headed by OIC representatives was created to oversee its implementation.

The First Mixed Committee Meeting and the Second Round of Formal Talks. The first Mixed Committee Meeting was held in Jolo, Sulu on December 20, 1993. This meeting was highlighted by the visit of the OIC Secretary General and other OIC and GRP officials headed by Ambassador Manuel Yan to the MNLF Headquarters in Timbangan, Indanan, Sulu to meet with MNLF Chairman Misuari. The Ad Hoc Working Group also met in Timbangan on December 28 while the five (5) Support Committees met in selected cities in Mindanao and Manila between January to April 1994. The second Mixed Committee meeting followed in Zamboanga City on April 4-5, 1994. The highlight of the meeting was the signing of the Ceasefire Guidelines and Ground rules.

The parties then came back to Jakarta for the **Second Round of Formal Talks** preceded by the **third Mixed Committee Meeting** from September 1-5, 1994. The product of the meeting was the Interim 1994 Agreement, which contained 37 consensus points. Additional agreements were also reached on the implementation of the Ceasefire Agreement, including the immediate dispatch of the OIC Observer Teams composed of Indonesian military officers.

The Fourth Mixed Committee meeting was held again in Zamboanga City from January 29 to 31. The meeting confirmed 31 additional consensus points on education and financial and economic systems.

The Fifth Mixed Committee meeting followed in Davao City from June 19-23, 1994. It was during this meeting that then Executive Secretary Ruben Torres met with Chairman Misuari. The meeting improved the level of mutual confidence between the two parties. It gave the GRP Panel enough confidence to present what they called the "two-track-approach" for consideration by the MNLF Panel. The MNLF, however, did not make any immediate reply but asked for time to conduct consultations. Nevertheless, the meeting came up with several consensus points including issues on Transitional Implementing Structures and Mechanisms (Provisional Government) and Shariah.

On July 19 then House Speaker Jose De Venecia, Jr. met with Chairman Misuari in Pagadian City. The Speaker informally presented certain proposals to the MNLF concerning possible political alliances, economic development programs and appointments of MNLF leaders or their recommendees in the national government. Then the **6th Mixed Committee** followed in General Santos City from July 26-28, 1995. Again, the GRP Panel reiterated their "two-track-approach" formula but the MNLF remained non-committal. Nevertheless, the MNLF Panel agreed to take up the GRP proposals in the MNLF Leadership meeting. But the MNLF meeting that followed in Jolo in the second week of August made a unanimous decision rejecting he GRP proposals.

The Special OIC Meeting in New York and the Third Round of Formal Talks. In the first week of October, the OIC Ministerial Committee of Six met at a special session in New York City and decided to invite the GRP and MNLF Panels separately for consultations. The MNLF Panel met with the OIC officials on October 25 in the Indonesian Consulate in New York City.[25] The GRP Panel even met earlier with the OIC officials also in New York City after coming from "warm, fruitful and constructive meetings"[26] with the Libyan leaders. These meetings led to the decision to push through with the Third Round of Formal Talks in Jakarta.

The Parties then, with renewed confidence as a result of the New York consultation meeting went back to Jakarta for the **Third Round of Formal Talks** from November 27 to December 1, 1995. The renewed confidence led to the signing of the **1995 Interim Agreement**, which contained 123 consensus points covering all the agenda items in the negotiations. By virtue of these accomplishments, it was the consensus of the participants that the "contours of the final peace agreement are irreversibly taking shape" as mandated by the 1976 Tripoli agreement.[27]

The 7th Mixed Committee Meeting then followed in Zamboanga City on March1, 1996. This was preceded by the so-called "Popular Consultation Meeting" with local executives of the Region. This consultation meeting was arranged by the GRP and the MNLF was invited together with the OIC representatives. But the "popular consultation" meeting did not help much in moving the talks forward. The 7th Mixed Committee Meeting failed to resolve the remaining contentious issues: the Provincial Government and the issue of plebiscite. President Ramos even admitted "the impasse remained; the difficulties seemed insurmountable. No fresh solutions were found."[28] The MNLF Panel left the negotiating table without any assurance of the positive outcome of the talks.

It was at this stage that the second meeting of Executive Secretary Torres and Chairman Misuari took place in Dubai, United Arab Emirates (May 39).[29] It was a critical meeting to save the talks from possible collapse. Ramos admitted later, "I tapped my Executive Secretary... to help in trying to find a meeting of minds with the MNLF."[30]

The Special OIC Meeting and the Final Round of Formal Talks.

Indonesia then initiated the holding of the Special OIC Ministerial Committee of Six meeting in Jakarta from June 2 to 4. Representatives from the GRP and MNLF Panels were invited to attend. The meeting resulted in the approval in principle of the GRP formula for the establishment of the Southern Philippines Council for Peace and Development (SPCPD) and the GRP offer for MNLF participation in the Autonomous Region in Muslim Mindanao election.

The 8th Mixed Committee meeting followed in Davao City from June 19-22, 1996. The meeting formalized the consensus reached in the previous OIC Special Meeting in Jakarta. But not all issues were resolved. A Special Working Groups was created and continued to discuss remaining unresolved issues on MNLF integration.

In the middle of July, Chairman Misuari agreed to register as a voter in Jolo and finally filed his candidacy for Regional Governor in the September 1996 ARMM election. On August 19, President Ramos and Chairman Misuari met in Malabang, Lanao del Sur. This meeting symbolized the finality of the Peace Talks and hastened the resolution of the remaining issues.

Then the parties finally made their "rendezvous with history"[31] for the **Fourth and Final Round of Formal Talks in Jakarta** from August 29 to 31. The parties signed the 1996 Interim Agreement and initiated the 1996 Final Peace Agreement in the Merdeka Palace in the presence of Indonesian President Suharto. The Final Peace Agreement was signed in Malacañang Palace on September 2, 1996 in the presence of President Ramos.

Analyses: The Negotiating Process and the Agenda of the Talks

Except in 1987[32], there was no direct negotiation between the GRP and the MNLF. The negotiations were always conducted with the active participation of the OIC. The involvement of the OIC is by way of "mediation" which is "a form of third-party intervention in a conflict. It is a mode of negotiation with the stated purpose of contributing to the conflict's abatement of resolution."[33]

Mediation differs from other forms of third-party intervention in conflicts because it is not based on the direct use of force and is not aimed at helping one of the participants win. The process involves the use of: **good offices** (helping the adversaries communicate, and **conciliation** (changing the parties' images of and attitudes toward one another).[34]

To accomplish its purposes, "mediation must be made acceptable to the adversaries in the conflict, who in turn must cooperate diplomatically with the intervener."[35] In addition, "mediation can suggest ideas for a compromise, and they can negotiate and bargain directly with the adversaries."[36] It is "basically a political process with no advance commitment from the parties to accept the mediator's ideas."[37]

The GRP-MNLF Peace Talks was basically a mediation process. Both parties accepted the participation of the OIC. Ramos, in fact, even before becoming President, already made contacts with Libya,[38] which was then believed to be MNLF's main backer in the OIC forum. Upon assuming the presidency, he outlined his programs in his first State-of-the-Nation Address where he announced a policy of peace and reconciliation with all armed groups, without any preconditions as to the status of their armed and political activities.[39] And in order to "find out what the other side's INTERESTS were,[40] " President Ramos initiated moves to contact the MNLF. One of such moves was this writer's first meeting with Congressmen Eduardo Ermita and Nur Jaafar,[41] which led to the holding of two Exploratory Talks.

On the other hand, the MNLF also had its own way of preparing for a possible resumption of talks with the GRP as always consistently called by the OIC in its various resolutions. They had a very clear agenda in mind: negotiations on autonomy based on the Tripoli Agreement, under the auspices of the OIC and in a mutually agreed foreign venue.

At this stage, communication was important and critical. "Conduct communication productively... communicate clearly, concisely and without exaggeration... knowing that not only the content is important, but also how it is said and when it is said."[42] The OIC's mediating role was still as "communicator... to act as conduit, opening contacts and carrying messages." "Tact, wording and sympathy... with accuracy and confidentiality are the necessary character traits of the mediator as communication."[43] This was the role initially played by the Libyan Ambassador to Manila, Rajab Azzarouq.[44]

In most successful negotiations, the manner of communication is done not in the form of **DEMAND, THREAT OR WARNING** but by way of an **OFFER.**[45] This is very clearly seen in the series of exchanges of formal communications between the GRP and the MNLF from start to finish, including even GRP communications in the form of aide memoires to concerned OIC countries.[46]

In addition to written communications, there were continued personal contacts particularly between the GRP and the MNLF and also with Ambassadors of concerned OIC countries. Later on, the OIC and the GRP also encouraged government officials to meet with Chairman Misuari which precisely achieved the effect of effectively "speaking and listening attentively[47] " and directly to him. Direct personal contact between parties is considered an important tool in negotiations called **PRESENTLY PERCEIVED CHOICE ANALYSIS**.[48] This tool allows the negotiators to identify who it is on the other side who really exercise the power to make the decision.[49]

The meetings held by selected officials of the Ramos Administration with Chairman Misuari (such as the Misuari-Ermita, Misuari-Torres and Misuari-De Venecia meetings) had the effect of this important and effective tool in negotiation, which led them "to understand the point of view" of the MNLF Chairman—"what factors will cause/influence him to make a decision."[50] Even in the early stages (1993) of the talks, President Ramos, more than any one else, was aware of the critical role of the MNLF Chairman in the outcome. He would write later, "the credibility of the peace process rested largely on our success in persuading Chairman Misuari himself to come to the negotiating table—since he was the recognized symbol of resistance in the region.[51]

Communication should not only be limited between and among the players in the negotiations but also with their respective constituencies. The matter of communicating to the public through the media or other forms of communication such as consultations became a very important issue in the talks. It in fact became an important feature in the negotiations so that after every end of the GRP-MNLF meeting, a Joint Press Statement is always prepared and issued to the media in order to avoid media controversy.

In addition, there were other sectors that demanded transparency in the talks. Some were motivated by certain political interests and the people in general were moved by the felt need for correct information on what was happening. The GRP responded to these demands through public consultations, dialogues, hearings and summits with all concerned leaders in addition to the official public pronouncements issued every now and then by concerned government agencies. The MNLF also held a series of consultations in various places in Mindanao, and even in Palawan. The

Diplomatic Community in Manila, particularly the Embassies of the United States and Japan were given briefings almost on a regular basis.

All of these actions added up to what Ambassador Yan referred to as the formation of a wide constituency of peace advocates in Mindanao and the country as a whole and in the global peace network as evidenced by the expression of support from the international community that poured in towards the end of 1995.

Another important element in negotiations is the matter of **AUTHORITY**. It is always helpful to check out early in the negotiations what is the extent of the other side's negotiating authority..."[52] In the GRP side, this is very clear—the Office of the President is the highest authority of the land. As regards the MNLF, its credentials were clear regardless of what the detractors would tell the President.[53] The MNLF is officially recognized by the OIC as the "sole and legitimate representative of the Bangsamoro People."[54] And since the GRP recognized the role of the OIC in the talks,[55] the GRP had to deal with the MNLF in resolving the autonomy issue in Southern Philippines. Even the MILF Chairman Salamat Hashim was reported to have said, "The MNLF actually negotiated for the *Bangsamoro* people."[56]

Former President Ramos cited "integrative negotiation," which he said is "the classic model of constructive, rather than adversarial encounters between parties not necessarily sitting across each other, but standing alongside each other in viewing the horizon of possibilities."[57]

This is also referred to as **PRINCIPLED NEGOTIATION**, "the paradigm of rationality and realistic problem solving" developed by the Harvard Negotiation Project and the Coverdale Organization.[58] It is a communication process in which both sides invest for mutual gain[59] and the participants are problem-solvers. This is what the Support Committees, the Mixed Committee and the Joint Ceasefire Committee did even in the level of the Formal Talks as always emphasized by Indonesian Foreign Minister Ali Alatas. And this problem-solving activity even went beyond the confines of the negotiating table. GRP and MNLF officials with the participation of Muslim Ambassadors[60] did not hesitate to sit together to come up with strategies on how to help solve peace and order situations like kidnappings and clan feuds in the area.

In addition, and as part of mutual confidence building measures, the MNLF and GRP Panels including the OIC mediators dined together, shared jokes with each other and became friends even after going through difficult and heated discussions on certain issues. President Ramos considered this as one of the "Lessons Learned" in the talks because "as friendships broadened and deepened, so did the will to push forward to win the peace."[61] Even the international community had observed that in those four years of negotiations, "both sides had overcome the antagonisms resulting from a lengthy war and the distrust arising from failures to implement previous agreements. Not only had the negotiators tackled these difficulties, but they also appeared to have become friends..."[62]

And as principled negotiation "is a paradigm of rationality," the parties "apply reason and are open to reasons; they yield to principle and not to pressure."[63] In the course of the GRP-MNLF talks, there were several instances when certain issues became intractable but as one party persisted with logical arguments, the other party yields. As the GRP showed flexibility by way of trying to "explore the constitutional universe," it finally came up with certain options that developed into what is now the SPCPD formula.

The MNLF also showed flexibility in the matter of the establishment of the Provisional Government, the most contentious issue in the talks. Because in principled negotiations, the parties "invent options for mutual gain, develop multiple options to choose from"[64] (like the GRP "two track" approach).

Based on the **HOWARD RAIFFA'S CONCEPT OF NEGOTIATION**[65] this writer believes that the negotiators, including the mediators/facilitators from the OIC fall under the category of **COOPERATIVE PARTNERS**. They recognized that both parties have different *interests* and also some common ones. The original position of the MNLF was complete independence[66] but it was scaled down to autonomy when they agreed to sign the 1976 Tripoli Agreement. Beneath this autonomy formula lies the core value of the MNLF struggle: the preservation of Islamic culture and tradition.

From the very beginning, President Ramos already recognized these *interests* of the other side as the GRP "approach was based on the assumption that all positions and courses of action being contemplated by the Government would be consistent with Islamic values."[67] On the other hand, the MNLF was cautious and sometimes intractable in the beginning refusing even to consider as part of the agenda any reference to the ARMM and other related implementations claimed by the Government to be in accord with the Tripoli Agreement. On many occasions, the MNLF declared its non-recognition of Philippine laws and Constitution. Later on, the MNLF allowed the GRP to take all the necessary constitutional processes as long as the Tripoli Agreement is implemented in letter and spirit. In the final phase, no less than the MNLF Chairman took the radical step of accepting the GRP offer to run as candidate for ARMM Governor in the 1996 regional elections paving the way for a political compromise that led to the signing of the Agreement.

But reaching this stage in the negotiation was not easy. **This was in fact the most crucial moment in the OIC mediation process.** In 1976, it was Libya through the "good office" of the OIC, who assumed the roled of "formulator" and came up with the autonomy formula. This time, the GRP, having formulated a proposal (the two-track approach) rested their case with the OIC. The MNLF did the same. Then Indonesia took the role of manipulator by "using its power to bring the parties to an agreement, pushing and pulling them away from the conflict into resolution"[68] (as when Indonesia initiated the holding of the Special OIC Meeting in Jakarta in June 1996).

The OIC then used its leverage. It had a "persuasive power" over the MNLF as seen earlier when they "persuaded" the MNLF to scale down their demand from independence to autonomy in 1976. The OIC's "persuasive power" was also used to pressure the GRP since 1974 to reach a negotiated political settlement with the MNLF. It came in the form of various OIC resolutions, OIC visits to the country including even unconfirmed reports of arms supplies to the MNLF by some OIC member states. This time, Indonesia, as Chair of the OIC Ministerial Committee of the Six, played its role effectively. Libya also continued its usual role. Chairman Misuari was in Libya in the middle of May (1996). It took the Libyan leaders 10 days to present to him the new GRP formula.[69]

This "persuasive power" of the OIC came with what Zartman and Touval also called "side payment". It was addressed to both parties in the form of "guarantees or financial aid in accomplishing changes required by the agreement." This was made very clear by the OIC from the very start of the talks. The "side payment" would make the agreement more attractive to both parties.

There was also one important element in the Ramos Peace Initiatives that was close to the heart, the core value of the MNLF and the Muslims. That was the Ramos declaration "to seek a peaceful resolution of armed conflict, with neither blame nor surrender, but with dignity for all."[70] Even the OIC officials kept invoking this principle in their official pronouncements as being consistent with the worldwide call for peace. "This is the PEACE OF THE BRAVE," declared Palestinian Leader Yasser Arafat after signing the Joint Israeli-Palestinian Declaration of Principles (DOP) in Washington, D.C. in the presence of U.S. President Bill Clinton. As Muslims, the OIC and MNLF leaders were guided by God's injunctions in the Qur'an which says: "*But if the enemy inclines towards peace, do (thou) also incline towards peace and trust in God.*" (Q VIII:61).

Consistent with this policy, the issue of "demobilizing" or "disarming" or surrender with the issuance of amnesty (as in the time of the late President Marcos) was never in the agenda of the talks because Ramos then believed that such "issue struck deeply into the honor and prestige of the other party."[71]

Ramos also mentioned "legitimacy and ethical conduct" in the negotiations as one of the lessons learned. "There is no substitute for candor and straightforwardness brought forward with courtesy, politeness and tact - untainted with personal, bigoted or condescending undertones. These latter qualities were abundant in both the GRP and MNLF Panles and infused the negotiation with greater trust and security."[72] Despite the occurrence of some incidents that threatened to scuttle the talks, such as the Ipil Raid in April 1995 and the movement of AFP troops in certain areas, no one from both parties ever got close to applying the principle of BRINKMANSHIP. This principle was made popular, some decades back, by a top U.S. official who advocated going back to the "brink of war" as a negotiating tactic.[73] The MNLF remained faithful to its commitment to "GIVE PEACE A MAXIMUM CHANCE."

The Agenda of the Talks

The MNLF and the OIC held on to the subject areas earlier defined in the Tripoli Agreement. These subject areas became the agenda of the talks with certain additions from the GRP in the form of an innovative formula at some stages of the talks. For a quick review on this subject, it should be helpful for us to look at it from a schematic presentation as follows:

The factors that contributed to the success of the negotiation including the difficulties/problems encountered and the remedies applied can be presented using a Schematic Success Analysis Format[76] as follows:

Table 1: Schematic Overview of the Agenda of the GRP-MNLF Peace Negotiations, (1992-1996) and the Results as Embodied in the 1996 Peace Agreement

AGENDA 1976 Tripoli Agreement	RESULTS 1996 Peace Agreement	REMARKS
Establishment of Autonomy (Article 1)	Autonomy to be established by phases: (Para 1-4): Transition Period: Phase 1	
Area: 13 Provinces and all cities and villages situated therein (Article II)	Establishment of SZOPAD covering 14 Provinces and 9 Cities (focus of intensive peace and development efforts for 3 years)	GRP established SZOPAD by Executive Order (October 1996)
Set up the Provincial Government (Article III Para 15)	Establishment of SPCPD	GRP created SPCPD by Executive Order (October 1996) with MNLF as Chairman; MNLF Chairman elected ARMM Governor (September 1996)
	Joining of MNLF elements with AFP and PNP (7,500 total force)	5,500 MNLF men integrated into AFP (85% of the agreed total) and 1,000 men into PNP members with last batch of 500 still being processed.[1]

AGENDA 1976 Tripoli Agreement	RESULTS 1996 Peace Agreement	REMARKS
Constitutional Process (Article III, Para 16)	A bill to be initiated in Congress (1996-1997) with approval including plebiscite expected in 2 years (1998) Amendment or repeal of ARMM law, through Congressional action, subject to approval by the people in a plebiscite to determine its establishment and the area. Phase 2: Implementation of the remaining provisions after the new Autonomy Law is enacted in Congress and approved in a plebiscite. These provisions shall be recommended by the GRP to Congress for incorporation in the new law	GRP initiated filing of the Bill in 1997. The 10th Congress was unable to pass it. GRP Administration changed in 1998. Bill still pending in both Houses of Congress but certified urgent by President Estrada[2] Bicameral Committee came up with consolidated version in January - February 2001 for signature by the President. There is no confirmation on whether the law been signed by the President Macapagal until now.
Article III:		
Para. 3: Shariah	Para. 152: Establishment of Shariah Courts	To be implemented in Phase 2 (1 provision)
Para. 4: Education	Paras. 94 to 125: Education	To be implemented in Phase 2 (32 Provisions)
Para. 5: Administrative System	Para. 62: Administrative system	To be implemented in Phase 2 (1 Provision)
Para. 6: Economic & Financial system	Paras. 126-151: Economic & Financial Systems, Mines and Minerals	To be implemented in Phase 2 (26 Provisions)
Para. 7: Representation & Participation in National Government	Paras. 63-72: Representation and Participation in the National Government and all organs of the State.	To be implemented in Phase 2 (10 Provisions)

AGENDA 1976 Tripoli Agreement	RESULTS 1996 Peace Agreement	REMARKS
Para. 8: Special Regional Security Forces	Paras. 73-93: Establishment of the Special Regional Security Force for the Autonomous Region	To be implemented in Phase 2 (21 Provisions)
Para. 9: Legislative Assembly and Executive Council	Paras. 21-22: Executive Council Para 23-61: Legislative Assembly	To be implemented in Phase 2 (2 Provisions)
Para. 10: Mines and Mineral Resources	Included in the Provisions under Economic & Financial System Paras 126-151	To be implemented in Phase 2 (39 Provisions)
Para. 11: Mixed Committee	Reactivated during the First Formal Talks and continued its work until the signing of the Agreement	Complied with and implemented during the Negotiations
Para. 12 : Ceasefire	1993 Interim Ceasefire Agreement was signed in Jakarta during the First Formal Talks with OIC Observers joining in 1994.	Complied with and implemented during the negotiations
Para: The Final Agreement to be signed in Manila	The Final 1996 Peace Agreement was signed in Manila on September 2, 1996	Now being implemented in accordance with its terms (though some provisions were not followed, particularly the time frame)
Additional Agenda: GRP offer of MNLF Participation in the ARMM until 1999, at which time the new law shall have been approved and the plebiscite conducted.		MNLF accepted the offer. Chairman Misuari was elected Governor in September 1996. Due to the non-passage of the new Autonomy Law, his term was extended until September 2000. Regional election for new officials was scheduled also in September 2000 but post-poned to May 14, 2001 by RA 8953

Table 2: Success Analysis GRP-MNLF Peace Negotiations 1992-1996 with OIC Participation on the Implementation of the Peace Agreement

As indicated above, the substance of autonomy will be implemented in Phase 2 when a new law is passed by Congress and approved in a plebiscite. What is being implemented right now is Phase 1 (Transition Period), which has the following main features:

- ✓ Establishment of the SZOPAD and the creation of the SPCPD
- ✓ Appointment of the MNLF or their representatives in the SPCPD and certain offices under the Office of the President (SPDA, Task Forces, etc.
- ✓ Passage of the New Autonomy Law to repeal/amend the existing ARMM law
- ✓ Continuing presence of the OIC in the Joint Monitoring Committee
- ✓ Provisions of the Agreement not requiring legislative action shall be implemented
- ✓ The joining of the MNLF into the PNP and AFP
- ✓ Special socio-economic, cultural and educational programs.

SUCCESSES	UNDERLYING CAUSES	DIFFICULTIES PROBLEMS	UNDERLYING CAUSES
Initial Contacts & Exploratory Talks	GRP initiatives through Third-Party Mediation (OIC and Libya and later on Indonesia); Acceptable initial agenda of GRP; MNLF acceptance of GRP initiatives.	Agenda Setting, Venue, military operations against suspected "MNLF Lost Command" and lawless elements that made the MNLF suspicious of GRP intentions	Confidence not yet established, venue not appropriate, no cease-fire agreement. Remedies: (venue settled by Indonesia using "shifting venue policy"; confidence building measured applied)

SUCCESSES	UNDERLYING CAUSES	DIFFICULTIES PROBLEMS	UNDERLYING CAUSES
Start of Formal Talks	Entry of Indonesia in the OIC Committee of Six as Chairman	Defining the Agenda	GRP intentions not yet clear (became clear in the final stage); Interim Ceasefire Agreement signed)
Start of Support & Mixed Committee Meetings in the Country	1993 Memo of Agreement; 1993 Interim Ceasefire Agreement	Security for the MNLF; slow movement of meetings; military operations against MILF and Abu Sayyaf	GRP policies against display of heavy arms in urban areas; military operations against MILF and Abu Sayyaf to uphold national security; GRP Panel limited authority; Remedies: (Activation of the Joint Cease-fire Committee; stop military operations but accordance with Cease-fire terms; GRP Panel given mandate by the President
Generation of local and international support	GRP and MNLF policies of public consultations and transparency	Rejection of GRP Constitution and laws	MNLF non-recognition of GRP constitution and laws: Remedies: (MNLF accepted constitutional process upon advise of OIC)
GRP formulation of innovative approaches within the	OIC appreciation of GRP formulation; OIC "persuasive		

SUCCESSES	UNDERLYING CAUSES	DIFFICULTIES PROBLEMS	UNDERLYING CAUSES
parameters of GRP Constitution and laws	power" over MNLF; MNLF acquiescence to GRP proposal in accordance with Constitutional process upon OIC advise; GRP and MNLF mutual need to attain peace through peaceful and negotiated settlement; MNLF acceptance of GRP offer to participate in ARMM Negotiation Techniques Applied: *Principle Negotiation: Third Party Mediation* (OIC with Libya and Indonesia); Negotiators as COOPERATIVE PARTNERS not as adversaries; *Confidence Building Measures* (CBM) well developed and nurtured throughout the negotiating period.		

Table 3: SWOT Analysis Implementation of the 1996 Peace Agreement

STRENGHT	WEAKNESSES	OPPORTUNITIES	THREATS
OIC Participation as signatory and the active involvement of Libya and Indonesia as Mediating States. Their continuing presence is provided in the Agreement through the GRP-MNLF-OIC Joint Monitoring Committee (JMC)	Constraints in the National Budget. Inherent defects in democratic and bureaucratic processes.	OIC support (financial and moral). Support from other countries (USA, Japan, E.U.) including international organizations in the UN and other donor institutions. Support from the peace advocates both local and international	Rejection of Agreement by the MILF, the MNLF-ICC and the Abu Sayyaf. The rising belligerency of the MILF and the increasing boldness of Abu Sayyaf Rise of disinterested parties and political oppositions.
Legitimacy of the MNLF (as signatory)	MNLF representation of the Muslims being questioned by other groups (MILF, MNLF-ICC, Abu Sayyaf) putting into doubt Chairman Misuari's ability as MNLF Chairman to provide unified leadership for the Muslims	MNLF combatants and families can return to normal life to avail of socio-economic development programs. Muslims in general will be encouraged to participate in socio-economic and political activities	Possible polarization of MNLF leaders and Muslims due to perceived failues in the ARMM and SCPDP. Instabilities in the ASEAN, particularly in Indonesia and Malaysia.
Majority support from the local Muslim population. Pending issues on autonomy stipulated in the Tripoli Agreement now completed	Ability of the MNLF leaders and those that they may invite to run the affairs of ARMM and SPCPD.	The right time to develop the material and human wealth of Mindanao (and the country as a whole).	Perceived political and economic instability at the national level.

Table 3: Situational Analysis (Problems) Implementation of the Peace Agreement

OBSERVABLE INDICATORS	PERCEIVED PROBLEMS	UNDERLYING CAUSES
Rise and increasing belligerency of the MILF	National Security Threat	Non-recognition of Peace Agreement; continuing belief in the legitimacy of struggle to put up Islamic State
Abu Sayyaf	Peace and order problem (kidnapping, extortion, murder)	Neglect by their leaders who are believed to be manipulated by foreign elements for certain agenda.
Rise of vigilantism	Potential Muslim-Christian conflict	MILF and Abu Sayyaf threats
Heavy military presence in Mindanao	Resumption of Muslim rebellion; militarization of the area	Presence of MILF and Abu Sayyaf
Drop in economic production/ agricultural production	Economic dislocation/ economic loss	Peace and order problem
Slowdown in foreign investments/donations	Economic dislocation	Peace and order problem

Conclusions

1. ***Principled negotiation proved to be the most effective way in coming up with a formula for peace in Mindanao , particularly with the Muslim rebels.***

Without the benefit of negotiation, the bloody conflict in Mindanao between the GRP and MNLF forces would have continued (as it did from 1972 to 1974) with no hope of settlement. Government policy of attraction, applied unilaterally, failed to address the root causes of the problem. The AFP may have won the battles but it did not win the war, because there was no war to be won. The Government cannot continue to engage in never-ending war against its own people. It is a violation of the basic principle upon which a government is founded as the Philippine Constitution renounces war as an instrument of national policy.[77]

The solution to the conflict in Mindanao cannot be found in the ruins of the rebels' *kuta* (camp) as Spain and America realized centuries earlier. MILITARY OPTION, as has already been proven many times in the past, is not the right approach to the resolution of a problem that has its root in the country's colonial history.

2. *Third-party mediation is necessary to resolve the Mindanao conflict, particularly with the Muslim Rebels (MNLF).*

The Mindanao conflict is no doubt a domestic issue but it has its political and security implications. The OIC recognized it as such as can be gleaned from the various resolutions issued after every OIC meeting. But when the conflict reached a "hurting stalemate" because one party "cannot resolve the problem by itself"[78] as what happened in 1974, mediation by a third party mutually acceptable to the parties in conflict is the best option. Because "conflicts over politico-security issues take place within a context of power politics, which has a major effect on international mediation."[79] The Mindanao conflict, even if it is admitted to be a domestic issue, has its regional and international ramifications. Its effects are felt within the ASEAN (particularly Malaysia and Indonesia) in many forms, like refugee problems and border security issues, not to mention the religious dimension of the conflict. As the other party (MNLF) is acknowledged to represent a sizable Muslim population, the OIC, an international organization of Muslim States, found it consistent with its charter to come in and help resolve the conflict.

Mediation (or facilitation) by the OIC with Libya as the leading mediating state came in 1975 that led to the signing of the Tripoli Agreement. In the 1992-1996 GRP- MNLF negotiations, the parties reached a deadlock on critical issues because the two conflicting parties could not reach an agreement without the participation of a mediating party as what happened in the 1986-1987 GRP-MNLF Peace Talks. Former President Ramos would say later, "Third party facilitation is indispensable if the parties are poles apart on fundamental political issues."[80]

Mediation therefore became necessary " as a mode of negotiation with the stated purpose of contributing to the conflict's abatement or resolution."[81] In the Mindanao Conflict, it is the mediation of the OIC. This was successfully applied in the case of the MNLF and will certainly apply in the case of the on-going conflict with the MILF.

3. ***Multi-level approach to negotiation is effective.***

Multi-level approach to negotiation applied in the GRP-MNLF talks proved to be effective. The modes used in different levels and stages of the negotiations "to marshal the interests of all the involved parties toward a mutually acceptable solution to the conflict... were communication, formulation and manipulation."[82]

In the GRP-MNLF negotiations, these modes were applied through the creation of different Technical and Working Committees (Support and Mixed Committees, Joint Ceasefire Committee and Secretariat) supplemented by personal, informal but official contacts not only between the two conflicting parties but also more importantly with the full participation of the mediating party/state (OIC, Libya and Indonesia). There were also "consultations and intensive dialogues, in all levels"[83] which reinforced the confidence of the parties to reach an agreement. This is because "mediation is basically a political process... and it is a triangular relationship."[84]

4. ***The GRP-MNLF Peace Agreement is the final agreement to resolve the Mindanao Conflict.***

The 1996 Peace Agreement is the "Final agreement on the implementation of the 1976 Tripoli Agreement... served as basis for a just, lasting, honorable and comprehensive solution to the problem in Southern Philippines <u>within the framework of the Philippine Constitution</u>.[85] (underscoring supplied). As shown in the SCHEMATIC OVERVIEW OF THE AGENDA, all the issues (in the Tripoli Agreement) have now been resolved and the provisions completed. The GRP can now confidently claim, "the Agreement has been hailed worldwide as a model for conflict resolution through negotiation and dialogue."[86]

It can then be said that the 1996 PEACE AGREEMENT stands today as an internationally acceptable document, legally and morally binding on the government and the MNLF (as the recognized representative of the Bangsamoro people in the OIC forum) in attaining peace in Muslim Mindanao. It is considered as the Final Peace Agreement on the implementation of the Tripoli Agreement. President Ramos then believed that "with the formal signing of this Final Peace Agreement... we bring to a close almost 30 years of conflict, at the cost of more than 120,000 Filipino lives."[87] Indonesian Foreign Minister Ali Alatas echoed the optimism of President Ramos by saying, "an arduous quest for peace that has lasted more than two decades has come to a splendid close"[88] The OIC Secretary General, Dr. Hamid Algabid, also expressed the same theme when he declared that "today, we seal the final act of the long way we have covered to reach a just, honorable and durable peace in Mindanao."[89] On the other hand, MNLF Chairman Misuari took the opportunity to make a passionate appeal for support to ensure the success of the Peace Agreement even as he declared that "if we fail... God forbid, we may not have another opportunity to talk peace for we and our children might be condemned to live in an atmosphere of perpetual war."[90]

Saturday, March 10, 2001

Endnotes

[*] The Author graduated from the National Defense College of the Philippines (NDCP) in July 2000 and was conferred the degree of Master in National Security Administration (MNSA) with a rank of Lieutenant Colonel in the Philippine Army Reserve Force. This is a summary of his thesis, which he successfully defended at the NDCP. He served as MNLF Special Peace Emissary, Chairman of the MNLF Secretariat and MNLF Spokesman during the GRP-MNLF Peace Talks, 1992-1996. He now serves as Consultant and a Research Fellow of the Strategic Studies Group at the NDCP.

[1] Mara Stankovitch, ed., *Compromising on Autonomy: Mindanao in Transition*, in **Accord (An International Review of Peace Initiatives)** (London: Conciliation Resources in association with the Research and Development Center, Mindanao State University, General Santos City and Peace Education Center, Notre Dame University, Cotabato City, Issue 6, 1999) p.5

[2] President Soeharto (Indonesia), Speech delivered at the Initialing Ceremony of the Peace Agreement. Merdeka Palace, Jakarta, Indonesia, August 30, 1996.

[3] Fidel V. Ramos, **Break Not The Peace: The Story of the GRP-MNLF Peace Talks, 1992-1996** (Manila: Friends of Steady Eddie, 1996). This book basically gives the Philippine government account of the negotiations. (Hereinafter referred to as Break Not the Peace)

[4] Soliman M. Santos, Jr. **THE PHILIPPINE-MUSLIM DISPUTE: INTERNATIONAL ASPECTS FROM ORIGIN TO RESOLUTION (The Role of the Organization of the Islamic Conference in the Peace Negotiations between the Government of the Republic of the Philippines and the Moro National Liberation Front).** A research paper in International Dispute Resolution in the Master of Laws Program at the University of Melbourne, Australia, (Unpublished, January 1999)

[5] President Ramos, *Break Not the Peace: We are all Victors* (Speech delivered during the signing of the GRP-MNLF Peace Agreement, Malacanang Palace, Manila, September 2, 1996)

[6] Richard Holbrooke, To End A War. (New York, USA: Random House Inc., 1998), p. Note to the Reader

[7] **Islamic Conference of Foreign Ministers (ICFM) Resolution No, 18 issued by the 5th ICFM.** (Kuala Lumpur, Malaysia, 25 June 1974). (MNLF Secretariat file)

[8] Fortunato U. Abat, **THE DAY WE NEARLY LOST MINDANAO: The CEMCOM Story.** (Fortunato Abat, Manila: 1993) p. 38

[9] ICFM Resolution No. 18... urging "the Philippine government to find a political and peaceful solution through negotiations with the Muslim leaders, particularly with the representatives of the MNLF in order to arrive at a just solution to the plight of the Filipino Muslims within the framework of the national sovereignty and territorial integrity of the Philippines..."

[10] IMPLEMENTATION OF THE TRIPOLI AGREEMENT (1984). Jointly published by the Department of Foreign Affairs and the Ministry of Muslim Affairs, Manila.
[11] Ibid. Annex 11, p. 52
[12] Ibid, Annex VIII, p. 58
[13] Aijas Ahmad, "Class and Colony in Mindanao," in **Southeast Asia Chronicle**, No. 82 (February 1982)
[14] Datu Michael O. Mastura, *The Crisis in the MNLF Leadership and the Dilemma of Muslim Autonomy Movement*, in **Papers on the Tripoli Agreement: Problems and Prospects** (International Studies Institute of the Philippines, U.P. Law Complex, U.P. Diliman, Quezon City, 1986) pp.34-70
[15] See Salah Jubair, Bangsamoro: A Nation Under Endless Tyranny, 3rd Edition (Kuala Lumpur, Malaysia: IQ Marin SDN BHD, 1999). Pp. 153-157
[16] From MNLF files, Nur Misuari, Chairman, MNLF, (Address delivered before the Plenary Sessions of the 19th ICFM, held in Cairo, Egypt, 31-July to 5 August 1990) *"The Tragedy of the Peace Process and What the 19th ICFM can do to help"*
[17] Jubair, Bangsamoro: A Nation Under Endless Tyranny... p. 156
[18] Ramos, Break Not the Peace... p. i
[19] MNLF Chairman Nur Misuari, **Official Statement**. (Delivered during the signing of the GRP-MNLF Peace Agreement, Malacañang Palace, Manila, September 2, 1996)
[20] Ramos, Break Not the Peace, p. ii
[21] This writer was part of the informal channel between the MNLF and GRP representatives as the MNLF Emissary
[22] **Statement of Understanding** issued by the GRP and the MNLF with the Participation of Libya representing the OIC during the First Exploratory Talks held in Tripoli, Libya, October 2-4, 1992.
[23] The OIC Summit in Dakar, Senegal in 1991 expanded the OIC Quadripartite Ministerial Committee created in 1973 (composed of Saudi Arabia, Senegal, Somalia and Libya as Chairman) to the OIC Ministerial Committee of the six to include Bangladesh and Indonesia with the latter as Chairman.
[24] **Statement of Understanding** issued after the GRP-MNLF Second Exploratory Talks, Cipanas, West Java, Indonesia, April 13-16, 1998
[25] Chairman Misuari headed the 7-member MNLF Panel. This writer was a member of the delegation. The Meeting was presided by Indonesian Foreign Minister Ali Alatas in the presence of the OIC Secretary General.
[26] Ramos, Break Not the Peace... pp. 71-72
[27] Joint Press Communiquè issued by the Third Round of GRP-MNLF Formal Talks, Jakarta, Indonesia, November 27 to December 11, 1995.
[28] Ramos, Break Not the Peace.... p. 79
[29] This meeting was arranged by this writer at the request of Secretary Torres
[30] Ramos, Break Not the Peace... p. 85
[31] Indonesian Foreign Minister Ali Alatas, Opening Statement, Final Round of GRP-MNLF Formal Talks, Jakarta, Indonesia, August 28-20, 1996
[32] The Peace Talks conducted by the Aquino Government with the MNLF, particularly the 90-Day Technical Committee meetings held in the country was without the participation of the OIC
[33] William Zartman and Saadia Touval, *Mediation: The Role of Third Party Diplomacy and Informal Peacemaking*, in **Resolving Third World Conflict: Challenges for a New Era.** Edited by Sheryl J. Brown and Kimber M. Schraub. (Washington, D.C., U.S.A., United States Institute of Peace, 1992) pp. 241-261
[34] Ibid.
[35] Ibid.
[36] Ibid.
[37] Ibid.
[38] Ramos, Break Not the Peace... p. 4
[39] Ibid.
[40] Gabriel Lopez, Coverdale Organization (Copyright, 1990). **Selected readings on Conflict Resolution, Principles Negotiation, Crisis Management and Brinkmanship.** (National Defense College of the Philippines).
[41] Congressman Eduardo Ermita is an elected Representative of the 3rd District of Batangas. He has been involved in the GRP-MNLF Talks since the 1976 Tripoli negotiations. Congressman Nur Jaafar is an elected Representative of the lone district of Tawi-Tawi. He enjoys the trust and confidence of senior MNLF leaders.
[42] Ibid.
[43] Zartman and Touval, Mediation: The Role of Third Party Diplomacy... p. 242
[44] Ambassador Rajab Abdelaziz Azzarouq was the Libyan Ambassador to Manila from 1991 to 1999. He played a very crucial role in the negotiations from the start to the finish and even went out of his way on many occasions to help negotiate for the release of kidnap victims in Sulu, Basilan, and Zamboaga. He is highly respected by the MNLF leaders. During criical times in the negotiations, he

gave counsel to the MNLF and suggestions to the GRP, when so requested. When ceasefire violations were reported (from both sides), he was the one person the MNLF and the GRP always listened to for advise to defuse the tense situation.

[45] Lopez, Selected Readings on Conflict Resolution...

[46] Ramos, Break Not the Peace... p. 99

[47] Lopez, Selected Readings on Conflict Resolution...

[48] Ibid.

[49] Ibid.

[50] Ibid.

[51] Ramos, Break Not the Peace... p. 27-28

[52] Lopez, Selected Readings on Conflict Resolution...

[53] Ramos, Break Not the Peace... p. 19

[54] Various Resolutions of the OIC beginning in 1977 when the MNLF was conferred the "Observer" status during the OIC Foreign Ministers Meeting in Benghazi, Libya.

[55] Ramos, Break Not the Peace... pp. 5 and 100

[56] Carolyn Arguillas, Interview with the MILF Chairman Salamat Hashim, Philippine Daily Inquirer, April 19-20, 2000.

[57] Ramos, Break Not the Peace... p. 97

[58] Lopez, Selected Readings on Conflict Resolution...

[59] Ibid.

[60] To be cited in particular is the role played by Ambassador Rajab A. Azzarouq, Libyan Ambassador to Manila from 1991 to 1999. He assisted, upon request from GRP and MNLF, in the negotiations for the release of kidnap victims in Sulu, Zamboanga, and Basilan.

[61] Ramos, Break Not the Peace... p. 101

[62] Stankovitch, Compromising on Autonomy.... Accord. p.5

[63] Lopez, Coverdale Organization (Copyright, 1990). Selected Readings on conflict Resolution...

[64] Ibid.

[65] Ibid. (taken from *The Art and Science of Negotiation* by Howard Raiffa)

[66] MNLF Manifesto,March 18, 1974 (MNLF Secretariat File)

[67] Ramos, Break Not the Peace... p.5

[68] Zartman and Touval, Mediation: The Role of Third Party Diplomacy and Informal Peacemaking...

[69] Santos, Jr, The Philippine-Muslim Dispute: From Origins to Resolutions...

[70] President Ramos' Memorandum to the GRP Panel dated April 26, 193. This is also found in "Break Not the peace..." p. 30

[71] Ibid. p. 103

[72] Ibid. p. 101

[73] Quoted in Lopez, "Selected Readings on Conflict Resolution...." From Jay M. Shafritz, Tood J.A. Shafritz, David B. Robertson, "Dictionary of Military Science", 1989

[74] The Implementation of the GRP-MNLF Peace Agreement, 1996-2000, prepared by the National Security Council Secretariat, March 2000, pp. 12-13

[75] Ibid. p. 15

[76] Prof. Gabby Lopez, "Notes on Strategic Management," in Selected Readings on National Security Management (NSA 207, MNSA RC 35, 1999-2000). Quezon City, National Defense College of the Philippines

[77] 1987 Philippine Constitution

[78] Zartman and Touval, Mediation: The Role of Third-Party Diplomacy and Informal Peacemaking... p. 251

[79] Ibid. p. 242

[80] Ramos, Break Not the Peace... p. 100

[81] Zartman and Touval, Mediation: The Role of Third-Party... p. 242

[82] Ibid. p. 252

[83] **Executive Summary**, Fourth Round of GRP-MNLF Formal Talks, Jakarta, Indonesia, August 28-30, 1996. Para. 94

[84] Zartman and Touval, Mediation: The Role of Third-Party Diplomacy and Informal Peacemaking... pp. 242, 243 and 253

[85] 1996 Peace Agreement (Title page and page 2)

[86] The Implementation of the GRP-MNLF Peace Agreement, 1996-2000... p. 3

[87] President Fidel V. Ramos, **Break Not The Peace: We are All Victors,** (Speech delivered during the signing of the GRP-MNLF Peace Agreement, Malacanang Palace, Manila, 2 September 1996.)

[88] Indonesia Foreign Minister Ali Alatas, **Official Statement** (Delivered during the signing of the GRP-MNLF Peace Agreement, Malacañang, Manila, 2 September, 1996.

[89] Dr, Hamid Algabid, OIC Secretary General, **Official Statement**. (Delivered during the signing of the GRP-MNLF Peace Agreement, Malacañang Palace, Manila, 2 September 1996.)

[90] MNLF Chairman Nur Misuari, **Official Statement.** (Delivered during the signing of the GRP-MNLF Peace Agreement, Malacañang Palace, Manila, 2 September 1996).

Impact of Religion on the Negotiation by and Between the Government and the MILF

HON. SAADUDDIN A. ALAUYA

HON. SAADUDDIN A. ALAUYA
Jurisconsult in Islamic Law

Saaduddin A. Alauya is an academician and public servant. He was a Professor at the King Abdul Azis University in Saudi Arabia and at the Mindanao State University, Marawi City. He was also elected Vice Governor of Lanao Del Sur during the Aquino Administration (1987 - 1992). Hon Alauya was responsible for the drafting of the Presidential Decree 1083 otherwise known as the Code of Islamic Personal Laws and has likewise written books on Sharia Law. Formerly a trial court Judge, Hon. Alauya is now a Jurisconsult in Islamic Law.

Apparently, two panels have different bases in pursuing their respective objectives. The GRP Panel has the constitution of the Philippines as their fundamental law, whereas the MILF has the Glorious Qur'an as their fundamental law. These two are contradicting each other. The Constitution provides: "Sovereignty resides in the people and all government authority emanates from them." (Sec. 1, Art.2). On the other hand, the Glorious Qur'an states:

إن الحكم إلا لله أمر ألا تعبدوا إلا
إياه ذلك دين القيم ولكن أكثر الناس
لا يعلمون (سورة يوسف ٤٠)

Meaning, "Sovereignty resides to none but Allah. He enjoined you to worship and obey none but Him; that is the (true) straight religion, but most men know not." (12:40, Qur'an).

The former is liable for amendment and the latter is absolutely not amendable. However, they agree on several principles despite the fact that the former is a man made law and the latter is not. Under this situation, I propose that we conclude the peace agreement on the precepts agreed upon. We will leave the issues not agreed upon for future discussion possibly by constitutional amendments, federalism, autonomy, or by other means.

The government of the Philippines will neither allow the dismemberment of its territory, nor the violation of its constitution. That is a non-negotiable issue to them. On the other hand, the Moro International Liberation Front (MILF) in particular and the Muslim Filipinos in general are strictly enjoined by their creator, Allah, to govern their affairs in accordance with what Allah has revealed to them. This is also a non-negotiable issue as far as they concerned. In fact, in case of conflict between the constitution or any other law in one hand and the Glorious Qur'an, in another hand, the Muslims are enjoined to make the latter prevail. The Qur'an is the most fundamental source of the *Shari'ah* (Islamic Law). The second most fundamental source of Islamic Law is the *Hadith*. There are other sources of Islamic Law emanating from these two fundamental sources.

To me, it is greatly a matter of reconciliation between these two systems of law. The government is not remiss in offering remedies. During the time of President Ferdinand E. Marcos, the Regional Commissions of Regions IX and XII were created, but with no legislative powers. The Tripoli Agreement was concluded but not implemented. During the term of President Corazon C. Aquino, the Autonomous Region in Muslim Mindanao was created with legislative powers in accordance with the constitution. Unfortunately, it has not yet enacted enough Regional Laws on *Shari'ah*. During the Ramos administration, the Peace Agreement was signed by the Government and the Moro National Liberation Front on September 2, 1996. Several stipulations of the agreement have not yet been implemented. During the time of deposed President Estrada, all-out war was declared. This has triggered the economic downfall of the Philippines that hastened the expulsion of Mr. Estrada.

All the aforesaid remedies offered are not acceptable to the MILF. What must be acceptable to them? Let it come from them. Let them spell it out. To meet them in a negotiation table at this precise moment will just aggravate the situation since the GRP Panel and the MILF Panel are not conversant on both Philippine Law and *Shari'ah* Law. Some are lawyers but not familiar in *Shari'ah*. Some are *Shari'ah*-knowledgeable but not lawyers at the same time. It is difficult to reconcile two systems of law when you only know one of them.

At this juncture, to abbreviate the negotiation, my suggestion is to offer the Organic Act of the ARMM as a working paper of the negotiation. The MILF Panel should be requested to comment on every provision of the Organic Act, having in mind not to violate the Philippine Constitution.

Thereafter, the working paper together with the comments and recommendations of the MILF shall be formally returned to the GRP Panel for study. By this, the GRP Panel must know the genuine demands of the MILF and the offers that can be acceptable to the Republic of the Philippines. After this exchange of notes, two panels may formally meet at the negotiation table. By then, they will not be preparing a peace agreement. They will instead be drafting a bill to be passed by the two Houses of the Congress of the Philippines, to be approved by the President.

SEA Regional Security and Mindanao Conflict

PROF. JULKIPLI M. WADI

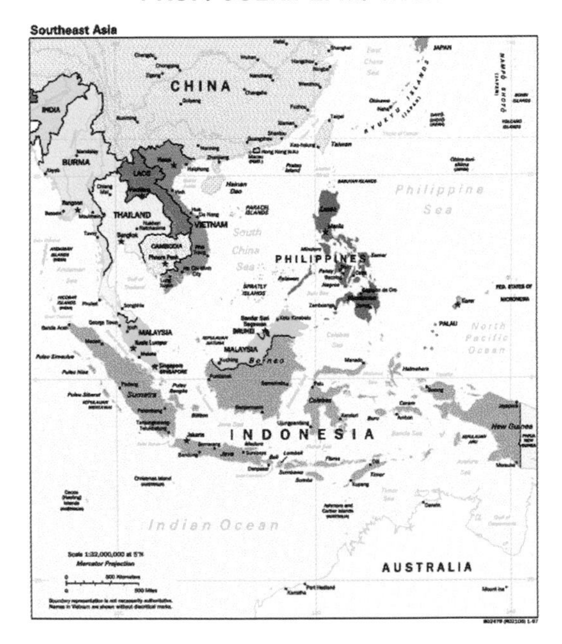

PROF. JULKIPLI WADI

Asst. Professor and Secretary
Institute of Islamic Studies, U.P.

Mr. Wadi is currently an Assistant Professor and the Secretary of the Institute of Islamic Studies at the University of the Philippines in Diliman. He earned his Bachelors Degree in Political Science from the University of the East and pursued a Masters Degree in Islamic Studies at UP Diliman.

He is a member of several organizations including the Association of Muslim Social Scientists in Virginia, USA, the Research Association of Islamic Social Sciences, Inc., the Philippine Political Science Association of UP Diliman, and Just World Trust in Penang, Malaysia.

Today, the "Mindanao conflict" reconfigures. It affects not just the Philippines but other areas of Southeast Asia (SEA). For quite sometime there has been a recurring spill-over of the conflict. It overarches age-old issues of territorial dispute, Moro separatism, migration, cross border security, among others. As the new Millennium dawns, the conflict takes new form characterized by "post-Moro nationalism" crystallized by unconventional politico-religious thought and fervor bordering on what Western political convention considers transnational crime and terror. The many faces of globalization define this kind of nationalism even as new economic factors and technological revolution emboss it. Certainly, they impact on Philippine foreign policy and SEA regional security.

The paper posits that the Mindanao conflict has reconfigured and converged with forces and factors that shaped the accumulating, unresolved political question of Mindanao whose spill-over affects national security, Philippine economy and international investment in the area. It also creates a stir in the larger frame of SEA regional security. Finally, the reduction of the Mindanao conflict as simply a discourse of Philippine interests and other economic forces in the region without taking into account the primary stakeholders of Mindanao diminishes the "holisticity" of the question and, as such, reduces the effectiveness of an approach in addressing the issue.

Signs of New Configuration

In order to drive a point, a number of major cases that happened lately are important to underline. They mark a new contour in the latest political configuration of the Mindanao conflict.

First, when then President Joseph Estrada callously dipped his finger on the "Anwar debacle," Philippine-Malaysia relation was put into a spin with enormous consequences on Philippine diplomacy in Malaysia, particularly on the almost 500,000 Muslim refugees and illegal Filipino immigrants in Sabah. In a demonstration staged by angry Malaysians, a placard written with "Pinoy go home" speaks the loudest voice. It also affected the cross border security arrangement between the two countries. Fully aware of the implications of the former President's misadventure in supposedly "hot water" of Philippine-Malaysia relation, Prime Minister Mahathir Mohammed practically rebuked the Philippine government by saying that if President Estrada does not stop his "interference" in Malaysian affairs he would fan the secessionist threat in Mindanao. The crestfallen President kept quiet since then.

Second, after issuing a warning against the Philippine government and even declaring the Moro National Liberation Front's (MNLF) intention to go back to its original objective in Qatar, Nur Misuari reiterated in Kuala Lumpur his charge against the Philippine government over the latter's failure to implement the 1996 Peace Agreement. Yet, many wonder why the MNLF continued to relish until these days the Autonomous Region in Muslim Mindanao (ARMM) and the Southern Philippine Council for Peace and Development (SPCPD). He also blamed the "fateful" Kuala Lumpur Resolution in July 1974 which is in fact the anchor of all agreements entered into by the MNLF with the government.

Third, after the capture of Camp Abu Bakar by the Armed Forces of the Philippines (AFP), the Moro Islamic Liberation Front (MILF) Chair Salamat Hashim declared "jihad" in Mindanao. A few days later, alleged MILF foreign sympathizers operating in Indonesia bombed the Philippine Embassy in Jakarta. This is not to mention a widely circulated report that a group of alleged Arab and Indonesian volunteers participated with the MILF in fighting against the AFP's "all-out war." Moreover, there were two bombs that exploded in a busy market of Sandakan in Sabah in relatively the same period. This form of participatory "linkage politics" is a new dimension in the history of the Mindanao conflict.

Fourth, the Abu Sayyaf's hostage-taking of 21 people, mostly foreigners, in Sipadan Island in 2000 brings to fore the vulnerability of areas that lie within the historic "Sulu zone." Few segments in Moro history display such "weird" tenacity of struggle that brought shock waves in Southeast Asia, Middle East and Europe. The cataclysmic effect on the Philippine economy and Mindanao investment, especially the country's image in the global community is enormous. Even if it appears expedient, the Abu Sayyaf's demand for the establishment of a "Sabah Commission" underscores the historicity and multi-faceted dimension of the conflict.

Fifth, like the MNLF in the 70s, reports of alleged flow of arms to the MILF and the Abu Sayyaf from their supporters and arms-dealers as far as Afghanistan and Peshawar course through the seas of Southeast Asia. Apart from Mindanao and Manila, Kuala Lumpur and Jakarta serve as their linkage entrepot with worldwide Islamic movements like the *al-Qaidah* of Osama bin Laden. Undeniably, the linkage of Moro Islamists with world Islamist movements alarms the Philippine government. The havoc they have wrought thus far is real and devastating.

Nature of Intersection

The above-mentioned cases, as noted, are simply "new" contours in the Mindanao conflict. How they reinforce the "old" or "constant" form of the issue is a crucial element in understanding the latest "intersection" of SEA regional security and the "Mindanao conflict." At first glance, it would appear off tangent to discuss the corollary relation between the regional security in Southeast Asia vis-à-vis the Mindanao conflict. They do not only belong to different "hierarchy of levels" of security concern, but they also represent a totally different structure in the web of "security complex" in the region. This means that SEA regional security is mostly shaped by its characteristic as a sub-system between the international system and the nation-state system whose main actors are states. On the contrary, the Mindanao conflict, in the perspective of the Philippine government, is simply a domestic problem within a national system and henceforth confines within the parameter of "national" not "regional" security. The binary relation between the two variables seems to appear incongruent.

However, it is also an accepted notion in regional security analysis that "specific patterns of amity/enmity may arise from local issues like border disputes and ideological alignments." Another is the level of cooperation, especially threat, affecting two or more states." As the concept of security is relational, "security complex" can be divided into *lower* and *higher* level "security complex". The former is "composed of local states whose power does not extend much, if at all." The latter concerns great powers whose powers "extend far beyond their immediate environment." Beneath the *lower* "security complex" is a web of domestic issues particularly ethnic resurgence and insurgency that cut across many areas of Southeast Asia.

In the post-Cold War era, analysts viewed the rise of ethnic conflicts as "ethnic nationalism" or "post-nationalism." Eager to make sense of the post-Cold War period to justify the role of the United States as a world policeman, Samuel Huntington advanced the "Clash of Civilization" by primarily painting Islam as a crusading force against the West. Incidentally, the Mindanao conflict remains one of the longest unresolved political questions that antedated many "hot spots" in the region even as Mindanao today is home to huge foreign investments and economic interests. Thus, an intricate tapestry of geopolitical, geo-strategic and economic significance in Southeast Asia weaves in the Mindanao conflict.

Regional Security in SEA, Philippine Foreign Policy and International Dimension of Mindanao

As in Europe and the Atlantic, the end of the Cold War brought new dimension of security in Asia including Southeast Asia. The war of ideologies receded into the background and globalization and economic development became the framework of international and regional cooperation. While military presence of the United States in the region decreased, the strategy of "strengthening of traditional elements of American policy" remained. This includes "the 100,000 troop forward presence, the alliance network, cooperation with friendly states and engagement with former and potential adversaries, and efforts to prevent and counter the proliferation of weapons of mass destruction." The Visiting Forces Agreement (VFA) illustrates the applicability of the U.S. "forward presence" policy.

The Asian financial crisis was a major concern of the United States but "the security relations with China and Japan and continuing uncertainty of the situation in the Korean Peninsula were seen as more direct and urgent significance for the US defense and security planning." While China is a major force to be reckoned with by competing states over the Spratly Islands, China's goal in maintaining an 8% annual growth rate in 1998 makes economic development, rather than security her primary concern. In the same vein, Japan's financial aid to countries affected by the Asian crisis amounting to US$75 billion in 1998 demonstrates Japan's priority concern in the region. However comparatively speaking, while these countries prioritize their economic development it does not mean security has been the least priority.

If at all, it is the Southeast Asian countries that continue to increase armaments and develop their weapon and defense system. For the past few years, there has been a sustained increase of military procurement among them. Although not a rule, countries with high Gross Domestic Product (GDP) have relatively developed military defense systems. Singapore, for instance, perceived the "necessity of deterring Malaysia, and possibly Indonesia" as "similar with the Israeli's." This is supposedly unusual considering the level of regional cooperation among the members of Association of Southeast Asian Nations (ASEAN). As noted by an Asia geo-political analyst, "while the rest of its ASEAN neighbors were still reeling from the financial crisis, cash-rich Singapore purchased 100 surface to air missiles from the United States to strengthen its military capacity." This development flies against the fact that Singapore is not like Indonesia, Myanmar and the Philippines. At any rate, it is "the long-term factor not the *threat* factor" that characterizes the level of security cooperation in the region.

As in the past, economic development and regional cooperation remain the primary thrust of countries in the region. Among others, through the careful arrangement adopted by ASEAN, Southeast Asia became one of today's dynamic regions. It was able to evolve steady economic development, political and diplomatic cooperation including "regional security" among its members. The ASEAN is able to represent a posture of confidence in the international community and has developed a relatively stable regional cooperation unaffected by domestic problems of each member. Since its humble beginnings in the Bandung Conference, ASEAN prides itself in forging other forms of regional cooperation like the Asian

Regional Forum (ARP), Asia Pacific Economic Cooperation (APEC), and the BIMP-EAGA (East Asia Growth Area).

During his term, President Fidel Ramos pursued "economic diplomacy." In fairness, the former President brought forth Mindanao's new image as "the food basket of the Philippines." Apart from taking off from President Ramos' foreign policy, the Estrada Administration planned to strengthen bilateral security arrangements particularly with the United States, ASEAN, and other Asian nations. Being one of the prime movers of the ASEAN, the Philippines benefited much from the "quite neat arrangement" adopted by the organization. It is shown in the ASEAN members' burgeoning investment in the Philippines especially with the formation of BIMP-EAGA, with Mindanao playing a crucial role.

Since 1997, for instance, Brunei remained a major supplier of oil in the country with a sustained Philippine export of US$52,310,677. Indonesia is ranked 15th among the country's largest export market and is also a major supplier of oil with Philippine exports amounting to US$142.45M. Malaysia remains the 9th biggest trading partner of the Philippines with exports amounting to US$498,210,949. For its part, Singapore is the 3rd largest export market of the Philippines at US$1,326,644,177, while Thailand is the 10th, with exports amounting to US$723,290,482. In the same year, Philippine exports to Vietnam amounted to US$76,057,667. Data on profile and specific amount of Southeast Asia investment in Mindanao is yet to be accessed by the author. In the meantime, it is presumed that the continuing packaging of Mindanao by the Philippine government to form part of the economic growth triangle in the region points to the vibrancy of Southeast Asian investment in the area.

It is, of course, the economic interest and investment by the United States, Japan, United Kingdom, Korea, World Bank, Asian Development Bank, European Union, and other financial giants that is heavily entrenched in Mindanao. Apart from numerous transnational corporations, these countries and foreign financial institutions implemented mostly long-term projects and provided loans amounting to billions of U.S. dollars distributed in many areas of Mindanao. As per report of the National Economic and Development Authority (NEDA) as of 31 December 2000, these projects are allocated in rural development, transportation, environment, education, telecommunication, air transportation, power, infrastructure, ports, social welfare and health. It also includes areas such as, rural finance, rural development, water supply and urban development, including special initiatives like the Southern Philippines Zone of Peace and Development (SZOPAD) Social Fund. The latter is an entity that calibrates peace and development projects in most of the areas covered by regional autonomy arrangement in Mindanao. As of SZOPAD Social Fund Project Accomplishment Report on 31 July 2000, of the 407 sub-projects, PhP237.08M were approved.

Dynamics of Configuration

Transformed into a discourse, the dominance of economy-based approach, albeit critical, reduces the Mindanao issue into a one-sided ideological prism based on wealth and economic development. While poverty is generally advanced as the primary cause of rebellion and restlessness in the area, Muslim reformists would contend that the quest for Mindanao development must be holistic, fair and just. They would argue that they do not wage the Moro struggle to become rich and to simply develop their lands. Their basis of struggle is ideologically anchored on their relatively distinct *welanschauung*. Hence, economic development and intervention in the area must be framed in the larger issue of the Moro's historical, political and human rights. Failure to do so would remind us the latest configuration of the Mindanao conflict.

Without rehashing the discourse on the origin of the Mindanao conflict as there are already voluminous works about it, what this paper would like to zero in is the impact of "constriction" of the conflict in the issue of reconfiguration. Like a chain, the Mindanao conflict is attached in the larger frame of Southeast Asian experience under colonial rule. Employing an amalgam of statecraft, diplomacy and war, colonial powers, e.g., Spain, United States, reduced the power of both Sulu and Philippines without the benefit of "plebiscitory consent" from the Moro people themselves. The logical issue that would spring then must be the so-called Sabah claim since it is intrinsically linked with the sovereignty of the Sulu over that part of North Borneo. Desperate, the Sulu sultans allowed the Philippine government to pursue the claim amid the intransigence of Malaysia. With the failure of numerous negotiations, then President Marcos made a bold decision to take Sabah by force that eventually engraved an indelible consequence on the Moros including the Muslim movements that emerged since then.

Central in the Mindanao issue at that time was the configuration of the Moro struggle from previously ethnic and collaborative strands in the early 1900s into revolutionary and nationalist lines in the 1960s onward. The rosary of Muslim movements that sprouted since then advanced the secessionist card against the Philippine government that ironically served the interests of Malaysia. The latter was not only saved from the venom of Tausug militants, but it also transferred the Moro threat to the Philippines. Indeed, Malaysians coddled the MNLF. However, Malaysia's help was highly calculated enough only to aid distressed brothers in times of need and not an all-out resolution of what they desire. Malaysia knows fully well the implication of an independent *Bangsamoro Republik*. It would not only mean a re-opening of the Sabah claim. It would be a floodgate for Moro's resurgence in the historic "Sulu zone" (Sipadan island included), a "sub-regional" area they once controlled. Moreover, Malaysia and the Philippines with their geo-political schism used the Mindanao conflict in pursuit of their respective interest: the first as buffer politics by Malaysia against the Philippines in constricting the Moro rebellion in order to mute the Sabah claim; the second as a source of legitimacy for whimsical national policy like the Declaration of Martial Law in 1972.

Hence, since the 1970s, Malaysia, supported by other Muslim ASEAN member countries, consistently maintained a "moderating influence" in the Mindanao conflict including the GRP-MNLF dispute. The Philippines and Malaysia gave premium to ASEAN "regional cooperation" because the stakes posed by the Mindanao conflict to both countries is extremely high. Thus, it can be said that the Mindanao conflict is "constricted" in three levels: first, by the Philippine claim of sovereignty and territorial integrity over Mindanao and Sulu; second, by the geo-political and geo-strategic interests by Malaysia; third, by the respect of national sovereignty and regional cooperation among ASEAN members.

With this indomitable hurdle, Nur Misuari had to find allies elsewhere like Libya and other Middle East countries including the Organization of Islamic Conference (OIC). Indeed, the support of these Middle East entities were strong in the early days of the MNLF rebellion. However, as they learned the

Realpolitik of the Mindanao conflict through time, Arab countries had to vacillate between the elusive, double-edged principle of national sovereignty and "Islamic solidarity." Unknown to many, the Arab support is more fundamentally framed by the paradigm of national sovereignty rather than "Islamic solidarity." The latter, if at all, is simply a façade for political expediency.

The Islamic Struggle

This brings us to the discussion on the emergence of the second wave of configuration (more specifically reconfiguration) of the Moro struggle. Feeling deserted by both their Muslim brothers in the ASEAN and the Arabs in the Middle East, the hard core amongst Moro struggles found Misuari's tactics in calibrating the peace agreement as illusory and fruitless. On the contrary, Misuari thought that he was just being practical given the circumstances surrounding the MNLF. Hence, the militants among them felt the need to form new groups and to ally with trans-Islamic groups. Since the late 1970s, Moro movements, like microbes, grew exponentially. Political rhetoric like "Islamic state," *shariah* and *jihad* became daily discourse among them. Correspondingly, Moro movements found allies in Islamic movements abroad. The latter have axes to grind against their respective Arab/Muslim governments because of their failure to go beyond the platform of "Arab nationalism" and weed out the neo-colonial hand in the Muslim world. This cleavage ushers the globalization of transnational Islam. It must be noted that few, Muslim countries today are spared of "Islamic" oppositions in many forms making "Islam" appear, according to Al Shariati, at war with another "Islam." Referred to by Bassam Tibi' as "politicization of the sacred" (known as political Islam), this cleavage eventually shapes the metamorphosis of the Moro struggle into a highly accentuated Islamist strand (e.g. MILF, al-*Harakak al-Islamiyyah*) since the late 80s.

Many analysts argue that the politicization of Islam is intrinsic to Islam itself. However, a close scrutiny of many Islamic reformers both militant and moderate shows that their reification of Islamic thought is anchored on deeply entrenched structural questions, power politics, social contradiction, and oppression. Hence, the harnessing of dogma and doctrine in political rhetoric and praxis is simply an effect of social contradiction. It is safe to say that the larger the social contradiction in the Muslim area, the more belligerent Islamists would become and, by logical extension, the larger the impact they can wreak. This observation is affirmed by continuing war and violence in Muslim Mindanao. A closer reading of the discourse and politics of the MILF and the *Abu Sayyaf* shows an overwhelming desire to carry an enormous responsibility honed by what they believe in and the accumulating social problem in the area. On the contrary, they may have the benefit of good intentions, but the end result is self-flagellation on the Muslim community as war, violence and destruction happened mostly in their areas. On this score, Islamists would argue, like many Muslim reformists, that self-sacrifice is the highest form of worship and political obligation as the Muslim community experienced what they believed as oppression and illegal occupation.

At this juncture, what we would like to impress is that in the twilight of the 20th century the discourse and politics in the Moro community has not only shifted from a Moro ethnic-collaborative strand but also from a nationalist line towards a highly accentuated Islamist divide. By 1990 onward, the *Abu Sayyaf* rampage became a threat to national security and even prompted the acceleration of the GRP-MNLF peace process. While Indonesia was considered as one of the prime movers behind the peace process, it was the *Abu Sayyaf* among others, that pressured both President Ramos and Nur Misuari to harness their political will and skill to forge an agreement. In this regard, the thought of President Ramos is instructive:

> "The most serious threat to the stability of the Mindanao area at that time was the emergence of extremist groups such as the Abu Sayyaf. Three facts had to be considered in facing the challenges of these groups. One is that the development of this new wave of Islamic extremism had an international character and was the concern of several countries, notably Algeria, Egypt and Pakistan. Second, it was not merely a passing fad in isolated parts of Mindanao, but a serious threat arising from a militant religious struggle against the purported evils brought about by "materialism

and corruption" in the modern world. Third, like the MNLF struggle, it was mainly rooted in the widespread poverty and deprivation that pervaded the area.

Reliable reports pointed out that Chairman Misuari was deeply concerned about the growing extremist threat. One reason for this was those groups like the *Abu Sayyaf* clearly posed an obstacle to a negotiated settlement for autonomy because terrorism further polarized the already contentious situation. The second reason was that the MNLF's own troops could very well be drawn into an extremist-instigated conflict. The third was that the OIC would surely look down with disfavor on any form of MNLF involvement in armed actions tainted with terrorist motives."

In another front, the MILF had gained its own political niche after the discouragement of Chairman Salamat on the MNLF leadership. The MILF was established to contain the continuing infiltration of settlers into the remaining Muslim dominated Mindanao. As a strategy, the MILF forged ceasefire agreements with the government while strengthening its organization and mass support. Before the "all-out war" last year, it was able to establish 46 camps in many parts of Mindanao and Basilan. It was only a matter of time before the MILF gained a foothold in the MNLF heartland of Sulu. Although in the eyes of the AFP, the MNLF, MILF and the *Abu Sayyaf* are the same, the MILF is an epitome of Muslim movement in Southeast Asia where Islamic political doctrine is calibrated to form the foundation for revolutionary struggle. Although it was not as politically pragmatic and expedient as the MNLF, the MILF is not as callous and fanatic as the *Abu Sayyaf*. Like the MNLF, its main challenge is how to get the support of non-Muslims in the area and how to portray Islam as a viable political alternative. In short, given the reconfiguration it is not far-fetched among Moro movements to take an unconventional route of struggle. The latest Sulu hostage-taking incident illustrates it.

Poverty and Armed Conflict in Mindanao

AMINA RASUL

AMINA RASUL

Research Fellow, AIM

Amina Rasul is currently a Research Fellow with the Asian Institute of Management Policy Center in the Philippines. She was a Senior Fellow with the United States Institute of Peace (2001-2002)

Rasul is an expert on issues relating to minority representation and democratic participation in the Philippines, focusing on the Muslim insurgency in Mindanao. She has a distinguished record of public service and of achievement in the field of development. In 1994-98, she has a distinguished record of public service and of achievement in the field of development. In 1994-98, she was the only Muslim member of the Cabinet of President Fidel V. Ramos. She served as Presidential Adviser on Youth Affairs and as Chair and CEO of the National Youth Commission. In 1990-98, she served as a Commissioner on the National Commission on the Role of Filipino Women. She has served on the boards of government institutions such as the Development Bank of the Philippines, Philippine National Oil Corporation, a founding director of the Local Government Guarantee Corporation, among others.

She holds a Masters in Business Management Degree from the Asian Institute of Management in the Philippines and an M.P.A. from the Kennedy School of Government at Harvard University.

In the past year, she has served as resource person for CNN, MSNBC, National Public Radio, Brooking Institution's Task Force on US Policy towards the Islamic World, the East West Center Study Group on Internal Conflicts in Asia, among others.

Introduction

When government and aid agencies look at our development potential today, they see the present situation as cast in concrete, and despair over how difficult it is to help Muslims help themselves. Few policy makers have a picture of the vibrant, prosperous Muslim communities that existed prior to Martial Law, with little help from central government. Muslim communities have suffered from the mistaken premise that it is difficult to introduce economic development to their areas. But this is not so. Years of armed conflict have largely been responsible for the debilitating conditions existing in Muslim Mindanao today.

Poverty has long been recognized as a likely consequence of armed conflict. Whether it lasts only for a year or persists for decades, war exacts its toll on the welfare of the people. It results in the loss of lives and the displacement of a significant segment of the population. The instability that accompanies periods of conflict stifles economic activity and discourages needed investments. Often, it results in the destruction of vital infrastructure and disrupts the delivery of basic social services. People in affected areas lose their homes, their properties and their means of living, not to mention the psychological harm war inflicts on them that may take years to overcome.

But poverty can just as likely cause conflict as result from it, particularly when it reinforces social inequities. Where a section of the population exists that feels marginalized, when the community feels excluded from the gains of social and economic development, there exists the precondition for armed struggle. When a community feels that it is being excluded from national development because it does not belong to the culture of the majority, then poverty provides the wick for violent ethnic conflict.

Every day, for the last decade, we have been bombarded with information on government programs to deal with the poverty and inequity suffered by the Muslim communities. We have been told of the billions spent for the Autonomous Region of Muslim Mindanao (ARMM). What is fact and what is rhetoric? How do developments in predominantly Muslim regions compare to that in other regions where there is no armed conflict?

Although it is true that poverty is still a major problem for the entire country, the national security situation dictates that Mindanao, especially the Muslim areas, needs to be prioritized. This is due to the aggravating impact of poverty and inequity on the ethnic conflict raging in the South. Thus, this paper will focus on—and is limited to—an evaluation of the poverty situation in Mindanao, specifically in the Muslim dominated regions.

The paper will look at the current status of Muslim communities and present data to find out if there has been any improvement in the situation after announced government programs for the Muslim provinces. The paper will also attempt to compare the status quo with the situation before Martial Law, with the limited data obtained. Finally, it hopes to show that, prior to the years of armed conflict, the Muslim provinces were not the basket cases they have since been reduced to. In fact, they were progressive.

The Mindanao Landscape

In the early years of Spanish rule, Muslims and Lumads co-inhabited Mindanao. In 1918, the Muslims were the dominant group comprising 49% of the Mindanao population while the Lumads accounted for 29% (Table 1). But attempts at integration pursued during colonial times and pro-migration policies continued under succeeding Philippine government administrations—a major strategy aimed at providing "land to the landless"—resulted in a thriving migrant population comprised mainly of Christians from Luzon and Visayas. The unfortunate Muslims and Lumads, who had no knowledge of land titling procedures, lost their ancestral lands. The ethnic conflicts in Mindanao erupted in no small part due to "land-grabbing."

Table 1 shows the dramatic transformation of the Mindanao population profile in merely 50 years, after 300 years of Spanish rule. American and "Filipino" colonial policies[1] supported the rapid expansion of Christian settlements in Mindanao and their share of the population skyrocketed at an average of 72% per annum from a minority share of 22% in 1918 to 68% in 1970.

Table 1. Mindanao Population Profile, 1918-1970 (Based on Official Data)

Sector	1918		1970		Average Annual Growth Rate (%)
	Total	% Share	Total	% Share	
Christians	159,132	22	6,119,026	68	72
Muslims	358,968	50	1,583,043	18	7
Lumads	205,555	28	1,269,660	14	10

Source: Prof Samuel K. Tan, "The Socio-Economic Dimension of Moro Secessionism", Mindanao Studies Reports 1995/No.I

Once its majority inhabitants, the Muslims, along with the Lumads who are indigenous to the island, are now considered a minority in Mindanao. Out of 24 provinces, Muslims today are the majority inonly five provinces: Lanao del Sur, Maguindanao, Sulu, Tawi-Tawi and Basilan.

In spite of these tensions, there was a minimum of armed confrontation between Christian and Muslim communities prior to the 70s. Although largely rural and undeveloped, the quality of life in the Muslim areas at the time did not lag far behind many Christian provinces. The gulf of inequities surfaced later.

Muslim Mindanao Prior to Martial Law

Data on economic activities in the Muslim provinces for the 60s and 70s are not easily obtained. For instance, it would have been valuable to analyze the business environment of the period, which benefited from economic activities such as barter trade. Barter trade[2] between Sulu and Borneo, Malaysia that had flourished for generations gave prosperity to Sulu although it gave headaches to the Bureau of Customs. In the 60s, barter trade was restricted to the Tausug and Sama tribes of Sulu and Tawi-Tawi not only due to their proximity to Sabah, but more because of historical antecedents. The Sulu Sultanate owned Sabah, a claim that has been languishing in the International Court of Justice for decades now.

Thus, the indicators used in this paper as a gauge of development are access to piped water and electricity. The quality of life of a community and its rate of development are positively influenced by the existence of basic necessities such as water and electricity.

In 1970, in terms of access of households to piped water, the Muslim provinces, out of a total of 67 provinces, were in the middle range. Manila, of course, topped the list with 95% of its households connected to a water system. Lanao del Sur ranked 28th with 19.6% access while Sulu ranked 37th with 15.5% of households having piped water. Interestingly, Lanao del Sur and Sulu were ahead of Pampanga, Nueva Ecija, Pangasinan, and Tarlac. Agusan del Sur had the least access, at 0.5%, (Table 2).

By 1990, the Muslim areas were already at the bottom of the ladder, (Table 3), with Tawi-Tawi occupying the bottom rung. While Agusan del Sur improved its share from 0.5% to 5.0%, Sulu's share fell from 15% to 11%. Maguindanao, Sulu and Lanao del Sur ranked 2nd, 3rd and 4th, respectively.

In 1970, Sulu was ranked 38th out of 67 provinces in terms of number of households with electricity. It was ahead of the Mindoro and Samar provinces, Capiz, Ilocos Sur and Bohol, among others. Sulu ranked 11th among 18 Mindanao provinces ahead of North Cotabato, Davao Oriental, Surigao del Sur, Bukidnon, Zamboanga del Norte and Camiguin, (Table 4). As mentioned earlier, Sulu's capital town benefited from the professional management by the Aboitiz group of Jolo's power generation and distribution system.

Twenty years hence, the Muslim provinces are the least electrified in Mindanao. Tawi-Tawi and Sulu ranked 3rd and 74th, respectively, out of 76 provinces (Table 5). Again, armed confrontations destroyed facilities in many Muslim areas and the intimidating peace and order condition has prevented the establishment of new facilities.

Other indicators for development most likely follow the same pattern, except military expenditures per province where the Muslim areas will be ahead.

Table 2. Ranking of Households According to Number of Households in Occupied Dwelling Units with Piped Water, 1970

Rank	Provinces	% HH with Piped Water	Rank	Provinces	%HH with Piped Water
1	Manila	95.3	35	*Agusan del Norte*	*15.7*
2	Batanes	87.6	36	Antique	15.6
3	*Camiguin*	*78.6*	*37*	*Sulu*	*15.5*
4	Mountain Province	69.9	38	Bataan	15.4
5	Rizal	68.6	39	Pampanga	13.3
6	Benguet	58.5	40	Ifugao	12.9
7	*Surigao del Norte*	*49.5*	*41*	*Misamis Occidental*	*12.6*
8	Southern Leyte	43.8	42	Oriental Mindoro	12.5
9	Laguna	39.0	43	Camarines Sur	11.9
10	Sorsogon	35.6	44	Masbate	11.7
11	Zambales	33.1	45	Ilocos Sur	11.4
12	*Misamis Oriental*	*32.7*	46	La Union	10.8
13	Marinduque	32.0	47	Palawan	8.0
14	Cavite	30.1	*48*	*Bukidnon*	*8.0*
15	Leyte	29.3	*49*	*Zamboanga del Norte*	*7.9*
16	Albay	28.5	50	Northern Samar	7.4
17	Catanduanes	28.1	51	Nueva Ecija	6.3
18	Cebu	24.8	52	Pangasinan	6.3
19	Quezon	24.5	53	Tarlac	6.0
20	Western Samar	23.8	*54*	*North Cotabato*	*6.0*
21	Bulacan	23.0	55	Camarines Norte	6.0
22	Bohol	22.9	56	Capiz	5.9
23	Negros Occidental	22.6	57	Davao del Sur	5.5
24	Abra	22.0	58	Nueva Vizcaya	4.7
25	Batangas	20.8	*59*	*Davao*	*3.3*
26	Negros Oriental	20.2	*60*	*South Cotabato*	*3.0*
27	*Lanao del Norte*	*19.7*	*61*	*Davao Oriental*	*2.5*
28	*Lanao del Sur*	*19.6*	62	Cagayan	2.4
29	Kalinga-Apayao	19.2	63	Eastern Samar	2.3
30	Iloilo	19.2	64	Aklan	1.9
31	*Zamboanga del Sur*	*19.0*	65	Occidental Mindoro	1.8
32	*Surigao del Sur*	*18.4*	66	Isabela	1.4
33	Ilocos Norte	16.6	*67*	*Agusan del Sur*	*0.5*
34	Romblon	16.5			

Note: Mindanao provinces are in italics
Source: 1970 Census of Housing and Population, NSO

Table 3. Ranking of Provinces According to Percent of Households with Own Faucet/Community Water System, 1990

Rank	Provinces	% HH with Own Use Faucet Community Piped Water	Rank	Provinces	%HH with Use Faucet Community Piped Water
1	NCR	54.5	39	Siquijor	15.3
2	Batanes	44.7	40	Ilocos Sur	15.1
3	Benguet	42.8	41	Cebu	15.0
4	Camiguin	42.2	42	Pangasinan	14.9
5	Albay	39.2	43	Occidental Mindoro	14.8
6	Laguna	37.6	44	La Union	14.1
7	Cavite	34.8	45	Negros Occidental	13.9
8	*Davao*	*32.1*	46	Ifugao	13.4
9	*Misamis Oriental*	*32.1*	47	Palawan	13.3
10	Zambales	31.7	48	Romblon	13.1
11	Rizal	31.1	49	Bohol	12.8
12	Bataan	31.1	*50*	*Bukidnon*	*12.8*
13	Mountain Province	30.3	51	Negros Oriental	12.2
14	Batangas	30.3	52	*Maguindanao*	*12.0*
15	*Davao del Sur*	*27.8*	53	Sulu	11.0
16	Pampanga	27.5	*54*	*Lanao del Sur*	*11.0*
17	Bulacan	27.1	*55*	*Basilan*	*10.7*
18	Biliran	27.0	56	Isabela	10.5
19	Catanduanes	24.2	57	Iloilo	9.2
20	Abra	22.5	58	Samar	8.7
21	*Surigao del Norte*	*20.2*	59	*North Cotabato*	*8.6*
22	*Lanao del Norte*	*19.3*	60	Nueva Vizcaya	8.5
23	*Agusan del Norte*	*19.1*	61	Aklan	8.4
24	Camarines Norte	18.2	62	*South Cotabato*	*8.3*
25	Sorsogon	18.2	63	Antique	8.0
26	*Misamis Occidental*	*18.0*	64	Northern Samar	7.3
27	Leyte	17.7	65	Quirino	7.3
28	*Zamboanga del Sur*	*17.4*	66	Kalinga-Apayao	7.3
29	Aurora	17.2	67	Eastern Samar	7.2
30	*Surigao del Sur*	*17.1*	68	Cagayan	6.7
31	Quezon	16.9	69	Guimaras	6.1
32	Ilocos Norte	16.8	70	Capiz	6.1
33	Southern Leyte	16.1	*71*	*Zamboanga del Norte*	*6.1*
34	Tarlac	15.7	72	Masbate	5.3
35	Camarines Sur	15.7	*73*	*Davao Oriental*	*5.2*
36	Nueva Ecija	15.5	*74*	*Sultan Kudarat*	*5.2*
37	Oriental Mindoro	15.4	*75*	*Agusan del Sur*	*5.0*
38	Marinduque	15.3	*76*	*Tawi-Tawi*	*4.1*

Note: Mindanao provinces are in italics.

Source: 1990 Census of Housing and Population, NSO

Table 4. Ranking of Provinces According to Percentage of Households with Electricity, 1970

Rank	Provinces	% HH with Electricity	Rank	Provinces	%HH with Electricity
1	Manila	94.6	35	Camarines Norte	7.0
2	Rizal	88.9	36	Catanduanes	7.0
3	Laguna	56.8	37	Nueva Vizcaya	6.8
4	Bulacan	55.1	*38*	*Sulu*	*6.7*
5	Cavite	53.9	39	Oriental Mindoro	6.7
6	Pampanga	44.0	40	Leyte	6.7
7	Bataan	42.9	*41*	*North Cotabato*	*6.4*
8	Benguet	41.8	*42*	*Davao Oriental*	*6.3*
9	Zambales	40.2	43	Occidental Mindoro	6.2
10	*Davao del Sur*	*25.9*	44	Sorsogon	6.0
11	Tarlac	22.8	*45*	*Surigao del Sur*	*6.0*
12	Batangas	18.9	46	Abra	5.6
13	Nueva Ecija	18.9	47	Palawan	5.5
14	*Agusan del Norte*	*18.6*	48	Aklan	5.4
15	Cebu	17.5	49	Capiz	5.1
16	Negors Occidental	16.7	50	Ilocos Sur	4.5
17	Quezon	16.1	*51*	*Bukidnon*	*4.4*
18	Pangasinan	16.1	52	Isabela	4.3
19	La Union	15.9	53	Southern Leyte	4.1
20	*Lanao del Norte*	*14.4*	54	Western Samar	4.0
21	*Misamis Oriental*	*14.1*	*55*	*Zamboanga del Norte*	*3.9*
22	*Misamis Occidental*	*11.9*	56	Bohol	3.8
23	Albay	11.2	57	Cagayan	3.8
24	Batanes	10.4	*58*	*Lanao del Sur*	*3.7*
25	Iloilo	10.3	*59*	*Camiguin*	*3.1*
26	Camarines Sur	10.1	60	Mountain Province	3.0
27	*Davao*	*10.0*	61	Masbate	2.8
28	*Zamboanga del Sur*	*10.0*	62	Northern Samar	2.3
29	*South Cotabato*	*9.3*	63	Romblon	2.1
30	Ilocos Norte	9.0	64	Antique	1.6
31	Marinduque	7.4	65	Kalinga-Apayao	1.2
32	*Agusan del Sur*	*7.4*	66	Eastern Samar	1.1
33	Negros Oriental	7.3	67	Ifugao	0.3
34	*Surigao del Norte*	*7.3*			

Note: Mindanao provinces are in italics

Source: 1970 Census of Housing and Population, NSO

Table 5. Ranking of Provinces According to Percent of Households with Electricity, 1990

Rank	Provinces	% HH with Electricity	Rank	Provinces	%HH with Electricity
1	NCR	91.9	39	Iloilo	40.1
2	Bulacan	90.9	*40*	*Surigao del Norte*	*39.8*
3	Pampanga	88.6	41	Albay	39.2
4	Cavite	87.6	42	Bohol	35.7
5	Laguna	86.1	43	Southern Leyte	35.6
6	Rizal	81.5	*44*	*Lanao del Sur*	*34.9*
7	Ilocos Norte	80.0	45	Leyte	34.7
8	Bataan	76.1	*46*	*Sultan Kudarat*	*34.6*
9	*Davao*	*74.1*	*47*	*Agusan del Sur*	*33.6*
10	Zambales	73.4	48	Catanduanes	33.2
11	Batangas	71.8	*49*	*Bukidnon*	*31.5*
12	La Union	70.3	50	Capiz	30.4
13	Ilocos Sur	69.8	51	Mohuntain Province	30.3
14	Nueva Ecija	67.4	52	Marinduque	29.6
15	Tarlac	64.3	53	Antique	27.9
16	*Misamis Oriental*	*60.0*	54	Negros Oriental	27.7
17	Pangasinan	58.6	55	Oriental Mindoro	27.2
18	Abra	54.5	56	Biliran	26.5
19	*Agusan del Norte*	*53.3*	*57*	*North Cotabato*	*26.4*
20	*Davao del Sur*	*51.5*	*58*	*Camiguin*	*26.4*
21	Cebu	50.6	59	Davao Oriental	26.3
22	Misamis Occidental	50.4	*60*	*Maguindanao*	*25.8*
23	Isabela	49.9	61	Occidental Mindoro	24.0
24	Batanes	49.7	62	Samar	23.9
25	Camarines Norte	48.7	63	Siquijor	23.6
26	*Lanao del Norte*	*48.0*	64	Palawan	23.1
27	Quezon	46.4	*65*	*Zamboanga del Norte*	*22.8*
28	Nueva Vizcaya	45.8	66	Ifugao	19.8
29	*South Cotabato*	*45.4*	67	Kalinga-Apayao	19.7
30	Camarines Sur	45.1	*68*	*Basilan*	*19.4*
31	*Surigao del Sur*	*43.9*	69	Romblon	15.5
32	Sorsogon	43.7	70	Guimaras	14.1
33	Aurora	43.0	71	Eastern Samar	13.2
34	Benguet	42.8	72	Northern Samar	11.3
35	Quirino	41.6	*73*	*Tawi-Tawi*	*10.0*
36	Cagayan	40.8	*74*	*Sulu*	*9.4*
37	Negors Occidental	40.6	75	Masbate	9.4
38	*Zamboanga del Sur*	*40.2*	76	Aklan	1.5

Note: Muslim provinces are in italics

Source: 1990 Census of Housing and Population, NSO

Muslim Mindanao in the 1990s

Economic Growth. ARMM's economic growth since its creation in the last decade followed a boom-bust cycle - a pattern that also characterized the growth path of the other regions in the country in this period (Figure 1). During its expansionary years, ARMM's Gross Domestic Product (GDP) grew by as much as 9.5 percent in 1995. The region, however, was unable to sustain such activity. In 1997, ARMM's GDP registered zero growth, an experience that was repeated in 2000.

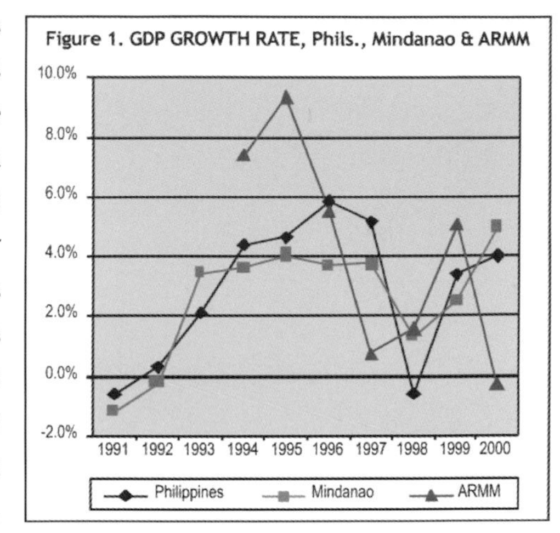

Source: NEDA Regional Indicators

Interestingly, official estimates of regional economic growth prior to 2000 suggest that during times of expansion, ARMM experienced a higher rate of growth than its neighboring areas and during periods of contraction[3], the effect was not as devastating in ARMM.

Despite this positive note, the fact remains that ARMM registered the lowest GDP among the six regions in Mindanao between 1993 and 2000 (Figure 2). During this period, ARMM's domestic product ranged from 6.9M to 9.2M Pesos. On the average, the region contributed only 5.4 percent of Mindanao's total domestic product. In contrast, the share of the other regions ranged from 38 percent (the highest) to 8 percent.

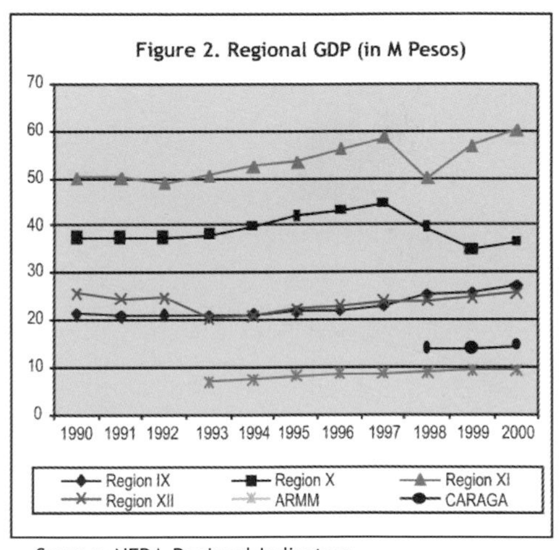

Source: NEDA Regional Indicators

Employment. As in the past, the families in Muslim provinces largely derived their income from agriculture. Based on the results of the 1997 Family Income and Expenditure Survey, 7 out of 10 families in ARMM depended on agricultural activities (such as farming, livestock poultry raising) for their income (Table 6).

Table 6. Total Number of Families by Main Source of Income, Mindanao Regions

Source of Income	Region IX	Region X	Region XI	Region XII	ARMM
			1997		
Total	5,568	5,281	8,904	4,495	3,561
Wages	1,946	2,456	4,11	1,802	453
Agricultural	419	510	1,174	388	39
Non-Agricultural	1,527	1,945	2,940	1,414	414
Entrepreneurial Activities	2,791	2,197	3,832	2,162	2,974
Agricultural	2,133	1,497	2,487	1,617	2,483
Non-Agricultural	658	700	1,345	544	491
Other Source of Income	831	629	957	531	133
			1994		
Total	5,088	7,342	8,871	3,952	3,300
Wages	1,876	3,245	3,933	1,481	369
Agricultural	347	796	1,312	506	6
Non-Agricultural	1,529	2,449	2,621	975	363
Entrepreneurial Activities	2,724	3,119	4,009	2,188	2,773
Agricultural	2,058	2,323	2,783	1,778	2,506
Non-Agricultural	666	796	1,226	410	268
Other Source of Income	488	978	929	283	158
			1991		
Total	4,788	6,855	8,300	3,673	3,108
Wages	1,618	3,090	3,223	1,215	297
Agricultural	299	1,024	1,012	323	16
Non-Agricultural	1,319	2,066	2,211	891	281
Entrepreneurial Activities	2,760	2,902	4,073	2,125	2,613
Agricultural	2,192	1,970	3,006	1,734	2,351
Non-Agricultural	569	932	1,068	391	263
Other Source of Income	410	863	1,004	334	198

Source: Family Income and Expenditure Survey, 1991, 1994 and 1997, NSO

This is not surprising given that Mindanao is largely an agricultural area. However, this heavy dependence on agricultural activities can be disadvantageous to families in light of the low level of productivity of this sector, and the impact of armed conflict on a family's capability to eake out a living. Simply said, no one farms when fighting is going on.

A greater prospect for earning higher incomes lies in the industry sector yet according to census reports in 1990 and 1995, the agriculture sector still absorbs the bulk of the labor force in ARMM. In 1995, close to 60 percent of age-eligible workers in ARMM are found either in agriculture, hunting or forestry.

Income Inequality. Total income in ARMM increased over the last ten years. By 1997, the Family Income Expenditure Survey (FIES) estimates that total family income in the region amounted to P26.7M. Most of the increase, however, was enjoyed by families belonging to the upper income decile as evidenced by the increase in the GINI coefficient[4] from 0.3198 in 1991 to 0.3406 in 1997 (Table 7).

Table 7. GINI Coefficient, by Region

Region	1985	1988	1991	1994	1997
NCR	0.4146	0.4258	0.4282	0.3967	0.4622
CAR		0.3741	0.4372	0.4100	0.4640
Ilocos Region	0.4011	0.3743	0.4039	0.3814	0.4257
Cagayan Valley	0.3856	0.3962	0.4172	0.4056	0.4130
Central Luzon	0.3992	0.3861	0.3986	0.3630	0.3638
Southern Luzon	0.4058	0.4034	0.4236	0.4016	0.4247
Bicol Region	0.3798	0.3876	0.3910	0.4116	0.4362
Western Visayas	0.499	0.4080	0.4031	0.4063	0.4412
Central Visayas	0.4537	0.4602	0.4604	0.4417	0.4750
Eastern Visayas	0.3904	0.4041	0.4149	0.4198	0.4457
Western Mindanao	0.3947	0.4087	0.4057	0.3861	0.4684
Noterhn Mindanao	0.4539	0.4424	0.4380	0.4157	0.4944
Southern Mindanao	0.3932	0.4019	0.4348	0.4114	0.4495
Central Mindanao	0.709	0.3583	0.4050	0.4280	0.4491
ARMM			0.3198	0.3125	0.3406
Caraga					0.4387

Source: 1997 Family Income and Expenditure Survey, NSO

Interestingly, ARMM registered the lowest GINI coefficient in the country during that period. This means that, while income distribution may have deteriorated over time in ARMM, the disparity between the lower and higher income deciles is not as wide as in the other regions[5].

While this could be seen as a positive development, its implication on the poverty situation in the region may be dampened by the fact that per capita income in ARMM remains the lowest not only in Mindanao but in the country. According to the 1998 Annual Poverty Incidence Survey (APIS), per capital income in the region for that year stood at P9,476—lower than the 1991 estimate of P10,780 (Table 8).

Table 8. Per Capita Income, by Region

Region	1991	1994	1997	1998
NCR	38,718	37,070	48,930	43,120
CAR	16,151	15,457	21,041	21,596
Region I	15,611	14,233	18,595	18,423
Region II	14,191	15,296	15,929	15,542
Region III	19,160	18,617	22,731	19,457
Region IV	18,458	19,756	23,677	21,622
Region V	10,019	11,227	12,821	12,217
Region VI	12,168	13,418	16,029	14,6259
Region VII	12,260	12,254	15,564	14,019
Region VIII	10,812	10,740	12,284	12,412
Region IX	10,729	10,402	14,768	12,213
Region X	11,214	11,754	17,149	14,871
Region XI	13,142	14,212	16,544	15,142
Region XII	11,375	12,170	13,954	13,023
ARMM	10,780	10,114	10,913	9,476
CARAGA			12,745	11,232

Source: Family Income and Expenditures Survey, 1991, 1994, 1997 Celia M. Reyes, Poverty of the Philippines, 2000

The Poverty Situation in Mindanao

Income Poverty

For the greater part of the last decade, the country enjoyed a steady decline in overall poverty incidence, defined as the proportion of the population living on incomes less than what is deemed adequate to fulfill basic needs. From 39.9 percent in 1991, the share of people in poverty fell to 31.8 percent in 1997, which translates into an average decline of 1.35 percent per annum.

In 1998, using estimates based on the results of the 1998 APIS, around 40.6 percent of the country's total population were officially considered poor, almost 10 percentage points higher than in 1997 (Figure 3).

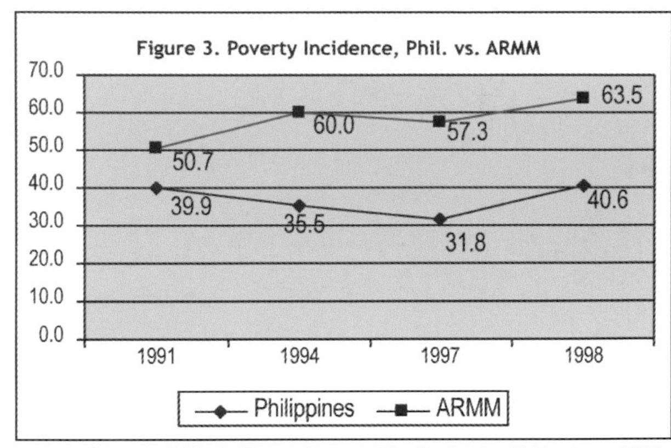

Source: Celia M. Reyes, Poverty Profile in the Philippines, 2000

These national developments, however, mask a wide range of experiences at the regional level. Marked disparities in the pace of economic growth across the regions resulted in wide variations in performance in terms of poverty reduction (Table 9). Between 1991 and 1997, most regions in Luzon and Visayas experienced significant reductions in poverty incidence. The decline was particularly substantial in Central Luzon and the National Capital Region

Table 9. Poverty Incidence, by Region

Region	1991	1994	1997	1998
NCR	13.2	8.0	6.4	13.7
CAR	57.0	51.0	42.5	48.0
Ilocos Region	48.8	47.9	37.8	47.3
Cagayan Valley	48.4	35.5	32.1	38.6
Central Luzon	43.3	25.2	15.4	27.4
Southern Luzon	31.1	29.7	25.7	32.9
Bicol Region	37.9	55.1	50.1	56.9
Western Visayas	55.0	43.0	39.9	50.6
Central Visayas	45.3	32.7	34.4	43.8
Eastern Visayas	41.7	37.9	40.8	47.1
Western Mindanao	40.1	44.7	40.1	54.9
Nothern Mindanao	49.7	49.2	47.0	48.6
Southern Mindanao	53.0	40.3	38.2	59.3
Central Mindanao	46.2	54.7	50.5	48.0
ARMM	50.7	60.0	57.3	63.5

Source: Family Income and Expenditures Survey, 1991, 1994, 1997 Celia M. Reyes, Poverty of the Philippines, 2000

(NCR) where the proportion of people living below the poverty threshold fell by at least half during this period.

In contrast, poverty incidence declined only slightly throughout most of Mindanao. **Poverty incidence, in fact, increased in the predominantly Muslim region of ARMM where the share of the poor rose from an already high 50.7 percent to 57.3 percent.**

In general, poverty incidence is higher in Mindanao than in other areas during this period - and often by huge margins. Table 10 shows the regional rankings in terms of incidence for 1991, 1994, 1997 and 1998 (where 1 indicates the lowest poverty incidence and 15 the highest). Three out of the five poorest regions in each survey year belonged in Mindanao. **Beginning 1994, ARMM registered the highest poverty head count in the country, which on average was almost twice that of the national estimate, and higher by at least 50 percentage points over that of the lowest ranked region.**

Table 10. Regional Ranking According to Poverty Incidence

Region	1991	1994	1997	1998
NCR	1	1	1	1
CAR	15	12	11	8
Ilocos Region	10	10	6	7
Cagayan Valley	9	5	4	4
Central Luzon	6	2	2	2
Southern Luzon	2	3	3	3
Bicol Region	3	14	14	13
Western Visayas	14	8	8	11
Central Visayas	7	4	5	5
Eastern Visayas	5	6	10	6
Western Mindanao	4	9	9	12
Nothern Mindanao	11	11	12	10
Southern Mindanao	13	7	7	14
Central Mindanao	8	13	13	9
ARMM	12	15	15	15

Source of Basic Data: Celia M. Reyes, Poverty Profile in the Philippines, 2000

Social Indicators

Health Outcomes. The last two decades witnessed a general improvement in the health status of Filipinos. In 1995, the average Filipino enjoyed a life expectancy of 68.1 years—8 years longer than the average life expectancy in 1990. One reason for this improvement is the steady decline in infant mortality rates in the country. From 57 in 1990, the rate of infant deaths nationwide fell to 49 per 1,000 live births in 1995. Child mortality rates likewise decreased over the same period, from an average of 24 deaths in 1990 to 19 deaths in 1995.

This improvement in the health status is also indicative of the increase in people's access to such basic services as safe water supply and sanitation. In 1997, 8 in 10 families had access to safe water supply and roughly the same proportion had access to sanitary toilet facilities.

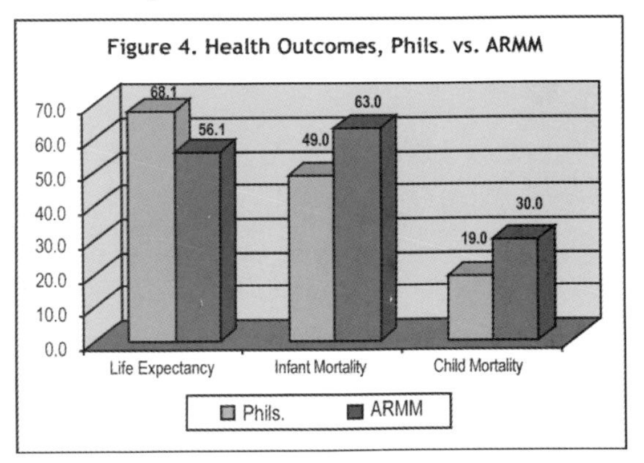

Similar trends are observed at the regional level - across regions life expectancies increased, mortality rates decreased and more families had access to basic services. But despite making the same progress, the Muslim areas still lag considerably far behind others in terms of health outcomes. In ARMM, for example, the average life expectancy in 1995 was only 56.1 years - 15 years less than in Central Luzon, which enjoyed the highest average life expectancy for that year. Infant mortality rates in this region from 1990 to 1995 were significantly higher than the national average and almost twice that of the lowest reported rates in the country. The disparity is even more glaring in terms of child mortality rates (Figure 4).

Also, a greater proportion of families in ARMM remain at risk of contracting an infection from drinking unsafe water—in 1997, only 3 out 10 families in ARMM had access to potable drinking water. In that same year, only a quarter of total households in the region had access to sanitary toilet facilities.

Education Indicators. There has also been a marked increase in literacy rates in the country over the last twenty years. The proportion of the population 10 years old and over able to read and write registered at 93.5 percent in 1990, an improvement of about 10 percentage points over 1980 estimate. By 1994, based on the results of the Functional Literacy, Education and Mass Media Survey (FLEMMS), this proportion stood at 93.9 percent. Additionally, the FLEMMS reported an increase in functional literacy rates among those aged 10 to 64 years (which measures numeracy skills along with reading and writing ability) from 75.6 percent to 83.79 percent.

This improvement in literacy rates is largely attributed to increasing access to education. In the country, primary and secondary education is compulsory and, as constitutionally mandated, offered free in public schools. In 1988, RA 6655 was passed into law, which strengthened the constitutional provision on free secondary education. Though still less than universal,

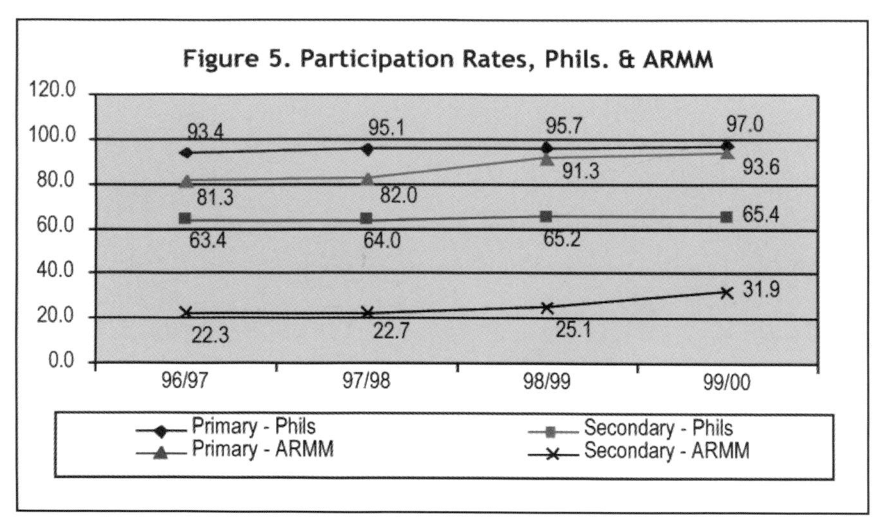

overall participation rates have been improving over time, particularly at the primary level (Figure 5).

At the regional level however, the indicators for the Muslim areas are dismal. While some regions achieved high levels, the predominantly Muslim areas have been unable to keep up—and the gap between them can often be quite glaring.

In 1994, simple literacy rates in the country ranged from a high of 99.5 percent in NCR **to a low of 73.82 percent in ARMM,** while functional literacy rates ranged from 92.41 percent in NCR **to just 61.12 percent in ARMM** (Table 11).

Table 11. Simple and Functional Literacy Rates, by Region

Region	Simple	Functional
NCR	99.50	92.41
CAR	91.26	78.55
Ilocos Region	97.33	86.42
Cagayan Valley	94.70	86.59
Central Luzon	97.36	87.28
Southern Luzon	97.52	88.01
Bicol Region	96.08	82.83
Western Visayas	93.62	80.94
Central Visayas	94.89	80.85
Eastern Visayas	92.56	79.72
Western Mindanao	90.69	75.38
Nothern Mindanao	95.64	83.41
Southern Mindanao	92.87	79.37
Central Mindanao	91.71	77.40
ARMM	73.82	61.19

Source: 1994 Functional Literacy, Educational and Mass Media Survey, NSO

The differences among the regions are particularly marked in terms of participation rates, especially at the secondary level (Tables 12 & 13). **On average, between SY 1996/97 and SY 1999/00, the participation rate of the lowest ranked region (often ARMM) was only one-third that of the highest ranked region (typically NCR).**

The low participation rates in Mindanao are compounded by high drop out rates during this period (Tables 14 & 15). **On average, roughly one-fifth of secondary students in ARMM leave school before finishing the level—this is double the national average and five times higher than the average rate in NCR.** The emerging picture is that of a growing number of families who are either not sending their children to school or taking them out of school.

Table 12. Participation Rates, Primary Level

Region	1996/1997	1997/1998	1998/1999	1999/2000
NCR	98.5	99.9	92.6	99.1
CAR	91.3	99.5	92.8	94.1
Ilocos Region	99.5	100.0	102.5	97.5
Cagayan Valley	98.6	98.7	101.0	96.5
Central Luzon	100.8	99.6	100.1	99.9
Southern Luzon	97.5	97.0	99.8	95.8
Bicol Region	92.5	94.1	96.0	96.5
Western Visayas	91.1	92.7	93.6	95.6
Central Visayas	91.1	92.7	93.6	95.6
Eastern Visayas	85.8	90.8	88.5	92.1
Western Mindanao	91.2	92.3	97.1	95.8
Nothern Mindanao	88.4	82.4	88.6	92.4
Southern Mindanao	88.4	88.6	88.6	92.4
Central Mindanao	91.3	99.5	92.8	94.1
ARMM	81.3	82.0	91.3	93.6
Caraga	85.3	90.3	94.5	92.7

Source: DECS Statistical Bulletins

Table 13. Participation Rates, Secondary Level

Region	1996/1997	1997/1998	1998/1999	1999/2000
NCR	80.8	80.2	82.1	80.3
CAR	72.2	73.2	84.0	79.2
Ilocos Region	65.0	66.3	67.1	67.3
Cagayan Valley	69.0	69.9	71.8	71.2
Central Luzon	66.5	69.5	70.8	71.7
Southern Luzon	61.3	62.7	65.4	65.5
Bicol Region	67.6	68.6	68.1	72.7
Western Visayas	60.6	61.9	66.1	65.6
Central Visayas	53.7	55.3	56.0	52.4
Eastern Visayas	50.7	51.8	48.4	50.5
Western Mindanao	56.4	46.2	48.2	50.0
Nothern Mindanao	55.4	56.3	49.1	50.9
Southern Mindanao	58.1	59.4	56.0	58.8
Central Mindanao	76.9	78.3	80.3	74.5
ARMM	22.3	22.7	25.1	31.9
Caraga	50.4	52.5	54.4	49.4

Source: DECS Statistical Bulletins

Table 14. Dropout rates in Secondary Level

Region	1996/1997	1997/1998	1999-2000
NCR	4.4	4.4	5.2
CAR	4.8	4.7	4.5
Ilocos Region	7.2	6.8	7.6
Cagayan Valley	4.8	5.0	4.6
Central Luzon	6.6	4.2	7.0
Southern Luzon	8.1	7.0	10.9
Bicol Region	9.9	7.3	11.3
Western Visayas	5.1	9.2	9.6
Central Visayas	11.4	10.6	11.7
Eastern Visayas	13.0	12.5	14.3
Western Mindanao	9.7	8.0	10.0
Nothern Mindanao	9.8	8.5	12.1
Southern Mindanao	12.2	11.7	12.6
Central Mindanao	6.6	8.1	10.4
ARMM	21.0	19.8	23.7
Caraga	7.4	11.7	12.8

Source: DECS Statistical Bulletins

Table 15. Dropout Rates in Primary Level

Region	1996/1997	1997/1998	1999-2000
NCR	8.3	8.4	13.3
CAR	6.6	7.5	12.7
Ilocos Region	6.1	6.7	14.7
Cagayan Valley	9.4	9.0	11.4
Central Luzon	8.7	11.4	8.6
Southern Luzon	11.5	14.1	12.8
Bicol Region	11.0	8.6	11.3
Western Visayas	13.1	8.5	12.2
Central Visayas	12.9	14.1	23.5
Eastern Visayas	7.6	11.1	13.4
Western Mindanao	11.4	11.5	15.2
Nothern Mindanao	9.9	8.7	14.8
Southern Mindanao	13.0	9.3	15.3
Central Mindanao	12.2	14.1	15.6
ARMM	16.4	16.1	12.9
Caraga	9.2	9.7	19.1

Source: DECS Statistical Bulletins

A recent report on the poverty profile of the country identifies two factors that could account for the low participation rates observed nationwide: the lack of adequate number of schools in the area, and the high opportunity cost of education. Previous studies have shown that the growth in secondary schools generally lags behind the growth in enrollment, particularly in the years following the passage of the Free Secondary Education Act.

The provision of free secondary education effectively freed families from the burden of paying for their children's tuition fees, at least when they are enrolled in public schools. However, there are other expenses to consider, such as allowance, cost of transportation, which could put a strain on an already limited budget. Thus, families often have to balance their children's need to gain an education (rewards for which will be enjoyed in the future) against the family's immediate needs. As a result, an increasing number of high-school age children are sent early into the workforce to augment family income. **Moreover, Muslim families are further burdened by insurgency and military operations in the conflict-ridden areas of ARMM and Central Mindanao, which prevent them from sending their children to school.**

Challenges

Poverty is still a major problem in the country. As of 1998, more than 5.8 million Filipino families nationwide—comprising roughly two-fifths of the total number of households in the country—continue to live on incomes less than what is deemed adequate to meet their basic needs.

While all regions share in this problem, the burden of poverty lies greatest on the Muslim areas. During the last decade, the regions in Luzon and Visayas (except perhaps for the Bicol Region and Eastern Visayas) have generally fared better in terms of poverty reduction and improvements in social conditions. In contrast, the progress in Mindanao has been slow and the regions here lag behind in many indicators. The Muslim provinces have fared worst of all.

Indicators such as access to electrification and water attest to the better quality of life existing in the Muslim provinces over twenty years ago. Whereas the Muslim provinces were better off than many Luzon and Visayas provinces prior to Martial Law, data has shown us that they have dropped to the status of "Poorest of the Poor." Destruction of infrastructure due to armed conflict as well as loss of confidence in the area due to continuing hostilities have prevented the Muslim provinces from recovering their pre-Martial Law status.

Together, poverty and conflict perpetuate a vicious cycle. Poverty fuels conflict—by magnifying the sense of marginalization and exclusion. Conflict, in turn, aggravates poverty—through its effects on people, institutions and the economy. Thus, they create the very conditions for their continuation.

National government, since the Aquino Administration, has trumpeted Mindanao economic development as a national priority. Moreover, economic development and poverty alleviation have been widely discussed as the major strategy to address the "Muslim problem." As has been shown in this paper, there is nothing to show over the last three decades except deterioration in the situation of the Muslim population.

For instance, barter trade used to drive the Sulu and Tawi-Tawi economies forward. In spite of the critical concerns raised by the Bureau of Customs over loss of revenue due to smuggling, national policy since Martial Law formalized and expanded the trade to allow operators from all over Mindanao to participate. Thus, national policy effectively took away from Sulu and Tawi-Tawi a major source of livelihood and replaced it with nothing.

Many Muslim leaders prefer to view poverty as the "Manila problem"—to highlight the fact that our poverty is not of our making and neither is it for lack of will to attain a better quality of life. We only have to look back and remember what and who we were thirty years ago. If the Muslim areas had been the poorest and most undeveloped then and showed no improvement today, then there is a "Muslim problem." But such is not the case. Progressive Muslim communities have deteriorated into "no man's land," rife with guns instead of plows.

Given the impact of the ethnic conflict in Mindanao on the island and the nation, fact should be made to match rhetoric. The crushing poverty in the Muslim communities should truly be made first priority in any national economic development and poverty alleviation program. Otherwise, the government's War against Poverty will yield little positive result to the entire country.

Endnotes

1 Pres. Manuel Quezon referred to the "colonization" of Mindanao during his June 16, 1936 speech to the First national Assembly of the Philippine Commonwealth.

2 Barter trade has ceased to be the exclusive domain of Sulu and Tawi-Tawi. During the Martial Law years, the center of trade was transferred to Zamboanga City. Today, what started as barter operations are now major international trading operations controlled by Manila and none-Muslim businessmen. Worse, it is suspected by local pundits that drug trade has been incorporated.

3 This pattern could stem from the very low GDP levels of ARMM to begin with.

4 A GINI value close to 1 indicates a higher degree of inequality; conversely, a value close to 0 indicates a high degree of equality.

5 Is this because there are very few rich residents or those who are well off are not rich enough to skew the distribution?

A Look at Corruption in the ARMM and the Role of Faith-Based Organizations in Fighting Corruption[1]

AMINA RASUL

Introduction

> *"Do not devour your wealth among yourselves through falsehood, and offer it not as bribe to the authorities that you may knowingly devour a part of the wealth of other people with injustice" (Qur'an, 2:189)*[2]

In an unprecedented event, the Philippine House of Representatives during the Eleventh Congress initiated impeachment proceedings against former President Joseph Estrada on charges of graft and corruption and betrayal of public trust. The case went as far as being tried by the Senate, but the proceedings were cut short by the walk out staged by the prosecutors. Events came to a conclusion in January 2001 year with "People Power 2" or "EDSA 2," a peaceful protest of Filipinos outraged by perceived manipulations of pro-Estrada senators to rig the outcome of the trial. EDSA 2 forced Estrada to step down, in a repeat of the 1986 People Power that forced strongman Ferdinand Marcos to flee the country.

The former president, charged with economic plunder, now languishes in "jail."[3] Plunder is classified in Republic Act 7080 as a non-bailable crime punishable by death. This law was passed in 1991, when Estrada was in the Senate.

The historic arrest of former President Joseph Ejercito Estrada on corruption charges leaves the impression that the Philippines is truly on its way towards reforming the bureaucracy. The fight against corruption is finally paying some dividends[4], snagging not just a police officer caught accepting bribes, or an employee asking for "grease money" to speed up processing of transactions. This was the president of the country, the biggest fish of them all.

Taking an anti-corruption stand is *de rigueur* among Filipino politicians. Of course everyone is against corruption. When he assumed office in July of 1998, Estrada made public morality one of his battle cries. Huge billboards sprang up outside government offices portraying a stern-looking Estrada with his fist clenched with the caption "Fight Graft and Corruption" printed in bold letters.

Transparency International (www.transparency.de) uses the Corruption Perceptions Index (CPI)[5] as a measure of transparency and good governance with 10 as the highest score. In 1999, the CPI for our country was at 3.6. Of the 99 countries rated, the Philippines came in as the 55th least corrupt country. But a year later in 2000, the CPI for the Philippines dropped to 2.8. The Philippines came in as the 69th least corrupt. This indicates a drastic mood swing towards perceiving the Estrada presidency as corrupt, just two years after he assumed office in 1998.

Table 1: CPI, 1980-2000

Region	1980-1985	1988-1992	1995	1999	2000
CPI	1.04	1.96	2.77	3.6	2.8

Source: Transparency International

But significantly enough, what led to the unseating of the president and his eventual imprisonment was not a result of a well-processed, systematic and institutional solution grounded on a moral foundation to combat graft and corruption.

Were it not for a falling out with his former gambling buddy, Estrada probably would still be President. If then Speaker Manny Villar of the House of Representatives did not abbreviate congressional proceedings, the impeachment resolution would not have been passed. If the prosecutors composed of opposition congressmen did not walk out of the trial when it became evident that Estrada's senatorial allies outnumbered the opposition, he could have been exonerated. The walkout triggered EDSA 2, which forced Estrada out of Malacañang. If these extraordinary events had not taken place, many believe that a simple denial of the accusation from the former president would have sufficed, and all would have been forgiven, and eventually forgotten.

What explains the pervasiveness and seeming acceptance of graft and corruption in the Philippine setting? Corruption has never been a novel topic. In fact one might say there is a surfeit of commentary on it[6]. All administrations over the past three decades have been smeared by it.

An investigative report released by Philippine journalists[7] details the huge scale of corruption in the country, even prior to Estrada. The report cites the anomalous sale of public land where an estimated P3-billion was lost to corruption in a single transaction (PEA-Amari deal). Other topics discussed the misuse of the public purse by members of Congress, collusion between government agencies with the private sector in siphoning public money in big contracts, how the electoral process perpetuates corruption, anomalies in privatization and liberalization transactions, and how regulatory agencies use their power to extract money from those they are regulating.

Some interesting arguments have been advanced defending Estrada. Some say that he is a "victim" of selective application of the law. They argue that if only he had been smart enough to finesse his corrupt acts, Estrada would not have been exposed and would still be in power today. Some say that at least Estrada mainly dealt with "illegal" money from gambling, and not with government funds, which makes it less of an evil.

The comments may indicate that there is a high subconscious tolerance for corruption. Desensitization to it may be a contributory factor, in that graft is so endemic that unless done blatantly, certain levels can be tolerated. Recent surveys show that, in spite of all charges, the poor still believe in Estrada. While the Macapagal-Arroyo Government was preparing to arrest Estrada, the latter's supporters—mostly from the urban poor—started rallying to support their idol. EDSA 3 was sparked by the arrest of Estrada and news footages later showing him forlornly standing against the wall for a mug shot. Hundreds of thousands of Filipinos, some estimates as high as 3 million, gathered before the EDSA Shrine to protest the government's treatment of Estrada. The protest ended in a violent confrontation when government troops and protesters, many armed with homemade weapons and rocks clashed in the Palace environs.

What conclusions can be drawn about corruption in the Philippines? Evidently, the roots of corruption lie in:

- The absence in government of a concrete, systemic, rational and determined effort anchored on a strong moral foundation to eradicate corruption; and
- The Filipino culture itself.

If the situation is thus in the national setting, what is happening at the local level? More precisely, how prevalent is corruption in areas occupied mostly by the Muslim minority in a country that is predominantly Catholic? Is their situation and attitudes toward corruption any better or worse, considering the attendant cultural differences? What accounts for the differences?

Role of Religion

More than three centuries of Roman Catholicism brought by the colonizing Spaniards redirected the indigenous native religiosity to Christianity. In the southern Philippine islands of Mindanao, Islamic influence grows stronger, and this influence stretches back to pre-colonial Philippines. Lately, various charismatic and prayer groups have been slowly eroding the once monolithic membership of the Catholic Church.

Every aspect of Philippine society is replete with religious imagery and influence, which sometimes blends Christian or Muslim beliefs and practices with indigenous traditions. In fact, a World Bank study cites a survey that 88% of Filipinos viewed themselves as "very religious" or "somewhat religious." Even in the political sphere, where the Constitution clearly mandates the separation of Church and State, it is unavoidable that religious leaders get involved, particularly (and this is usually the case) when issues tackle morality and ethics.

Faith and religiosity provide the Filipino a source of optimism and psychic energy when faced with difficult obstacles and a source of solace when tragedy strikes. By and large, the average Filipino has yet to stop ascribing negative events to "the will of the Almighty." As a basic social institution, religion plays a vital role in all interactions of Philippine society. Its main function is to spiritually nurture its adherents, and create a set of moral values and beliefs that bind people together.

Religion also galvanizes people to action as the various groups founded on religious principles are getting organized to take a more positive and activist role in actualizing the teachings of their religion. Prime examples are the role of faith-based organizations during the People Power demonstrations at EDSA and the role of the Ulama League of the Philippines in supporting peace efforts in the Muslim areas.

Surveys also indicate that Filipinos are religious and do not accept corruption. However, there seems to be a split between the ideals and morality espoused by religious groups and the average Filipino and the norm resignedly accepted by the people.

Special Focus: Autonomous Region of Muslim Mindanao (ARMM)

Mindanao, in the southern Philippines, is the traditional homeland of Filipino Muslims, or "*Moros*." Comprising about 15% of the 76 million population, Muslims are the largest minority group in the country. The majority of the Muslim population[8] resides in Basilan[9] and the ARMM—a special political subdivision in the Philippines created by law to serve as a solution to decades of conflict in the area arising from the clamor of the Filipino Muslims for self-determination. ARMM is comprised of four non-contiguous Muslim-dominated provinces[10] that opted to be included in the autonomous region during a plebiscite[11] held in 1989.

The poorest provinces are in the Muslim-dominated areas of ARMM. This is attributed to neglect by central government and a poor peace and order situation aggravated by corruption, inefficiency, and outright incompetence of officials.

Muslim children have the option to attend the "*madaris*" or the Islamic educational system. A separate set of personal laws also operates in the area, with the implementation of the Muslim personal code called the "*Shari'ah.*" Thus, given the differences in religion, education, and culture, there are definite differences in the worldview of the Filipino Muslims with the rest of the country.

Added on to these divergences is an overlay of historical events, which markedly divides the histories of Mindanao and the rest of the Philippine islands. Only in the 20th century can it be said that there was a merging of historical experiences in the entire country to include the Muslims.

Islam is the dominant faith of 99% of ARMM residents, which makes it unique in a country of predominantly Christian faith. Mindanao, which used to be primarily Muslim, today has a Christian majority. The Muslim tribes, living according to their culture and religion in conditions of poverty find themselves increasingly alienated from the majority.

The provinces of ARMM are the poorest in the country. ARMM has the lowest development indicators—lowest literacy rate, lowest life expectancy, and one of the lowest average family incomes[12]. The annual average family income in ARMM (1997) is P74,885, compared to the national average of P123,168.

The Functional Literacy, Education and Mass Media Survey (FLEMMS) of 1994 show that the predominantly Muslim areas are clearly disadvantaged. In simple literacy, ARMM rates are way below at 73.5% compared with the national rate at 93.9%. The functional literacy rates show the same trends, with the ARMM rate at a low of 61.2% and the national functional literacy rates pegged at 83.8%.

The life expectancy in ARMM for males is 55.5 years, compared to the national average of 66.9 years. On the other hand, life expectancy for females in the region is at 59.3 years while the national average is 72.2 years.

THE NATIONAL ANTI-CORRUPTION FRAMEWORK IN THE PHILIPPINES

Despite all of these manifestations of a system-wide problem that has tainted the highest office of the land, the Philippines does possess the necessary structures to combat graft and corruption. Early in 1999, Estrada himself asked the World Bank to conduct a study on corruption[13] and make recommendations on how to address it.[14] The World Bank study resulted in the creation of a National Anti-Corruption Framework and Strategy, as well as a National Anti-Corruption Commission (NACC) last July, which was to serve as the government "super body" to combat corruption.

The country also has an Ombudsman, a constitutional and therefore independent body that serves as the investigative and prosecutorial agency for criminal charges against public officers. We also have a special court that deals exclusively with these charges against high public officials, called the "*Sandiganbayan.*"

Two other constitutional bodies are tasked with oversight functions on the government. These are the Commission on Audit (COA)—which reviews all financial transactions of government—and the Civil Service Commission (CSC), the personnel agency of government, which enforces standards of hiring and performance of government employees.

In 1994, the government established the Presidential Commission Against Graft and Corruption (PCAGC). This institution deals with the administrative cases filed against officials at the director level and above. Then there is the Inter-Agency Anti-Graft Coordinating Council composed of the Commission on Audit, the PCAGC, the Civil Service Commission, the National Bureau of Investigation, the Ombudsman and the Department of Justice.[15]

In terms of laws, we have an "Anti-Graft and Corrupt Practices Act" and a "Code of Conduct and Ethical Standards for Public Officials and Employees Act," Other complementary laws exist, such as the reclassification of the penalty for plunder, as well as the usual efforts to streamline government operations for efficiency and to minimize opportunities for corruption. The Transparent and Accountable Governance (TAG)[16] has a website (www.tag.org.ph) that enumerates the complete set of laws, dating back to 1946 to as recent as a year ago.

Apart from the criminal justice system, these institutions serve as the main pillars for Philippine government and society in addressing the endemic problem of corruption.

On the surface, there seems to a formidable array of institutions and laws to keep graft and corruption in check. Even if ARMM is an autonomous region, it is still governed by all these laws, and all these national institutions are supposed to operate in the area as well. But given the national experience and the local ARMM situation, all these instruments are weak against invisible forces that make corruption flourish.

Institutional Weaknesses

The institutional and legal framework in the Philippines has failed in combating corruption. This can be partly due to institutional weaknesses buttressed by widespread political immaturity, thus creating an environment conducive to corruption. Analysts enumerate such weaknesses as:

1. Failure to establish an independent judiciary and a framework of enforceable laws to impose accountability;

2. Failure to create an honest and efficient administration (e.g. equitable and efficient tax and customs collection);
3. Failure of legal structures and institutions to enforce transparency in governance and delivery of public service; and,
4. The marketplace is still not a level playing field - thus control in the hands of a few allow for pressure to be exerted favoring so called friends or "cronies."

Despite the existence of interlocking institutions to address corruption, no important public officials have been charged or jailed through the normal legal process.

The Ombudsman himself, who ideally should be a person of probity and high ethical standards, was summoned to a Senate hearing on anomalies in his office and had faced impeachment proceedings in the House of Representatives on charges that he, himself, was corrupt. While successfully fending off the charges, a cloud of suspicion and mistrust has been cast over the premier anti-corruption institution of government.

To date, no high-profile case has been resolved and no important official has been convicted in the Sandiganbayan. Common complaints of a snail-paced adjudication process and inefficiency cast doubt on the Sandigan's intent, interest or effectiveness to fulfill its role.

Law enforcement agencies such as the Philippine National Police (PNP) and National Bureau of Investigation (NBI) have long been tainted with graft and corruption, with the public harboring generally negative perceptions about their role in combating crime. Media has provided a constant stream of complaints against the police, although in recent times, they enjoyed a more positive image due to reforms instituted[17].

The criminal justice system in the country also leaves much to be desired. With thousands of cases backlogged at the lower courts, justice is most likely to be denied because it is most likely delayed. The TAG website has a special feature on how the judiciary in the Philippines has been tainted by corruption at all levels, with the problem even reaching all the way to the Supreme Court.

The newly founded National Anti-Corruption Commission was a failure as well[18]. Credible and eminent people from government and civil society refused the invitation to join the NACC upon realizing they would be directly under the Office of the President and hence, had no independence.

ROOTS OF CORRUPTION

Filipino sociologists[19] enumerate several "roots" of the Filipino character, and their specific effects particularly in promoting corruption.

Foremost among these traits is that the Filipino is highly personalistic, due to the value of *"pakikisama."* This person-orientedness gives rise to hospitality, helpfulness and generosity in times of need, and a heightened sensitivity to others' feelings. Thus, the value placed on smooth interpersonal relationships supersedes other values that may be deemed important in other societies, such as being openly honest, or acceptance of constructive criticism.

This also prevents the Filipino from being able to easily deal with "impersonal stimuli", such as the bureaucracy founded on the Weberian principles of impartiality and standards. Conflict is often mediated through intercessors, with direct confrontation eschewed to preserve the *"samahan"* or relationship. Everything is personal.

The Filipinos are also said to typically possess strong family ties. The family gives the Filipino a sense of "rootedness" and identity. The family serves as the main source of emotional and material support, which explains the preeminence of the family in an individual's decision-making process. The definition of the family does not end with the parents and siblings, but extends to cousins and grand uncles, in-laws, and godparents through *compadrazgo*[20]. Since the Filipino uses "binary kinship ties" (using both the father and mother side) to trace family lineage, adding on to that the ceremonial kin, it makes for plenty of relatives. An old joke goes, "Power is relative. Where there is power, there are relatives."

Then there is also the very powerful dimension of Filipino political culture, which is the high level of societal trust. This extensive mutual trust is manifested in *"utang na loob"* or debt of gratitude.[21] *"Utang na loob"* motivates individuals to repay favors with the expectation that others would reciprocate given the same circumstances. Sometimes these debts can never be repaid, such as when one gives selfless aid in times of crisis. When one has a debt of gratitude to another, it does not matter what the reciprocal favor is, one has to pay or lose face.

Philippine society is also said to be hierarchical, where respect for authority is ingrained early on in the family (translated as respect for elders), and reinforced in the education system (where obedience to the teacher is highly valued).

These traits of person-orientedness, family orientation and "*utang na loob*" are, however, often taken to the extreme in Philippine society and culture. In fact, these very same strengths of the Filipino character are often the very same weaknesses.

When extreme personalism and family-centeredness is present, the very idea of a common good cannot surface. Clans take precedence over the greater community, with individuals generally identifying with people in degrees—first as family members, as fictive kin, as belonging to the same ethnic grouping, and last and least, as belonging to one nation.

Everything is seen as personal, which extends to the idea that a public office is a private domain and not a public trust. Family interests and honor have to be advanced, debts of gratitude have to be paid, and maybe then, the larger community is thought of. This attitude is not limited to the people who are in power or try to acquire positions, but to the masses as well.

The blurred distinction between public and private spheres is said to be an extension of the feudalistic structures that exist to the present day. Philippine society is still largely feudal in nature, with huge gaps between rich and poor,[22] landlord and tenant, elite and masses. Hence, the basic relationships in a feudal system remain pervasive as exemplified by patronage politics in the Philippines. The further away from urbanization and development, the more deep-seated feudal structures are.

Hence, all of these values converge into the dominant patronage politics in the country, where poverty and the inability of government to deliver basic services impels the client to seek remedy from the patron, who normally has extraordinary public and private resources at his or her disposal.

From cradle to grave, constituents line up for all kinds of assistance in their leader's house. This puts tremendous pressure on the patron to produce or face the risk of losing his followers, thus weakening his political base. It is both urgent and easy to give a few thousand pesos for the burial of someone's relative, rather than to work on a better climate for investors. Besides, the former is more personal, concrete and speedily achievable.

This need to cater to the various personal needs of the constituents that are not items in the budget brings forth the attraction to augment personal sources from public funds.

Corruption in the ARMM

Do these national assumptions hold true for the Muslim population of the ARMM? Apparently, a resounding yes. Decades of neglect by national government, the continuing conflict between secessionist and government troops, and the perennial failure to alleviate the situation in ARMM have all contributed to the problem.

From the way government is run in the ARMM, it could be said that Filipino Muslims are extremely person-oriented and family-centered. One look at the roster of elected officials clearly shows that politics is a family business. It is one area of the country where blood feuds called "*rido*" still rage.

If ever there were a more feudalistic society in the Philippines, it would be the ARMM. The recent elections have once more highlighted this situation as clans go after one another in securing the plum post that would give honor and resources to the candidate and his supporters.

This can be traced to the sultanate and datu system, where office and person were one and the same. Members of royalty and *datus* are now the elected baranggay (village) captains, mayors, congressmen, and governors. Thus, the imposition of a western-style democratic government did little to change the system of governance—the sultanate and datuship is still alive in spirit.

Economic and political isolation for centuries since the Spanish arrived has marginalized the role of Muslim Mindanao in the growth of the Philippine Republic. The Muslim communities have suffered neglect by the government for decades. Moreover, government has given their ancestral lands away to the landless peasants of Luzon and Visayas resulting in conflicts between the Muslims and the Christian settlers who started occupying Mindanao in the 50's.

This feeling of isolation and neglect is clearly reflected in the attitude of the Maranao tribe towards national government. The *Maranaos* have always described national government as "*Beberno a Saroang-a-tao*"[23] (a government of foreigners or aliens). This attitude makes corruption acceptable: it is but right to take the money of an oppressor, the unwanted foreign government. That these funds are earmarked to improve the lives of the people is forgotten.

The feeling of neglect and cultural and religious persecution grew strong in the South. Three decades ago, the Moro National Liberation Front (MNLF) headed by Nur Misuari rose in arms against the Philippine government.

The MNLF insurgency has since been resolved in a peace agreement brokered by the Organization of Islamic Countries[24]. The law creating the ARMM was passed and Nur Misuari was elected as the 3rd Regional Governor. However, conflict continues in the area, between government and other armed Muslim groups (such as the Moro Islamic Liberation Front (MILF)). These groups still seek that elusive goal of self-determination or secession, particularly as they see no significant progress in their lives.

The ARMM regional government has been criticized as inefficient and corrupt, with leaders hiring people based on loyalty or kinship, which is totally contrary to civil service regulations. Although the same description would fit the poorest provinces of the Visayas and Luzon, there is a fascination to correlate Muslim Mindanao with corruption and inefficiency, as if to underscore religion as a major contributing factor. It must be noted that the ARMM structure has been criticized as flawed.

In an article[25] assessing the ARMM seven years after its creation, the authors claim that the "ARMM is widely perceived as corrupt, wasteful and riveted by internal wrangling" and that with "its oversized, demoralized and mostly inept bureaucracy of more than 19,000 employees, it is an example of how not to run an autonomous government." The study then cites how billions of funds have been poured into the area with no great effect.

In 1990, the first ARMM governor, Zacaria Candao, was elected. He organized the bureaucracy from scratch, and after a bid for re-election three years hence, he lost to Liningding Pangandaman. It was under Pangandaman that the bureaucracy bloated to 19,040 people. It was described as an employment agency for family members and those with political connections.

And now it is Nur Misuari's turn. After having spent five years as concurrent chairman of the MNLF, the Southern Philippines Council for Peace and Development and governor of the ARMM, one would think that he had sufficient clout to effect the necessary reforms, particularly in controlling corruption. But on April 28, 2001, the MNLF's highest policy-making body—the Central Committee—declared its total loss of confidence in Misuari after his dismal failure to solve the myriad problems of the region.

The MNLF Vice Chair for Foreign Affairs[26] stated that Misuari "wasted too many opportunities for ARMM's development amid signs of nepotism, corruption and incompetence in his leadership."[27] Despite all these allegations, a formal complaint has yet to be filed, and judging by history, such a complaint would have never seen the light of day.

All three governors have been accused of tolerating corruption, but few formal charges have been filed, and for those filed, none prospered.

The grinding cycle of poverty and ignorance, and the dependence of the people on informal structures are permanent fixtures in the near-absence of governance in the area. There is a failure to deliver basic services and a general breakdown of government institutions. These function dismally or not at all, or are misdirected to serve the personal interests of those in power. Any delivery of services must go through the local kingpin. The feudalistic patron-client relationship remains the norm.

It must be noted, though, that the ARMM structure has been criticized as ineffective. Governor Misuari has been vocal about the lack of real autonomy, specifically in the area of revenue sharing. There should be a study conducted to evaluate the effectiveness of the present structure, especially today when many Mindanao leaders are pushing federalism.

Perhaps Filipino Muslims, for these reasons, are more personalistic than the average Filipino. They are also more clannish because reliance on the family, or the clan, is essential to survival. Necessarily, unquestioning loyalty and obedience are given to those who control the resources by the sheer logic of survival.

This further leads to the corruption so necessary to perpetuate the local leaders in power. That corruption comes in many forms — public funds siphoned off to pet projects or personal gain, excessive spending in elections to secure the gold mine that is the public office, nepotism, warlordism, and mismanagement of resources. The vicious circle continues.

Given the general absence of governance where state institutions fail to work, the only alternative is seeking remedies beyond the state, or into the very moral fiber of the people. Religion is where Filipinos, particularly the Muslims, can relate as it is the tie that strongly binds the different ethnic groups of Filipino Muslims together.

Islam on Corruption

Islam is one of three scriptural religions, along with Judaism and Christianity. On the fundamental questions on morality there is no marked difference among the three faiths. Any form of corruption, abuse, and extreme love for worldly possessions is condemned by all three religions. Any personal gain made at the expense of others is likewise condemned, and helping the less fortunate in life is encouraged. For Muslims, charity is not merely encouraged but mandated by the fourth pillar of Islam which is the "zakat" or giving of alms. This may be analogous to the tithe, with an established formula for computing how much is due to God and to the less fortunate.

Islam has very specific injunctions against corruption. A *hadith*[28] states: "When I appoint someone among you to public office and he puts away by stealth a needle or something else, that is embezzlement, and he will be called upon to produce it on the Day of Judgment." [29]

Earning one's own living and making money are legitimate quests, wasting wealth is unlawful, and spending extravagantly on lawful things is prohibited. It is also unlawful to abuse others' wealth. It is prohibited to possess other people's property illegally, which explains why the thief's hand is amputated as a punishment. Usury is likewise prohibited.

Hâdimî, in a publication for Waqf Ikhlas, tackles the subject matter in ethics in Islam where he states that in Islam, the third malady of the heart is the greed for wealth, property, or a leading position in the society.

Islam is not merely a religion. It is a complete system that has prescriptions for areas that other religions leave to the secular State—such as politics. Thus, despite the Constitutional principle of the separation of Church and State, this cannot realistically be followed in an Islamic milieu such as the ARMM.

Given these religious injunctions against excessive accumulation of wealth or the illegal acquisition of it, and the nature of Islam as an overarching ideology that includes both spiritual and secular matters, corruption should be held at a minimum in the ARMM. But that is assuming that Islam and its teachings are not influenced by other factors.

Thus, despite the formal framework of Islam, which clearly condemns corrupt practices, the informal relationships and customs in society play an important role that sometimes subverts the teachings of Islam. This is also true for the majority of the Christian population who are deeply religious and moral, yet constantly turn a blind eye to practices that are clearly immoral. A good gauge of this attitude is voting patterns[30], where obviously corrupt or immoral officials continue to be elected, and there is continued support for a disgraced president.

But all is not lost.

Role of Islamic Groups in Combating Corruption

There is a resurgence of religious organizations calling for a return to Islamic ways that serve to strengthen the moral fiber of the populace. Two powerful, loosely organized faith-based movements propagated Islam. Over the last two decades, the "Tableegh"[31] movement has grown in strength in Mindanao. The "Sabbab" group based in Lanao del Sur has caused the election of clerics to 19 posts. Muslim missionaries spread at the grass roots level, re-educating the people on the true ways of Islam. Although the focus of the teachers/missionaries is not specifically on corruption, their admonitions to live according to the tenets of Islam serve as a deterrent to corrupt practices.

Annually, thousands of Muslims from all tribes come together in a gathering called "huruj" to gain spiritual strength. Organized by an informal network of religious leaders, the *huruj* changes venue each year and has become a major activity of Muslim communities. Religious leaders from other countries—Pakistan, Malaysia, and Indonesia—join the *huruj* in the Philippines.

In the political arena, Islamic groups have been formed to specifically address this problem within the political arena.

The first was the establishment of *Ompia* ("reform") party in the late 80's, a creation of Muslim clerics (*Ulama*) of the Maranao tribe of Lanao del Sur supported by the Sabbab. It ran on a strong anti-corruption platform and secured important elective posts[32]. Ompia Party, with little funding, secured the election of Mahid Mutilan, a highly respected Ulama, to the position of Mayor of Marawi City. He later ran and won as governor of Lanao del Sur[33].

Mentioned earlier, the Ulama League of the Philippines is an organization of Muslim religious leaders and teachers who are active in promoting peace and development in the area. The League works with local government officials in Peace and Order Councils to reduce criminality and resolve conflicts within the community.

The MILF is also headed by an ulama in the person of Salamat Hashim. He sends a strong signal to be emulated by others, that one must adhere to Islamic principles even in the midst of a war with the government. Hence, the MILF disavows kidnap-for-ransom groups and other criminal activities perpetrated by their members. Crimes conducted by MILF members are tried according to the *shari'ah*[34] and justice is executed without going through the Philippine criminal justice system.

Admittedly, the fight against corruption is not a major concern among Muslim communities, survival is. However, Muslim religious and leaders of civil society in Mindanao have acknowledged corruption as an issue, and are using the strong moral foundation given by Islam to address it.

Role of Civil Society

Morality in governance is one important solution to the problem of corruption. However, we cannot expect morality to surface in governance and in business overnight—not even with a string of peaceful EDSA People Power revolutions. We have to look into educating our people, especially our young, on issues—enabling them to better discern what is wrong from right. The education process geared towards moral recovery may take time but it must be undertaken. An educated people, aware of political and moral issues, are the best solution to corruption for they will demand accountability of their leaders. Thus, education—whether formal or non-formal—is a priority.

In an underdeveloped area such as ARMM where government institutions are malfunctioning and where the business sector has yet to establish a presence, the only alternative service delivery mechanism is the so-called "Third Sector" of civil society, composed of non-governmental organizations, people's organizations, and other advocacy groups, including faith-based organizations.

This is where my organization, the Magbassa Kita Foundation Inc. (MKFI) comes in. The organization sees literacy and education, coupled with livelihood opportunities, as the foundations for a self-sustaining and politically aware community. Our goal is to help give the people a voice in the decision-making process and thus have a hand in governance over their communities.

Over thirty years ago, a Muslim mother of 6 decided to do something about the crippling illiteracy and poverty oppressing the Tausug and Sama tribes of Sulu. She developed a literacy-training program ("Magbassa Kita" or "Let Us Read"), which today is implemented nationwide. This lady since then has been twice elected Senator of the Philippine Republic, the only Muslim woman to be elected and the only Muslim ever to be re-elected by a Christian majority.

Senator Santanina Rasul saw education and livelihood training as the permanent solution out of the cycle of poverty and ignorance oppressing the Muslim communities. Thirty years ago, she already saw that the Muslims of the Philippines could not be empowered without the foundation of education and economic development.

We have also organized Muslim women. The Muslim Professionals and Businesswomen's Association of the Philippines (MPBWAP) implements seminars to empower women, that they may help in conflict resolution and establish a culture of peace in their communities. The Association has a Women's Center in Zamboanga City, which is used for training seminars and as home to a children's library.

We established an agricultural high school, which incorporates Islamic education in the program. Unfortunately, the school is temporarily closed. Funding has become a problem due to armed conflict in our province.

Civil society has become more active in the Muslim provinces. These organizations generally do not focus on the fight against corruption.

However, their work serves to empower the citizens so that the Muslims may become more aware of their oppression and do something about it. One organization in Sulu, supported by UNICEF, runs a community radio station which airs educational programs. The Catholic school, Notre Dame, has non-governmental organizations (NGOs) that provide livelihood training, literacy and credit programs in the Muslim communities.

Leaders and members of NGOs in the Muslim provinces have become more politicized and vocal, criticizing corruption in their local government units (LGUs). We in civil society believe that change must come from the grassroots level, if change is to be permanent.

Corruption will continue if the citizenry will not challenge corrupt officials. The citizenry cannot become a force for change if they themselves are easily manipulated because of ignorance and poverty. Thus, NGOs like MKFI and the MPBWAP are focused on empowering the individual members of the Muslim community.

RECOMMENDATIONS AND CONCLUSION

Given the nature of corruption in the Philippines and particularly the ARMM, there can never be a solution until the fundamental issues of poverty and ignorance are addressed. People who have to worry about where to get the next meal will not think about the corruption behind political dole-outs, as long as they receive what they need.

The systemic nature of the problem means that isolated efforts at addressing it—even one as powerful and dramatic as People Power demonstrations—will never succeed unless the foundation itself is strengthened. Rhetoric, exhortations and appeals to morality are certainly the weakest strategies to employ when dealing with corruption. The institutions created to precisely address corruption do not work.

Culture can be overestimated as the root cause of corruption. However, in the Philippine and ARMM cases, the prevalent negative attitudes of the people are further reinforced by the twin cycles of poverty and ignorance. While Muslims are a highly religious people, there seems to be an overriding element in our culture that makes it possible to accept someone obviously corrupt and immoral in a position of authority.

For the people in the fringes of development particularly the ARMM, governance remains an abstract concept, but the datu/mayor is the reality. Hence, he is the government. There can be no separating the person from the office, particularly if the clan of this person has been in the leadership role for generations.

Morality has taken a back seat to the stark reality of surviving in the poorest areas of the country. Therefore, a moral high ground is essential to the new government if only to avoid the fate that befell the previous administration. People have become more politically and socially aware. In fact the almost 90% voters' turnout in the May 14, 2001National Elections is a very good indicator of rising civic engagement.[35]

Hence, leaders and politicians are more wary of being blatantly corrupt, at the national level at least. It will take some time before this attitude and awareness seep into the less developed regions such as the ARMM.

That is why civil society organizations are so necessary in a developing country such as the Philippines. They are neither profit-oriented, nor encumbered with the burdens of bureaucracy. The resurgence of religious groups and the strengthening of civil society offer a positive outlook for the future of the country and the ARMM in addressing corruption.

Corruption takes on added importance as leaders look at federalism as a viable political solution to the ethnic conflict in Mindanao. Where the local government units and civil society are weak, decentralization allows graft and corruption to flourish. Thus, we need to focus attention now on how to deal with this endemic problem. For instance,

1. Studies should be conducted on the extent and nature of corruption in ARMM in order to provide for effective safeguards. Perhaps the UP Institute of Islamic Studies, the Mindanao State University (MSU) and other Islamic institutes can be brought together with institutions which have experience on the subject such as the Policy Center of the Asian Institute of Management, TAG and Transparency International (TI). A collaboration of these institutions to address the problem should produce proposals which are culturally sensitive, thus more likely to succeed.
2. Strengthen the Ulama League and other faith-based organizations (FBOs) so that they can play a more visible role not only for peace-

building but also for the fight against corruption. During the Anti-Corruption Global Forum II at The Hague, the FBOs organized the International Network of Faith-based Organizations Against Corruption (INFOC)[36] composed of organizations representing the faiths of the world. The Ulama League and other FBOs can be linked up with such networks. INFOC will be meeting at the next international conference on transparency in governance organized by TI in Prague this October. Perhaps representatives of the Ulama League and other Muslim FBOs can be sponsored to attend.

3. As part of the Judiciary Reform Program, fully implement and strengthen the Shari'ah Courts. This will not only help decongest the Philippine judiciary, it will also place in the Muslim communities a visible symbol of justice. However, the codified Muslim personal laws need to be reexamined. First, laws that impinge on women's rights were put in place without inputs from women legal experts. Second, there is a growing demand from Muslim communities to allow the Islamic courts to cover more than family and personal laws.
4. Give voice to the people. Build up the capacity of local NGOs and people's organizations, especially those managed by the Muslims themselves. Aggressively implement literacy programs outside of the public educational system to reduce, if not eradicate, the 40% illiteracy rate in the Muslim areas.
5. Design and implement training programs for LGU officials of Muslim communities on good governance, within the context of Islam and the local cultures. On a positive note, the ARMM LGUs seem to be more receptive now to concepts of transparency and good governance. During a CIDA-funded training seminar for newly-elected ARMM mayors recently, some mayors of Sulu asked that such training seminars on governance be organized for them.
6. To complement the above, create an awards mechanism for the LGUs in the Muslim provinces, similar to the "*Galing Pook*", setting as examples those with effective delivery of public service. A similar mechanism can be created for civil society to include outstanding individuals.

In the end, the interlocking approach will still be the best model for governance, where government focuses on administering the region and delivery of public services, where business focuses on economic development, and where civil society bridges the gap in empowering the citizens. In the meantime, the groundwork must be built. The winds of change are blowing in the right direction. However, the cycle of poverty must be broken. Education- civic, political and moral - must become widespread. Only then can we become an empowered people with full control over our own lives.

Table 2: Statistics on Autonomous Region in Muslim Mindanao

Indicator	ARMM	Philippines
Family Income and Expenditures (as of 1997)		
(in Philippine Peso, at current prices)		
Annual Average Family Income	74,885	123,168
Annual Average Family Expenditures	57,546	99,537
Annual Average Family Savings	17,339	23,631
Education (as of 1994)		
Simple Literacy Rate (10 yrs. old and over)	73.5	93.9
Functional Literacy Rate (10 to 64 yrs. old)	61.2	83.8
Vital Statistics (as of 2000)		
Crude Birth Rate (per thousand population)	28.2	26.78
Crude Death Rate (per thousand population)	8.6	5.89
Crude Rate of Natural Increase (per thousand population)	19.6	20.89
Total Fertility Rate (number children per woman)	3.5	3.38
Life Expectancy at Birth (in years)		
Male	55.5	66.33
Female	59.3	71.58

Source: National Statistics Office, Philippines

SOURCES:

Coronel, Sheila S., Editor. Pork and Other Perks: Corruption and Governance in the Philippines. Philippine Center for Investigative Journalism: Quezon City, Philippines. 1998.

Gutierrez, Eric et al. Rebels, Warlords and Ulama. Institute for Popular Democracy: Quezon City, Philippines: 2000.

Licuanan, Patricia. Amoral Recovery Program: Building A People, Building A Nation. Ateneo de Manila University Press: Quezon City, Philippines. 1988.

National Statistics Office. "NSO Quickstat." Electronic posting. http://www.census.gov.ph/data/quickstat/index.html. 2001.

Pazzibugan, Dona. "MNLF: Misuari did nothing for years". Philippine Daily Inquirer. May 09, 2001. Electronic posting available at http://www.inq7.net.

Romero, Segundo E. "Civil Society-Oriented Measures for Enhancing Transparency and Accountability in Governance and the Civil Service". Electronic posting. http://www.fes.or.kr/Corruption/papers/Philippines.htm.

Translations of the Holy Qur'an. Electronic posting. http://www.dawn.com.

Transparent Accountable Governance. "Philippine Laws on Corruption". Electronic posting. http://www.tag.org.ph/phillaw/default.htm.

World Bank. Combating Corruption in the Philippines. World Bank Philippine Country Management, Unit, East Asia and Pacific Region: Manila, Philippines. 2000.

Wurfel, David. FILIPINO POLITICS: DEVELOPMENT AND DECAY. Ateneo de Manila University Press: Quezon City, Philippines. 1991.

Transparency International. "2000 Corruption Perceptions Index". Electronic posting. http://www.transparency.de/documents/cpi/2000/cpi2000.html.

Endnotes

1 Based on paper presented at the Panel of Faith-Based Organizations Against Corruption during the Global Forum on Fighting Corruption and Safeguarding Integrity II, The Hague, May 28-30, 2001.
2 Translation, http://www.dawn.com
3 The former President and his son, former Mayor Jinggoy Estrada, are confined on the premises of a government military hospital.
4 In a separate incident a month earlier, an officer of the Bureau of Internal Revenue (government's tax collection agency) was jailed for economic plunder.
5 For the Philippine case, the CPI is a composite index of 12 different polls and surveys.
6 Even media is accused of corruption, of "envelopmental journalism" wherein news or commentaries are for sale.
7 "Pork and other Perks: Corruption and Governance in the Philippines", edited by Sheila S. Coronel, PCIJ, 1998.
8 Large Muslim communities also reside in the rest of Mindanao provinces especially Lanao del Norte, Sultan Kudarat, North Cotabato and South Cotabato, Zamboanga City, Zamboanga del Sur and del Norte, Davao City.
9 Basilan is an island province in Western Mindanao.
10 Composed of 4 provinces: Sulu, Tawi Tawi, Maguindanao and Lanao del Sur.
The plebiscite was conducted in 17 provinces, which were considered the traditional homeland of Muslim tribes. The MNLF campaigned for a boycott of the plebiscite, resulting in a low vote. Only four provinces voted for inclusion.
12 National Statistics Office
13 Published in May 2000, the World Bank study is entitled "Combating Corruption in the Philippines".
14 Estrada commissioned the study at the same time he was reportedly receiving funds from illegal gambling, kickbacks from stock market manipulation, and a personal share of excise taxes from tobacco.
15 Combating Corruption in the Philippines"
16 TAG is an aggrupation of major civil society and research institutions which includes the Social Weather Stations, Makati Business Club, PCIJ, Philippine Center for Policy Studies and the Asia Foundation.
17 It is interesting to note that the Philippine National Police head responsible for its positive image, Gen. Ping Lacson, is being accused with criminal involvement.
18 According to an article by Dr. Segundo Romero, senior consultant of the Development Academy of the Philippines, which recommended the creation of the NACC.
19 Patricia Licuanan in her study for the Moral Recovery Program in 1988.
20 Ritual or ceremonial relatives: surrogate parents chosen to witness baptisms and weddings.
21 "Filipino Politics: Development and Decay" by David Wurfel (1998)
22 Licuanan, "Moral Recovery Program", 1988
23 Observation made by Commissioner Nasser Marohomsalic, Commission on Human Rights.
24 GRP-MNLF Peace agreement was finally signed in 1996.
25 Gutierrez and Danguilan-Vitug "ARMM After the Peace Agreement" in Rebels, Warlords and Ulama.
26 Dr. Parouk Hussin is now Presidential Adviser for Muslim Affairs.
27 Pazzibugan, "MNLF:Misuari did nothing for 5 years," Philippine Daily Inquirer, May 10, 2001
28 These are the recorded traditions of the Prophet Mohammed, which along with the Holy Qur'an comprise the sources of Islamic Law.
29 Translation from www.dawn.com
30 Although it is hoped that the results of the May 14 elections will show a trend of support for capable leaders with integrity, the election thus far is being described as one of the most fraudulent and violent in our history.
31 Tableegh movement came from Pakistan and has grown in Muslim Mindanao. Its membership includes not only the masses and religious leaders but also many political leaders.
32 Gutierrez et al., "Rebels, Warlords and Ulama"
33 Governor Mutilan won three terms as governor. Unfortunately, charges have been filed against him for graft and corruption.
34 Islamic law
35 The counting or canvassing of votes is another matter entirely. Ed.
36 Author is a member of the executive committee.

The Status and Impact of Education and the Madaris Among Muslims in Mindanao

DR. CAMAR A. UMPA
AND PROF. SALIPADA S. TAMANO

DR. CAMAR A. UMPA

President, MSU

Dr. Camar Umpa, who is currently the President of Mindanao State University (MSU), specializes in the field of science and technology education, national development, political development and the integration of national communities, as well as peace research and conflict resolution.

Dr. Umpa obtained a degree in Political Science from MSU, a Doctorate of Philosophy and Master of Arts in Political Science from the University of Hawaii, and Post-graduate International Training on Peace Research and Conflict Resolution in Uppsala University in Sweden.

PROF. SALIPADA S. TAMANO

Prof. Tamano is a candidate for the degree of Doctor of Philosophy in Education, Ain Shams University, Cairo, Egypt. She obtained her Master of Arts and Special Diploma in Education at the same university.

Prof. Tamano has been in several government positions, most notable of which is being Assemblyman/Member, Consultative Assembly, Southern Philippines Council for Peace and Development (SPCD) from 1996 to present. She was also the Regional Secretary, Department of Education,Culture and Sports, Autonomous Region in Muslim Mindanao (DECS-ARMM), from 1994-1996.

Introduction

Education is an investment for economic development, for social progress, for cultural preservation and enrichment as well as for harnessing science and technology for the benefits of man. It provides skilled manpower, managers and entrepreneurs, agriculturists, aquaculturists, implementers, government employees, social workers, peacemakers, and other professionals needed for nation building.

In Mindanao, particularly in areas predominantly populated by Muslims, education, when examined within the context of the above-mentioned educational ends, is found wanting. For one thing, it remains a mediocre social institution, unable to make a tenable impact on their socio-economic life. Due to poor education, the Muslims are not able to participate actively in regional and national development. They need a comprehensive realistic and relevant education so that peace and development can be put in place in this impoverished land of plenty.

This paper reviews the status of education in Muslim Mindanao including the madrasah. It emphasizes the four provinces of the Autonomous Region in Muslim Mindanao (ARMM) - Lanao del Sur, Maguindanao, Sulu and Tawi-Tawi. It also offers recommendations to solve the educational ills in the region.

Educational Performance in Muslim Areas

Performance indicators of basic education (elementary and secondary) in Muslim Mindanao are poor, most especially in areas directly affected by the Mindanao armed conflict. These indicators include participation rate, cohort survival rate and literacy rate.

The participation rate (the ratio between the enrollment of the school-age children 6-7 years old or above and the total population of that age range) for Muslim Mindanao in both public and private elementary schools shows that ARMM has 91.32% in SY1998-99. This is quite high compared to other regions in Mindanao. However, high schools have only 22.66%.

The cohort survival rate (the percentage of enrollees at the beginning grade or year who reach Grade VI or senior high school) of ARMM is 31.28% in the elementary level and 59.32% in the secondary level (SY1998-99). This means that while the participation rate in elementary schools is high, its cohort survival rate is very poor, allowing only about 31 pupils to reach Grade VI out of 100 Grade I enrollees. In high school, on the other hand, at least 59 students out of 100 freshmen graduated during the same period. This implies that the level of educational attainment in Muslim Mindanao is poor.

Table 1: Participation and Cohort Survival Rates for Public, Private Basic Education in ARMM and Regions IX, XII. SY1998-99

Regions	Participation Rate		Cohort Survival Rate	
	Elementary	Secondary	Elementary	Secondary
National	--	--	68.56	71.36
Mindanao	89.46	49.26	55.54	65.97
Region IX	88.46	51.76	53.14	65.37
Region XII	79.26	59.37	54.80	70.77
ARMM	91.32	22.66	31.28	59.32

Source : PBSP & MEDCo, 1999

In terms of functional literacy rates, ARMM and Regions IX and XII in Mindanao fall below the national literacy rate of 87.80%. The ARMM is the lowest with only 61.19% in 1997.

Table 2 Functional Literacy Rate (1999)

Region	Fanctional Literacy Rate
National Average	87.80
Reion IX	75.8
Region XII	77.40
ARMM	61.19

Source: PBSP, 1999

In addition, the educational performance indicators in the conflict-ridden areas of Lanao del Sur are much lower than those in the unaffected areas. Considering that most of the areas in Muslim Mindanao have been affected by the conflict, it is expected that most provinces in Muslim Mindanao lag behind in all educational indicators compared to those in Luzon and Visayas.

Table 3: Mean Performance Educational Indicators at the Secondary Level in and Unaffected Areas in Lanao del Sur (2001).

Indicators	Affected Areas	Unaffected Areas
Enrollment Rate	47.92	51.46
Participating Rate	72.08	74.20
Drop-Out Rate	17.76	11.72
Survival Rate	87.74	95.84
Promotion Rate	80.66	88.26
Cohort Survival Rate	45.96	61.64
Completion Rate	64.20	73.62
NSAT Weighted Men	83.56	86.46
Mean Percent Teacher Absenteesim	3.79	2.71
Teacher Performance Rating	7.04	8.36

Note: Data in this table are mean ratings from 1996 to 1999.
Source: Sarip, 2001

The Problems of Education in Muslim Mindanao

The inefficient educational system in Muslim Mindanao can be attributed to a host of problems. The Comprehensive Mindanao Education Program (CMEP) has identified some serious problems of education. First is the physical facilities. The lack of physical facilities, such as classrooms, chairs/ desks, laboratories, among others, as well as books and instructional materials, have adversely affected the performance of pupils and students at the basic and secondary levels. The lack of culturally sensitive instructional materials may have also contributed to the low performance of Muslim students in standardized achievement tests.

Second, there is a perennial inadequacy of financial support for basic education in Muslim Mindanao that has contributed to low educational indicators. This inadequacy cannot find a viable rationale in a nation whose Constitution has mandated the allocation of the highest financial priority to education and which that has also legislated free basic education.

Third, there is a lack of mutual understanding and the absence of common unifying identity among the varied Muslim cultures in Mindanao (e.g. Maranao, Tausog, Maguindanao, Samal, Yakan, etc.). For education to address the various cultures of the Muslim Mindanaoans in a common government-prescribed curriculum is by itself impossible for the most people to totally understand and appreciate.

Fourth, there are two discrete systems of education for the Muslims in Mindanao, which individually, cannot fully answer their educational needs. These are the public school system and the *madrasah* system. The Muslims are caught in a labyrinth of two incomplete educational systems, each of which does not meet their spiritual aspirations and their material needs. And in order to receive the benefits of both systems, Muslim children have to attend both schools. This is a problem that continues to face Muslims today.

The Public School System. The public school system is supported by the Philippine government and provides for the education of the youth from the primary to secondary levels. Basically, the curriculum prepares the child to grow up educationally adequate, emotionally equipped, and mentally ready to face the duties and responsibilities of adulthood and citizenship. But while public schools teach morality, it is not based on the spiritual bedrock of Islam. As such, this system has found resistance from the Muslims since its introduction by the Americans in the early 1900's because they are concerned that the children would abandon their spiritual upbringing as Muslims. The values and attitudes inherent in this system are western and alien to Muslim culture.

The *Madrasah* System. The *madrasah* refers to a traditional religious school which teaches Arabic language and Islamic theology. It prepares the Muslim child spiritually from the primary to the secondary levels of Islamic education. Beginning with the coming of Islam in the Philippines, the *madrasah*, in the course of its evolution, took the form of a "formal" school adopting the curricula of the old Middle East religious schools. These curricular offerings encourage students and graduates to seek scholarship grants for higher education. Since not all the graduates of the *madrasah* can be given scholarships in the Middle East, there arises the problem of finding employment for them or having them pursue further studies. Unemployment is exacerbated by lack of skills or technical know-how necessary for competitive government or private enterprises among the *madrasah* graduates. Furthermore, children are not taught skills for gainful living. And because English and Filipino languages are not offered in the *madrasah*, its graduates have difficulty finding work in the government services. They are also ineligible for further studies in Philippine public schools due to the non-recognition or non-accreditation of *madrasah* schools by the government. Subjects offered in these schools cannot be accredited because they do not advance national educational aspirations. Their subjects deal with history, literature, geography and the heritage of Middle Eastern countries and not of the Philippines. So while the Muslims are trained in their faith in the *madrasah*, the system deprives them of finding their rightful role in the economic stream of Philippine society. To have a complete education, a child has to enroll in both systems of education.

The *madrasah* is both an educational and socio-political institution. Its primary concern is to enhance progress, unity and understanding among Muslim peoples. It is an institution of learning that molds and shapes Muslims to serve as agents of change, helps the people in the performance of their community and religious duties, and also serves as a depository of Muslim written literature, forms and Muslim sacred texts and objects.

In an attempt to have a complete education, some Muslims enroll in both the public school and the madrasah. It is very taxing, however, for a Muslim child to attend the public school for five days a week, from Mondays to Fridays, and attend the *madrasah* during weekends. The primary school adage is very applicable in this situation: "All work and no play makes John a dull boy." Yet, the vast majority of Muslim children in Muslim Mindanao, particulalry those in the primary and elementary levels, are forced to attend both schools if they want to have their share in the Philippine socio-economic and political milieu and at the same time maintain their Islamic upbringing.

Fifth, there is an absence of a determined effort to develop science and technology programs among Muslims in Mindanao to support Mindanao's role as a the new food basket of the Philippines.

The new millennium is a very challenging one. It is in this century that scientific advancements and technological progress proceed at an exponential rate. Often, we are caught in amazement and sheer wonder by the speed with which scientific discoveries are being put into practical use. Electronics and information technology, plastics and synthetics, nuclear energy, to name a few, are just some of the areas which illustrate how fundamental scientific discoveries are immediately translated into processes and products used in daily life.

The impact of modern technology cannot be underestimated in the new knowledge-based world economy. Due to the shift in the forces of production, knowledge has become the primary wealth-producing resource, superceding labor and capital in the post-industrial society. Raw materials and cheap labor no longer represent the commanding trade leverage it once enjoyed during the days of mercantilism and colonialization; rather it is the rapid and continuous improvement in products and technologies, coupled with aggressive marketing strategies, which give industries and nations their competitive edge.

However, in Muslim Mindanao, the level of science and technology education is dismal. There is only one science high school in the region and only a few subjects in this area offered by tertiary institutions. Most of them are not well-equipped and lack the facilities necessary to build skills needed in the knowledge-based economy.

Sixth, there is a low internal efficiency in the educational system. Improvements in the internal efficiency of basic education in the region leaves much to be desired. This is perpetuated by unqualified faculty members, lax supervision and an over-staffed system with high levels of absenteeism. This results in the high cost of basic education in the Muslim areas.

Unqualified teachers are able to enter the teaching force because of a distorted selection and recruitment system. Rampant political patronage goes in the appointment of teachers, accompanied by the tale of vacant items and lack of information on vacant teacher items. This is aggravated by hiring inefficient teachers on the pretext that there is a lack of civil service- eligible applicants.

Lastly, the tertiary educational institutions in Muslim Mindanao are suffering from poor access and quality. In the state universities and colleges (SUCs), not all students seeking admission are admitted because of the entrance examination requirement. Due to the poor quality of education in barangay and rural high schools, very few of their graduates pass the entrance exams, while the rest of the slots are filled up by those coming from science high schools, provincial high schools, and sophisticated private high schools.

Those who are not admitted to standard higher education institutions seek admission in private colleges, where most faculty members and facilities are substandard resulting in poor quality college education.

These Problems Need Solutions with Dispatch

The educational ills in Muslim Mindanao have been here since the 1950's. For the past few decades, these problems may have persisted to weaken the intellectual, moral and physical fiber of the Muslim Mindanaoans. Now that we are focusing on them to pull the socio-economic cart of the country in this new millennium, these educational problems should be solved with dispatch and finality. Following are a few suggestions offered by Muslim Mindanaoans to address these issues:

Improving Physical Facilities

The lack of physical facilities as well as the absence of Muslim instructional materials should be addressed. School buildings, science laboratories, libraries as well as culturally-sensitive materials should be provided. Books with distinctive Muslim Mindanao elements should be written and distributed to students in Muslim areas. The Department of Education, Culture and Sports (DECS) should allow the writing and printing of text books and reference materials by the Muslim themselves.

Funding Assistance

Funding for basic education in Muslim areas should be increased at a level similar to that given to Luzon and Visayas. A proportionate share of educational funds for basic education should be allocated. Muslim areas in Mindanao receive very limited portions, hence the deterioration of education in the area, especially in Muslim Mindanao. This should be increased at levels necessary to put Muslim education in Mindanao at par with that of Luzon and Visayas.

Madrasah System of Education

There is a need for the *madrasah* schools to secure an official permit to for operation as an educational institution using a DepEd-approved reconciliatory curriculum. This revised curriculum will incorporate the teaching of subjects offered in the public school system alongside topics on Islamic tenets and Muslim cultural heritage. So far, less than 10 *madaris* have availed of the accreditation scheme implemented by DepEd-ARMM.

Three success stories of accredited *madaris* can be reviewed: 1) Jamiatu Muslim Mindanao (JMM) located in Matampay, Marawi City. It used to be a madrasah operating as an educational institution without government permit. In the early 1990's, it sought accreditation by organizing an English Department and using the *madrasah* reconciliatory curriculum. Now, JMM has evolved into a large sectarian Islamic institution of learning in Marawi City offering various college courses; 2) Jamiatu Marawi Al-Islamia Foundation (JMIF), Moncado Colony, Marawi City, was originally a *madrasah* until 1995-96, when it sought government permit to operate as a sectarian Islamic college. It is now a fast-growing college offering the three levels of education using a curriculum enriched with Arabic language and Islamic studies at all academic levels; and, 3) Shariff Kabunsuan College (SKC), Cotabato City, was established as a sectarian Islamic college using a curriculum enriched with Arabic language and Islamic studies. It began as a high school and is now one of the fastest growing private colleges in Cotabato City.

Science and Technology

We should strengthen Infomation Technology-related courses in Muslim Mindanao by empowering tertiary-level institutions to offer these programs. Support for infrastructure building should also be provided by the government, at the same time, more science high schools should be established in Muslim areas.

Increasing Internal Efficiency

Political interference, hiring of unqualified teachers, overstaffing and teacher item mercantile should be eradicated in schools in Muslim Mindanao. The DepEd should improve the training of school managers and teachers to improve their performance and boost internal efficiency in the entire system.

Tertiary Education

The SUCs should lead in improving access and quality of tertiary education in Muslim Mindanao. It should spearhead teacher in-service training, teacher graduate education programs and college bound projects.

At the Mindanao State University, a College-bound Program was established to allow students who did not qualify for the System Admission and Scholarship Examination (SASE) to have receive remedial instruction in Science, Mathematics and English. The outstanding students qualify for entrance into college while those in the border lines can continue their remedial instruction in a pre-university program in the first semester and may qualify for admission in the second semester, depending on their academic performance. It is expected that other SUCs will implement similar schemes.

Concluding Remarks

These proposed interventions will make education in Muslim Mindanao relevant and a wise investment for national and regional development. A good education will be a powerful instrument in strengthening Muslim Mindanao, in terms of contributions to the national economy and producing skilled workers. If implemented correctly, these proposals can empower Muslim Mindanao to become the new economic forefront of the country. When development, growth and stability take place, long-term peace and harmony in Muslim Mindanao is reachable. Together, we can make these proposals work.

The Moro Woman: Herstory and Role

AMINA RASUL

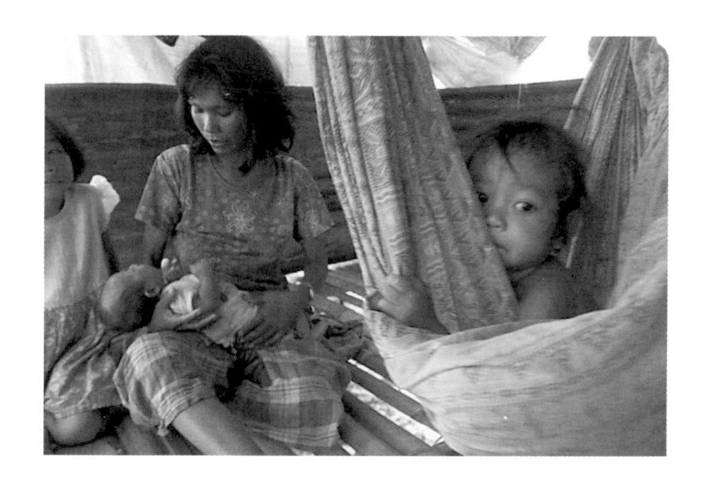

Introduction

Women in the Philippines face conflicting realities. We live in a patriarchal society, yet at the same time possess rights and privileges that contradict the very notion of a male-dominated culture. We have a strong tradition of women participation and empowerment even in pre-colonial Philippines, yet majority of our women are still treated as second-class citizens.

What is the situation of the Muslim Filipina? Belonging to a different religion, with a different set of personal laws, many having gone through basic education in a different system in the "Madrassah", it is inevitable that Muslim Filipinas shall possess other norms, standards of morality, and worldviews than Filipinas who profess a different faith. The general situation for Filipino women may not hold true for the Muslim Filipina.

In the Philippine context, Islam must be viewed in a setting where it is neither the state religion nor even the dominant faith. Hence, the lives of Filipina Muslims are circumscribed by a larger context, that of the national Filipino history and culture.

Of interest to policy makers is the plight of women in the Autonomous Region of Muslim Mindanao (ARMM). As conservative religious movements gain in strength, there is the fear that the condition of Muslim Filipinas will deteriorate. The concern revolves around the loss of equal opportunities for development as well as diminution of their status as political discussions focus primarily on providing greater autonomy for ARMM.

This paper will first look at the global context of women in Islam, then discuss the situation of the Muslim Filipina, particularly in the ARMM.

Islam in a Global Context

Being the state religion of around a billion people in many nation-states in the Middle East, Southeast Asia and Africa, Islam encompasses both the spiritual and secular aspects of life of a stunningly diverse group of people, collectively called the Muslim *ummah*.

The resurgence of Islam today brought in its wake a tide of criticisms aimed against it. The questions on Islam as a way of life continue to be asked, brought about by the initial impetus of wanting to learn about the people who control the world's oil, to recurring crises that involve Muslims worldwide—whether on the state level, or on the level of ethnic minorities.

With human rights being pushed into the forefront of world economics and politics,[1] conservative societies—which most Muslim communities are considered part of—are being forced to accept certain conditions by the dominant world economic players of the world to enable them to partake of the benefits of this economic exchange. These conditions call for the promotion of egalitarian principles and the breaking down of static social conditions as requisites for participation.

The stress on rights puts the spotlight on societies that are unwilling or unable to accept democratic and libertarian concepts such as equality of the sexes. Hence, the renewed criticisms against Islam—perceived to be one of the strongest countervailing forces against "progress".

A Muslim feminist scholar explains, "minorities, women and slaves are the groups that have historically constituted a challenge and a limitation to Islam's claim to universality and equality. . . The Islamic state thus rested on the contradiction between the legal inferiority of some groups and the philosophical principle of equality of all beings, which is central to Islam as a universal religion. . . This is why most of the debate on democracy in the Muslim world circles endlessly around the explosive issue of women's liberation, and also why a piece of cloth, the veil, is so loaded with symbolic meaning and so powerful as a source of violence within, and now also without, Muslim territories."[2]

Arguments that these practices violate the Muslim woman's human rights have their basis in religion arise because in some Muslim countries, women today still are regarded as less than equal to men. And the farther away the community is from urban centers and economic development, the more deep-seated the ideas and practices of male dominance get.

However, it is useful to find the root causes of Muslim attitudes towards women, if only to be armed with the right knowledge to initiate change and begin a transformation. Hence, the question still begs: do these practices and teachings have any basis at all in the teachings of Islam, as codified in the Qur'an? Or are these merely remnants of a feudal order of things that have remained intact after so many centuries of isolation and misinterpretation?

It is particularly important for Muslim Filipinos, who do not have a history of women oppression. In their quest for further unity with the Muslim ummah, there might be an indiscriminate adoption of practices from Islamic countries that might prove to be detrimental to the situation of Muslim Filipinas.

There has been a constant seesawing in the battle for Muslim women's rights. Egyptian women in the 1920's started taking off the veil. Afghanistan in 1921 had abolished the veil, Iran in 1936. While there was a serious backlash to these attempts, reforms continued. It was the years between the 1950's and 1970's that is considered a watershed period in this struggle, where the feminist movement in Islamic countries made great inroads towards the promotion of women's rights.[3]

As early as the 1950's, a number of Arab states had female ministers long before some Western states did.[4] The world has already seen the ascendancy of the first female leader of a modern Muslim state in the person of Benazir Bhutto (1988-90, 1993-96). Turkey elected a female Prime Minister, Tansu Çiller (1993-95). Sheik Hasina was elected the first female Prime Minister of Bangladesh in 1996. Megawati Sukarnoputri was recently elected President of the most populous Muslim country in the world—Indonesia.

In the Philippines, the first Muslim woman governor was Princess Tarhata Lukman of Lanao del Sur elected in 1971. Governor Lukman defeated the brother-in-law of Ali Dimaporo, one of the most powerful political leaders of Lanao del Sur. In 1987, Santanina T. Rasul was elected to the Philippine Senate, the first Muslim woman to occupy the post. Senator Rasul was re-elected in 1992, the first Muslim Senator to be reelected. Two Muslim women were recently elected to the House of Representatives (Representative Soraya Jaafar of Tawi-Tawi and Representative Fayzah Dumarpa of Lanao del Sur).

In the ARMM, women have been elected to the Regional Assembly since its inception.

However, despite these solid gains, the situation today is said to be reversing with the trend towards conservatism.[5] With Muslims increasingly seen as a "target" for modernization, there is a corresponding reaction—that of going back to their roots and fortifying their identity from the "invasion of Western decadence".

Can this situation be truly attributable to Islam? What does the Qur'an say about women's participation in economic endeavors? Are there any proscriptions for women to work, hence the low GDP output? What about education? Or political participation? Are women prohibited by Islam to actively engage themselves in political exercises in the community? Is it why many Islamic countries have no women in their legislative bodies?

There are also the more obvious aspects of the Islamic way of life that continue to be subjects of controversy and debate, such as the compulsory wearing of the veil and the practice of polygamy. Hence, the primary source of Islamic law and way of life—the Holy *Qur'an*—must be scrutinized.

Women (and Men) in Islam

> ***"And for women are rights over men,***
> ***similar to those of men over women."***
> ***(2:226, Qur'an)***

Women of the Islamic faith are being deprived of their rights, and most do not even know it, mainly because they perceive this as "natural". This situation has come about as a carryover from centuries of female subordination. However, this is not unique to Islamic societies. Even today, in the most democratic societies, there is still the continuous struggle to break down the male-dominated structures of society. As the Human Development Report states, all countries measured have given less opportunities to women than to men. These countries include the highly industrialized, libertarian societies of the west.

What can we expect of women in the Islamic countries? Reforms have generally been slower in coming to conservative Islamic countries. Some analysts claim that the slow pace, or lack, of reform is due to practices perceived to violate women's human rights that have their basis on the *Qur'an*. Hence, the reluctance to make changes that might actually be going against God's will. Accordingly, "Islamic legislation regarding rules that influence and control women's lives has been maintained more rigorously than other parts of the Islamic law-complex in modern times."[6]

In this issue of divine prescriptions, the women's rights question has been compared to that of slavery. Slavery is no longer acceptable in our community of nations. Albeit late in comparison to the rest of the world, Saudi Arabia had abolished slavery in the 1960's.[7] While there are some guidelines for the treatment of slaves in the *Qur'an* and other sources of Islamic teachings, no one apparently uses them to justify slavery's revival. And so should it be with women's rights.[8]

The best solution is to scrutinize the primary source, and view it in light of present-day context, as many scholars have done. If one has to rely solely on interpretations done many decades or centuries past, it must be noted that these previous interpretations of the books that guide our religions have, by and large, been done so by men. Add to this the fact that those who were studying the passages were doing so in the societal and cultural context of patriarchy.

These interpretations are now being redefined, both by men and women, with the enlightenment brought about by centuries of progress and development. However, like many questions of religion, these debates may not be settled at all.

Despite strong arguments to the contrary, it is possible to challenge archaic notions of human rights as advanced by some Islamic leaders since "the Shari'ah is merely a historically conditioned human understanding of Islam" and hence, alternative interpretations in the modern context which are conducive to the human rights of women are possible . . . ."[9]

The Holy *Qur'an*

In pre-Islamic societies of Arabia, the practice of female infanticide was prevalent. Yet there was a woman who was very much in control of her life, was publicly visible, economically independent, and had initiated her marriage to a man many years her junior. This woman was Khadija.[10] Maybe she was the exception, but the significance of it is that she was to be the wife of God's messenger on Earth, and was the first to be converted to Islam.

In the preface to his book "The Rights of Women in Islam", Ali Ashgar Engineer states "Islam is one of those religions which has discussed in detail women's rights both in the *Qur'an* and the formulations of the *Shari'ah* (Islamic law)." In fact, it is "the only religion to formally outline the protection of women's rights. . . ."[11]

According to Khan, "God clearly defined and guaranteed the rights of women in *Qur'an*, so that they could no more be subjected to those wrongs, injustices, and oppressions which had been inflicted on them since the beginnings of the human species."[12]

Scholars have scrutinized the *Qur'an* and have advanced their arguments that present practices that are clearly prejudicial against women have been merely reified after centuries of having been customary practice, with very flimsy basis from the Holy Book. Even the *Sunnah*, or the "normative model behavior of the prophet"—the second source of Islamic law consisting of Muhammad's statements and sayings, his deeds, and tacit agreement, as recorded in the *hadith*[13]—indicates the opposite.

The very creation of Adam and Eve is a revelation in itself of women's position vis-à-vis men in Islam. Eve and Adam, in the *Qur'an*, were created from a single soul (*nafs*), signifying equality, having come from a single essence. In the Christian tradition, Eve was created from the rib of Adam, which gave dubious proof of subordination of woman to man in earlier debates.

This is the passage in the *Qur'an* (4:1): "...fear your Lord, Who created you of a single soul, and from it created its mate, and from the pair of them scattered abroad many men and women".[14]

The Prophet Muhammad himself on various occasions always emphasized the importance of women. In his final public address on the Mt. of Mercy at Arafat near Mecca for the Farewell Pilgrimage, he commanded 124,000 of his fellow Muslims to treat their women well, be respectful, and be kind to them.[15]

When asked if there was a shortcut to Paradise, he replied "paradise lies under the feet of the mother." It is also reported that when a man asked Prophet Muhammad: "O Messenger of Allah, who is the person who has the greatest right on me with regards to kindness and attention?" Muhammad had replied: "Your mother." He was asked a second time: "Then who?" He replied, "Your mother." And for a third time: "Then who?" He still replied, "Your mother." And the fourth question: "Then who?" Muhammad finally replied: "Your father."[16]

The Prophet Muhammad was a social reformer. More than that, his ideas were revolutionary for the 1st century. He had abolished female infanticide, slavery and levirate (marriage between a man and his brother's widow), while introducing concepts guaranteeing women the right to inherit and bequeath property, and the right to exercise full possession and control over their own wealth.[17]

These are only some of the passages in the *Qur'an*, as well as in the hadith, which unequivocally indicate the importance given by the Qur'an and the Prophet Muhammad to women.

Cultural norms and beliefs in various Muslim societies, while varying from country to country, share similar practices that are interpreted as discriminatory and prejudicial against women. The most noticeable and obvious of these practices are the wearing of the "*hijab*" or covering for the head and face for the Muslim women, polygamy, and suppression of political and economic participation of women.

The Veil

Wearing of the veil as a prerequisite to becoming a moral woman is viewed as a constraint against the freedom of the person to choose even the mode of clothing, and hence goes strongly against basic human rights of freedom of expression and choice. This is often interpreted to mean discrimination since their male counterparts are not obliged to so.

While there are many Muslims who wear the veil as the sign of their adherence to the Islamic teachings for modesty, the religion in general is criticized as being too inflexible since the justification for the veil is to prevent men from being tempted by women. Hence, women must be covered. As a consequence, the veil has become equated with the very morality of a woman. What about the woman who sees compulsory veiling as an abridgement of her rights? Is she actually violating any Islamic teaching?

The answer seems to be "no." Studies on the subject of women in Islam reveal that "the wearing of the veil has no, or at best questionable, support in the Qur'an; it has never been common practice in the Muslim world...." "These verses on the seclusion of women deal with the Prophets' wives and it is questionable whether it should be binding for all women."[18] In fact, the traditional veil did not exist during the lifetime of the Prophet.[19] It had merely originated from Persia as a fashion trend to distinguish the elite from the masses.[20]

Niazi cites the chapter in the *Qur'an* entitled "*Nur*" which is identified as the *Qur'anic* injunction for the veil: "Say to the believing men that they should lower their gaze and guard their modesty...And say to the believing women lower their gaze and guard their modesty; that they should not display their beauty and ornaments except what (must ordinarily) appear thereof (xxxiv. 30-31)."[21]

Hence, all that the *Qur'an* requires of women is that they not display their sexual charms, and dress in a dignified manner.[22] In Saudi Arabia, the covering of women from head to toe was recent. It was not required before the discovery of oil. Even Bhutto began veiling only when she started to campaign for office[23] as she had to attract the more conservative vote to ensure victory.

Polygamy

Polygamy is another Islamic custom that is perceived as discriminatory against women. In most modern societies today, polygamy is either illegal or immoral. Of course, there is serial polygamy brought about by legalization of divorce, but that is another matter. Where does polygamy find its basis in Islam?

"If you fear that you will not act justly towards the orphans marry such women as seem good to you, two, three, four; but if you fear you will not be equitable, then only one, or what your right hands own, so it is likelier you will not be partial" (The Qur'an, 4:3).[24]

This is the verse that is cited in justifying the existence of polygamy. But as it stands, in full context, there is a condition attached to marrying more than one wife, which is, to give justice to orphans, and that one must treat the women equitably. The third verse states "If you fear you that cannot be equitable to the several wives, then have only one, or marry a slave woman." But in verse 129 of the same chapter, it is stated "You will not be able to be equitable between your wives. . . ."[25]

Nothing could be clearer in meaning. If a man cannot give equal attention and justice to his wives—and the Qur'an states that he never can—then there should only be one wife. Maulana Muhammad Ali states that "this passage permits polygamy under certain circumstances; it does not enjoin it, nor even permit it unconditionally."[26]

Injunctions for polygamy had a very compelling reason, but the rationale was historical, and not spiritual. In the battle of Uhud, the newly converted Muslims numbering around 700 went to war against the pagans. They saw their ranks decimated when 70 men were killed in the battle. This posed a problem as the widows and children of the slain men would not have anyone to provide for them.

Abdur Rahman Doi in his article states:

> "The worst calamity for a woman is when her husband passes away and, as a widow, the responsibility of maintaining the children falls upon her. In the Eastern World, where a woman does not always go out to earn her living, the problems of widowhood are indescribable. The Prophet Muhammad (peace be upon him) upheld the cause of widows. Most of his wives were widows. In an age when widows were rarely permitted to remarry, the Prophet encouraged his followers to marry them. He was always ready to help widows and exhorted his followers to do the same. Abu Hurairah reported that the Prophet said: "One who makes efforts to help the widow or a poor person is like a mujahid (warrior) in the path of Allah...."[27]

Hence, polygamy satisfied a social obligation towards these people by allowing a man to care for more than one wife or family.[28]

And as an example to be emulated, all of the Prophet Mummahad's wives were widows, with the exception of Aisha, who was a child-bride.[29] The Prophet Muhammad lived with his wife Khadijah for 25 years until her death. His other marriages were for purely religious, political and social considerations.[30]

Given that the situation many centuries hence has drastically changed, are justifications for polygamy still present? The answer is clearly "no". Tunisia had prohibited polygamy in 1957 citing the very same verse, variably stated as "have it not in your power to deal equally between wives, however much you may wish it...." Turkey has also outlawed polygamy, although it is still being practiced.[31]

Political Leadership and Economic Participation

The issue of women holding positions of leadership and economic participation follows the very same path as that of the discussions on the veil and polygamy. With the advent of Islam, women were very much involved in decision-making processes in the society. It was only after the death of Muhammad when interpretations began to be slanted against women.

In today's world, Islamic women's position in society and the influence that they can exert over their own lives vary considerably from country to country. This in fact belies the argument that women's inferior position in Muslim countries has theological or religious basis. There is a wide variance in interpretations, even in the core Islamic countries of the Middle East.

When one goes outside this core area and moves into Asian Islamic countries, the variance is greater. This is due to the totally different history and culture of these countries, which exerts an influence that can never be overestimated. Hence, any generalization about Muslim women must be advanced with caution.[32]

As regards Muslim women and their political and economic participation in society, the women surrounding the Prophet were by no means docile and subjugated. This is exemplified by no less than Khadija, and the role that the other wives of Prophet Muhammad, particularly Aisha, played in the development and growth of Islam.

While the *hadith* states "The nation which gives the supreme control of its affairs in the hands of women cannot prosper," other hadith indicate that women could and did participate in society. Islamic scholars also interpret this to mean that this was merely in the context of the old Caliphate, not in the modern nation-state. Muhammad had stated that "a woman is the steward over the property of her husband and she will be held responsible for her subjects."

Scholars have made some inquiries into this matter, and Fatima Mirnissi discovered that there have been queens who ruled in Muslim countries but their names have been relegated to the dustbins of history.[33] In the modern context, we have the aforementioned Benazir Bhutto and Megawati Sukarnoputri's ascendancy to leadership positions.

The Moro Woman

In the Philippine context, there is a growing trend among Muslims to lean towards conservatism. It is feared that this conservatism may spell disaster for the fight for women's rights, once scripture is quoted to justify female subordination.

But what about the history of the Moro woman? While materials are scant, Dr. Carmen A. Abubakar of the University of the Philippines - Institute of Islamic Studies had made a study on the lives of the Moro women during the period of colonization, which indicates that these women were less than the docile, subjugated females of other Muslim countries. In her research, Dr. Abubakar cites descriptions made by foreigners on the women of Sulu, from the late 1600's to the late 1800's. The physical description of the Moro women indicated that there was, in fact, no veiling.[34]

Even in their fight to repel the colonizers, women were very much at the center of combat - not as nurses or in other "support" roles - but as warriors themselves. Former Senator Rasul recounts the exploits of her great grandmother, Panglima Hatima of Tandubas in Tawi-Tawi, who led the troops of her slain husband to victory against their Spanish enemies. Then there is the story of the Battle of Bud Datu, where the American Governor General Forbes made a comment about not being able to distinguish men from women who fought side by side in their bombardment of the area in Jolo. Vic Hurley is cited by Dr. Abubakar as he states that the women were "more desperate and determined than the men, with her child suspended to her breast or slung across her back, the Moro woman enters the fight with the ferocity of a panther."[35]

This very active role that the Moro woman played during that period included occupying positions of leadership and power, such as Inchi Jamila, Dayang Dayang Hadji Piandao, and Sultana Nur Al Azam.

While Abubakar grants that prejudice against women was present (women were not given education at the time), they were not prevented from participating in public life, as some present-day conservatives want to assert.[36]

> ***"The State recognizes the role of women in nation-building and shall ensure the fundamental equality before the law of women and men"*.** (Art. II, Sec. 14, 1987 Philippine Constitution)

No less than the fundamental law of the land—the 1987 Philippine Constitution—embodies the principle of women empowerment. However, the separate set of personal laws that govern the Muslim population in the Philippines constrict women's freedoms and rights. In 1977, the Muslim Personal Laws were codified and issued as Presidential Decree No. 1083 by then President Ferdinand E. Marcos. Unfortunately, the codification was conducted by men, with no inputs whatsoever from women experts. Used as basis for *Shari'ah* decisions, the code has the following features which violate women's rights:

1. A Muslim woman cannot exercise her profession or occupation, engage in lawful business, acquire property by gratuitous title without the consent of her husband;
2. She is not legally recognized as a partner of her husband in providing for her family;
3. In case of disagreement in parental authority over the children, the father's decision prevails;
4. The wife does not have equal rights in the matter of divorce since this right is dependent on whether the husband desires to divorce her or not; and
5. The woman is not entitled to as much share as the man in legal succession.

Since the *shari'ah* is recognized and accepted by Philippine judiciary, the code should be revisited and evaluated. Various laws have been enacted at the state level to make the aspiration for women empowerment a reality. How can Muslim women benefit from these laws if the code has conflicting features?

Interestingly, a Muslim woman, Senator Rasul, was the principal author of significant laws to empower women. One of the most important of these laws is Republic Act 7192 of 1992 or "An Act Promoting the Integration of Women as Full and Equal Partners of Men in Development and Nation-Building and for Other Purposes".

RA 7192, or the "Women in Nation Building Act" as it is known, enumerates concrete interventions. The first of these is to decree that "a substantial portion of official development assistance funds received from foreign governments and multilateral agencies and organizations shall be set aside and utilized by the agencies concerned to support programs and activities for women."

The law also decrees the following: that government instrumentalities will ensure women participation and involvement in the development programs and projects of these agencies from the planning stage, all the way to the evaluation of these activities; that these agencies review and revise all regulations, circulars, issuances and procedures to remove any bias against women; that they assist women in activities that are of critical significance to their self-reliance and development; that women be given equality in their capacity to act and enter into contracts; equal membership in clubs; and voluntary social security coverage for full-time household managers.

Probably the most high profile of these interventions in RA 7192 is Section 7 of the law which allowed women for the first time in history, to be admitted, train, graduate and be commissioned in the Philippine Military Academy and Philippine National Police - thus effectively liberalizing these heretofore male-dominated institutions.

A Situationer on the Muslim Women in ARMM

The Moro woman, while circumscribed by the bigger national policy environment, still has to contend with harsher realities in her immediate community. Harsher, because the poorest provinces in the entire country are in the ARMM.

Unlike her counterparts in the generally more developed areas of Luzon, Visayas and other parts of Mindanao, the Filipina Muslim has to contend with an environment that is the least empowering in the entire nation, with the least resources and capabilities for any development initiatives. The economic and social realities in the ARMM make the various empowering laws almost moot and academic.

The national life expectancy rate for males is 66.93 years, while that for the women is 72.18 years. Juxtapose these figures with the average ARMM rates, and it is very evident how poor the quality of life in these predominantly Muslim areas is. For males in ARMM, life expectancy is at 56.5 years, while that for women is at 60.3.[37]

The 10 to 12-year difference in life expectancies speak volumes for the health care, nutrition and for the other basic services that have direct impact in the quality of life of the people in the region. This difference is a shocking number, considering that all figures come from one country.

Other economic indicators show the same disturbing trend. For example, the annual average family income in ARMM as of 1997 is only P74,885.00, compared to the national average of P123,168.00. With just slightly over half of what the average Filipino family earns, it is not surprising how the families in ARMM have such low life expectancies.

As of August 1999, the predominantly Muslim region had 0 cities and 84 municipalities. The fact that not a single municipality in the ARMM has been converted to a city indicates that development in the region, even in the relatively progressive areas, has yet to reach the level where a municipality has achieved the necessary requirements for it to become a city. Hence, urbanization is something that remains elusive.

Table 3: Comparative Table for Literacy Rates in the ARMM

	National Rate	ARMM Rate	ARMM Male	ARMM Female	ARMM Male (Rural)	ARMM Female (Rural)
Simple Literacy	95.02%	71.77%	75.88%	71.77%	73.43%	68.12%
Functional Literacy	83.79%	61.19%	63.24%	59.14%		

Source: FLEMMS94 from the National Statistic Office

In terms of education, the Functional Literacy, Education and Mass Media Survey (FLEMMS) of 1994 quite clearly indicate how the predominantly Muslim areas are clearly disadvantaged. And for the women in ARMM, the contention that they are doubly disadvantaged holds true.

In simple literacy, as compared to the national average, ARMM rates are way below, with a disparity of more than 20 percentage points. When broken down by gender, the disparities are even more glaring especially in the rural setting. The functional literacy rates show the same trends, with only slightly over half of the women being able to use their literacy for their day-to-day lives.

The extremely low literacy rates pose a great problem since education is the single most important factor in developing the human resources in the area, and is the great equalizer as it serves as a vehicle for social mobility.

In terms of political power, a survey of the statistics (Table 4) for the past four elections in the ARMM may indicate to what extent women are accepted as leaders in their community. The mayoralty post is probably the most important in local elections, since the municipality or city is the frontline government unit in the delivery of basic services.

Table 4: Comparative Figures for Male and Female Mayors in ARMM from 1992 to 2001

Province	1992		1995		1998		2001	
	M	F	M	F	M	F	M	F
Lanao del Sur	38	0	35	3	27	7	33	5
Maguindanao	19	2	18	0	18	1	20	1
Sulu	18	0	18	0	14	3	16	2
Tawi-Tawi	10	0	9	1	9	1	9	1
Total	85	2	84	4	80	12	87	9
% To Total	97.7	2.3	95.2	4.8	85.0	15.0	89.7	10.3

Source: Commission on Elections

The Commission on Elections (COMELEC) figures show that while women local chief executives in the ARMM local government comprise only a small percentage of the totals (which is also true for the national levels, [illegible] credence to the argument that Philippine politics is still male-dominated), there has been a steady increase in the number of women mayors in the ARMM.

While there has been a slight downturn for the most recent elections (the results of which are still to be fully known in the region) the sharp increases (doubling from 1992-1995, then more than tripling from 1995-1998) is an indication that women in the Muslim-dominant ARMM can, and do, lead their communities.

There may be other factors for these women to have been elected as mayors, but the assertion that Muslim Filipinas cannot hold positions of leadership because Islam forbids it is clearly an invalid one. With the strong folk tradition of women in leadership positions, it may be concluded that this up-trend will continue.

Conclusion

That women in Islamic countries have been marginalized cannot be argued with. That much is clear from the United Nations Human Development Report. However, to assert that it is Islam itself that subordinates the women to the men is erroneous. There is, in fact, sufficient support in the *Qur'an* and the hadith for equality of men and women.

But through the centuries, there has been a subversion of the true spirit of the *Qur'an* through the misinterpretation of passages as read through the looking glass of patriarchy. Cultural practices arising from these misinterpretations have, over time, been understood to be the true meaning and spirit of the *Qur'an*. They have remained thus for centuries, unquestioned.

Today however, with the rising tide of discourse on human rights at the forefront of global debates, the true spirit of equality between men and women in the *Qur'anic* passages is finally allowed to surface, interpreted by both male and female scholars. However, there is the backlash of conservatism, arising from the defensive posture of cultures which are feeling threatened by the wave of western concepts of liberalism, egalitarianism and democracy.

One would think that in the Philippines, with a strong tradition of women participation, Muslim Filipinas would be facing a different situation. But looking at the poor indicators of their situation in the ARMM, one may conclude otherwise, and say that Muslim Filipinas are more disenfranchised, and that their situation mirrors that of other women in Islamic countries.

The marginalization of Muslim women in the Philippines arises not from the fact that they are Muslim. Marginalization occurs because the entire region itself is suffering from neglect and exclusion from mainstream society. It occurs because lack of education prevents both men and women from emerging from "backward" practices associated with a highly feudal structure. This dates back to the period of Spanish colonialism, and has been compounded by the failures of modern-day Philippine governments to adequately address the unique needs and demands of the Moros.

Hence, it is now the region with the poorest quality of life in the country, with the lowest human development indicators. It is also the region that has witnessed constant conflict between secessionist forces and government troops for the past three decades. Then there are recent terrorist activities of a small group of bandits wreaking havoc within the region.

Given this environment, it is not surprising that Muslim Filipinas face a daunting task in rising above their condition. Since they are the homemakers, the mothers and the caregivers, they mostly face the brunt of poverty and conflict in the region.

But it cannot be argued that the Muslim Filipina has distinct advantages over other women in Muslim countries. This advantage lies in the fact that the national policy environment for all Filipinas is an empowering framework. The success of other Filipinas (the two women presidents, a Muslim woman as a senator, Muslim congresswomen) can serve as a benchmark for the women in ARMM.

As mentioned earlier, there is only the need to guard against the danger of indiscriminate emulation of practices from Islamic countries, particularly those practices that will reinforce the concept of women subordination.

The paradox of women empowerment in the Philippines continues to this day. There is no denying the strength of Philippine traditions and the present policy environment for women empowerment. Yet it is quite obvious that men still dominate the political, economic and social fields. Maybe it is only the inertia of centuries of male domination. But then again, given the trend of increasing women participation, it may be only a matter of time until the situation is reversed. The more important issue lies in the fundamental attitudes of people, and in this aspect, it may be argued that women in our country are more equal than others.

The twin problems of being a Muslim and a woman weigh heavily on the Moro women. She has to transcend the gender bias existent in almost every country, and more importantly, she has to guard against the preaching of reactionary people who hark back to the medieval ages as their model.

Then there is the more difficult task of transcending illiteracy and poverty. The constant conflicts in Mindanao, specifically in ARMM, make it almost impossible for development initiatives to take root and grow. Hence, the Moro woman has to make do with less than half of what her sister-Filipinas enjoy in other parts of the country.

But despite all these obstacles, there is genuine progress in addressing her problems. The policy framework exists. As Congress and the Executive study the demands of the Muslim communities for meaningful autonomy, the welfare of half of the Muslim population - the women - should not be set aside in favor of quick fixes.

Bibliography

Abubakar, Carmen A. "Wither the Rose of Yesteryears: An Exploratory Look into the Lives of Moro Women During the Colonial Period". **Review of Women's Studies**. Vol. VIII No. 2. Edited by Albina Peczon Hernandez. (University of the Philippines Center for Women's Studies, RoMA Graphics: Diliman, Quezon City). 1998.

An-Na'im, Abdullahi. "The Dichotomy Between Religious and Secular Discourse in Islamic Societies". **Faith and Freedom: Women's Human Rights in the Muslim World**. Edited by Mahnaz Afkhami (I.B. Tauris Publishers: London, New York). 1995.

Busran-Lao, Yasmin. "Gender, Reproductive Health and Women's Rights in the Autonomous Region in Muslim Mindanao (ARMM) in the Philippines." **Report on the Proceedings on the Regional Workshop: Islam, Reproductive Health and Women's Rights**. (Sisters in Islam: Kuala Lumpur, Malaysia). August 20-23, 1998.

Dery, Luis Camara. **Remember the Ladies and Other Historical Essays on the 1896 Philippine Revolution**. (M&L Licudine Enterprises: Las Piñas, Metro Manila). 2000.

Doi, Abdur Rahman I. **Women in Shari'ah.** Centre for Islamic Legal Studies, Bello University, Zaire. Electronic posting. **wwww.WomeninShariah.com**).

Engineer, Ashgar Ali. **The Rights of Women in Islam**. (C. Hurst & Co., Ltd: London, United Kingdom). 1996.

Esposito, John L. **Women in Muslim Family Law: Contemporary Issues in the Middle East**. (Syracuse University Press: Syracuse, New York). 1982.

Feliciano, Myrna "Legal and Political Issues Affecting the Status of Women, 1985-1993" **Review of Women's Studies**. Vol. IV, No. 1 1993-1994. Edited by Thelma B. Kintanar (University of the Philippines Center for Women's Studies: Diliman, Quezon City). 1994.

Feliciano, Myrna "The Political Rights of Women in Philippine Context" **Review of Women's Studies**. Vol. I, No. 2 1990-1991. Edited by Thelma B. Kintanar (University of the Philippines Center for Women's Studies, San Anton Printing and Publishing: Quezon City). 1991.

Goodwin, Jan. **Price of Honor: Muslim Women Lift the Veil of Silence on the Islamic World**. (Penguin Books: New York, USA). 1994.

Hjarpe, Jan. *"The Attitude of Islamic Fundamentalism Towards the Question of Women in Islam"* in **Conference Proceedings of "Women in Islam": Scandinavian Institute of Asian Studies**. Edited by Bo Utas. (Woolnough Bookbinding: Great Britain). 1988.

Implementing Rules and Regulations **REPUBLIC ACT 7192 "WOMEN IN DEVELOPMENT AND NATION BUILDING ACT**".

Khan, Qamaruddin. **Status of Women in Islam**. (Sterling Publishers Private Limited: New Delhi, India). 1990.

Mendez, Policarpio Paz, et. al. **The Filipino Family in Transition: A Study in Culture and Education**. (Centro Escolar University Research Center: Sison's Printing Press, Philippines). 1984.

Mernissi, Fatima. "Arab Women's Rights and the Muslim State in the Twenty-first Century: Reflections on Islam as Religion and State". **Faith and Freedom: Women's Human Rights in the Muslim World**. Edited by Mahnaz Afkhami (I.B. Tauris Publishers: London, New York). 1995.

National Statistics Office figures in "Quikstat", **www.census.gov.ph**. 2001.

Niazi, Kausar. **Modern Challenges to Muslim Families**. (Hafeez Press: Kashmir Bazar Lahore, Pakistan). 1976.

Nicolaisen, Ida. "*Introduction*" of the **Conference Proceedings of "Women in Islam" : Scandinavian Institute of Asian Studies**. Edited by Bo Utas. (Woolnough Bookbinding: Great Britain). 1988.

United Nations Development Programme. **1999 Human Development Report.** (Oxford University Press: Oxford, New York). 1999.

Endnotes

[1] The 1999 United Nations Human Development Report's final chapter is actually entitled *"Putting human concerns and rights at the centre of global governance"*

[2] Mernissi, Fatima, "Arab Women's Rights and the Muslim State in the Twenty-first Century: Reflections on Islam as Religion and State" in "Faith and Freedom: Women's Human Rights in the Muslim World", p. 44

[3] Goodwin, Jan, "Price of Honor: Muslim Women Lift the Veil of Silence on the Islamic World", pp. 31, 34

[4] Ibid., pp. 30-31

[5] It did not help the status of Muslim women in ARMM when MNLF Chair and Regional Governor Nur Misuari took a young bride for a second wife in a highly publicized betrothal. Media focused on the news that it was the unwilling bride's father who arranged the engagement.

[6] Ibid., p. 7

[7] Hjarpe, Jan, "The Attitude of Islamic Fundamentalism Towards the Question of Women in Islam" in "Conference Proceedings of Women in Islam", p. 13

[8] Engineer, Ashgar Ali, The Rights of Women in Islam, p. 2; 10-11

[9] An-Na'im, Abdullahi, "The Dichotomy Between Religious and Secular Discourse" in "Islamic Societies in Faith and Freedom: Women's Human Rights in the Muslim World", p. 57

[10] Op. cit., Goodwin, pp. 35

[11] Ibid., pp. 34, 26

[12] Khan, Qamaruddin, "Status of Women in Islam", p. 13
[13] Esposito, John L., "Women in Muslim Family Law: Contemporary Issues in the Middle East", p. xi
[14] Op. cit., Khan, pp. 16-17
[15] Doi, Abdur Rahman I., "Women in Shari'ah"
[16] Op. cit., Goodwin, p. 41
[17] Ibid., p. 30
[18] Op. cit., Hjarpe, pp. 19-20
[19] Niazi, Kausar." Modern Challenges to Muslim Families", p. 33
[20] Op. cit., Goodwin, p. 30
[21] Op. cit., Niazi, p. 30
[22] Op. cit., Engineer, p. 14
[23] Op. cit., Goodwin, p. 31
[24] Op. cit., Khan, p. 19
[25] Ibid., pp. 21-22
[26] Quoted in Engineer, p. 155
[27] Loc. cit., Doi
[28] Op. cit, Khan, pp. 19, 21
[29] Op. cit., Goodwin, p. 38
[30] Op. cit., Khan, p. 23
[31] Op. cit., Goodwin, p. 34
[32] Op. cit., Nicolaisen, pp. 2-3
[33] Abubakar, Carmen A., "Wither the Rose of Yesteryears: An Exploratory Look into the Lives of Moro Women During the Colonial Period" in "Review of Women's Studies", p. 119
[34] Ibid., pp. 120-121
[35] Ibid., pp. 124-125
[36] Ibid., p. 130
[37] Statistics found in National Statistics Office website www.census. gov.ph

Conclusion: Issues and Recommendations

Policy Workshops on Mindanao Peace and Development

AMINA RASUL

Childhood Revisited

Growing up in Jolo, Sulu in the 60s was idyllic. On moonlit nights, we played in the streets while my father would look out from the windows of our house, watching over us. My best friends, Catholic and Muslim, would be with us playing patintero, strumming the guitar (it seemed like everyone played the guitar), telling stories.

*I remember my father's Manila friends flying down to Jolo in their private plane to have lunch with us then fly to Tawi-Tawi to hunt wild boars - without bodyguards. American tourists visited Jolo and sampled our white beaches, haggled over antiques at my mother's shop. The Philippine Air Lines flew from Zamboanga City to Jolo twice a day. My cousins, UP graduates, opened "Serendipity", a bookstore. Jolo **had** running water and electricity twenty-four hours a day. The Aboitizes of Cebu ran the electric cooperative and enjoyed a high collection rate. I remember being able to call Manila through a working local telephone system, connected by a local phone operator.*

On February 7, 1974 the MNLF occupied the capital town of Jolo. In an attempt to recapture the town, the Philippine military bombarded Jolo weeks later. Jolo was recaptured but 80% of the town burned to the ground. I remember those painful days. My parents were attending an Islamic conference abroad as we lost our home in the conflagration. They returned immediately only to find out my three younger brothers - Cheng, Jun and Pop - had been missing for days. They were spirited away to the mountains for safety by our relatives. My parents found them physically unhurt but scarred by their experience of war at such a young age. Cheng, hunger overruling his fear, came back to town to scavenge for food. He remembered where the bakery was located and dug around the ovens, locating barely edible bread. Thus they managed to survive until help came.

Our idyllic world disappeared overnight. Martial law and the armed confrontation between government forces and the Muslim secessionist movement changed the political and economic landscape into the bleak scenario of today. Sulu, like the other Muslim provinces, became mired in poverty and hopelessness such as I had not experienced, growing up in Jolo. Migration of longtime residents took capital, professional and entrepreneurial talents away from Sulu and into Zamboanga and Cebu, even crossing into Sabah, Malaysia. In Central Mindanao, the Maranaos started their own migration away from Lanao del Sur and del Norte to Manila and other provinces as far away as Ilocos Norte. Today, you will find a Muslim community - mostly Maranaos - in any capital town of the Philippines including Greenhills.

Government and the Moro National Liberation Front signed an historic Peace Agreement in 1996. The Muslims of Mindanao expected much from their leaders, both local and national. They expected the leaders to bring peace and, if not prosperity, at least give them a space within which they could finally live. Unfortunately, most Muslim residents of ARMM are disenchanted with the "peace dividends". From the refugess of the "all-out-war" policy of former President Estrada to the victims of the Abu Sayyaf encounters, the residents of ARMM have suffered from poor governance, poor education, poor health, low incomes, and breakdown of peace and order. In Sulu and Basilan,tensions are rising due to the frequent military operations to eliminate the ASG threat.

And yet the majority still hope to benefit from their peace dividends. This concluding chapter summarizes their aspirations and proposals on how to finally live in peace within the embrace of the Philippine State.

After the March 15 plenary discussions on the history and extent of the Muslims' armed struggle, the assessment of the negotiations undertaken by both government and the insurgency groups for the past thirty years, the participants focused on specifics. On March 23, the conference participants broke up into five (5) workshops on subjects that define the aspirations of the Muslim communities and influence the nature of the Southern conflict:

- The Islamic State
- Impact of Religion

- Poverty and the Lack of Business Development in Muslim Areas
- The Role of Women in Islamic Society
- Impact and Status of Education and the Madaris

The workshop discussions were lively, at times passionate, as the participants grappled with issues many had never before considered as pertinent to a national program for development of the Muslim areas. The proposed recommendations were comprehensive.

In the interest of consensus building, two workshops were conducted in Mindanao on April 28 and April 30 (2001). President Camar Umpa of the Mindanao State University hosted the first workshop in the Marawi City campus. The second was conducted in Zamboanga City in coordination with Ateneo de Zamboanga. Administrator Randolph C. Parcasio of the Southern Philippine Development Authority, who was particularly concerned about poverty and business development, provided financial support. Executive Director Zamsamin Ampatuan of the Office on Muslim Affairs also supported the activities, his interest perked by the workshops on religion and the *madaris*.

Whereas the leaders who attended the Marawi discussions were all Muslims, half of the conferees in Zamboanga were Christian, reflecting the population mix of the city. The leaders, NGO heads and scholars gathered spent a day studying the proposals recommended by those who participated in the Asian Institute of Management workshops, after making pointed observations about "Imperial Manila" and its top-down approach to finding solutions. It had to be clarified that first, Muslim Mindanaoans were responsible for the articulation of the proposals; second, the Mindanao workshops would serve to validate those recommendations.

The validated recommendations and issues discussed are detailed in this section.

I. THE ISLAMIC STATE

Muslims have not been given the chance to exercise fully their right to self-determination.

- The Sultanate system in the Philippines, unlike those in Malaysia and Indonesia, was not allowed to flourish by colonial rulers and the eventual Philippine government.

- The unitary system which replaced the Sultanate system suppressed the Muslims right to self-determination and caused frictions among Muslims
- There are questions/doubts on the efficacy of the current autonomy set-up
- There is no sincerity/seriousness on the part of the Philippine government to implement an effective autonomous system based on the peace talks.

The main policy recommendations are:

- To operationalize the Muslims' aspiration for self-governance based on Islam and to determine how to accommodate MILF, MNLF aspirations, individual histories, cultures. Will it be through independence, greater and more meaningful autonomy or federalism?
- This would necessarily require a referendum to determine whether: (1) Muslims want autonomy; (2) Muslims want a federal state within the Republic of the Philippines; or (3) Muslims want independence.
- The proposed referendum should involve only Muslims from the provinces cited in the Tripoli Agreement and should be held as a separate activity from the upcoming plebiscite deciding the New Organic Act. The latter should involve all sectors and communities, not just the Muslims, from the provinces in ARMM.
- In the short-term, there is a need to initiate focused group discussions on the issue of self-determination, i.e., what this means exactly and what it entails, in order for this to be understood better by all, not just by Muslims.
- In the long-term, lobby for the appropriate constitutional amendments based on the results of the referendum.

II. IMPACT OF RELIGION AND CULTURE

Social friction between Muslims and Filipino Christians stems from their different socio-cultural backgrounds and religious beliefs.

- There are fundamental differences in how Muslims and Christians view such basic concepts as sovereignty, religious freedom and the separation of church and state. For example in defining sovereignty, the Muslims turn to the *Qur'an*, which states that sovereignty rests in Allah alone whereas Filipino Christians refer to the Constitution according to which sovereignty resides in the people.

- These differences contribute to the tensions between these two communities as Muslims try to practice faithfully their culture and religion.

There is therefore a proposal for:

- Constitutional amendments to resolve these differences. A federal structure would allow for diverse cultures to co-exist as one nation. Such an action plan should be premised on government's clear understanding of the sincerity of the Muslims to be faithful to their religion as well as to the Filipino nation.

Lack of awareness resulting in social stratification, biases and prejudices against non-Christians.

The recommendations include:

- Information dissemination and the promotion of awareness among the Christian community. Education should start not from the college level but from the elementary and high school levels to prevent biases and prejudices from setting in.
- Change the curriculum at the different levels to allow the teaching of Islamic history and culture. If necessary, enact a law to ensure that this is carried out. However, to fast track the implementation of these changes, the issuance of an Executive Order is suggested.
- Relatedly, look at enacting laws that will institutionalize these measures (e.g., the Comprehensive Mindanao Education Plan) at the national level, not only in Mindanao.
- Tap the private sector and the non-government organizations to support programs that promote the concept of kinship among all Filipinos and understanding of brothers and sisters of a different faith and culture.
- Reassess the writing of history with particular focus on how Muslims have been portrayed thus far. This would involve the media,

including the movie and entertainment industry, which has often portrayed Muslims in a less than favorable light.

III. POVERTY AND THE LACK OF BUSINESS DEVELOPMENT IN MUSLIM AREAS

The peace and order situation in the area promotes an environment that is hostile to business.

- Peace and order is a vital component of business development. The lack or small number of businesses in Mindanao is credited to the peace and order problem in the region, particularly in the Muslim areas, which has experienced a large share of the armed fighting and kidnappings.
- The increased presence of the military in these critical areas as a result of the continued threat from rebels has only compounded the problem.
- The peace and order problem does not only stem from the armed conflict between the government and rebel troops. The old problem of "goons, guns and gold" still persists in Mindanao.

Given this, the following are recommended:

- Resume the peace negotiations with the Moro Islamic Liberation Front (MILF). A speedy and fair agreement with the MILF is a concrete step towards restoring peace and order in Mindanao.
- Minimize the militarization of Mindanao or increase its re-civilianization. Where military presence cannot be avoided, greater vigilance from civil society and the local government units is necessary.
- Implement a gun ban in Mindanao.
- Implement measures to make the police and the military less beholden to corrupt local officials. This would include recommending to the Philippine National Police to regularly re-shuffle its police force in these areas.

The poor physical infrastructure and lack of logistics facilities discourages investments in the area.

- Profit remains a paramount concern in business. Mindanao is rich in natural resources and in that sense it has a distinct comparative advantage over other regions. However, the poor state of its physical infrastructure and the lack of adequate logistics facilities discourage businessmen from putting up businesses in the area.

- This is not limited to businessmen; even the farmers in these provinces face the same problems. The high cost of transporting their goods to the market brought on by the poor road conditions in the area has forced a number of them to turn to subsistence agriculture.

There is therefore a need to:

- Secure a commitment from the National Government to prioritize infrastructure projects (roads, ports, power, water, etc) in Mindanao. In particular, government must work to complete all road networks and highways in Mindanao especially in neglected areas like Sulu and Tawi-Tawi to effectively link all areas in the region.

- Increase budgetary allocation for infrastructure projects (roads, ports, power, water, etc.) in Mindanao, especially in the Muslim areas to a level commensurate to its population needs as well as its contribution to the country.
- Develop a coherent develop plan for the whole of Mindanao taking into account the different existing regional development plans and inequities.
- Increase the efficiency in operations of major support industries crucial to businesses in Mindanao, such as the shipping industry.

Poor governance at the local level negatively affects the development of these areas.

- The lack of competency of Local Government Units (LGUs) to govern adequately is a deterrent to development in the area. The high level of graft and corruption among local government officials compounds this.
- "Absentee" local officials who spend most of their time outside their locales also exemplify poor governance.

The recommendations include:

- Initiating basic mandatory trainings for government officials. In the case of Muslim leaders, such trainings should focus on modern as well as traditional governance based on the tenets of Islam. Creating an institute that trains/re-trains Muslim leaders in all aspects (e.g., leadership, governance, business) is also seen as a necessary innovation to improve the competencies of local government officials.
- Creating an advocacy cum pressure group to initiate and sustain efforts calling for greater accountability and transparency among local government officials. As two of the most recognized and organized Muslim groups, the Moro National Liberation Front (MNLF) and the MILF should be mobilized towards this end.
- Initiating a moral recovery program, with particular focus on individual accountability.

Low productivity of the agricultural sector is a major factor of poverty in Mindanao, especially the Muslim areas.

- Low agricultural productivity is attributed to poor irrigation of farmlands in Mindanao and the poor technology still being used by farmers.
- This problem is also tied up with the unresolved issues on land ownership and control. Muslim and indigenous modes of ownership are not properly documented and are not recognized by Philippine laws. Yet these groups continue to invoke these laws in claiming ownership over the land.
- The lack of clarity as to who has say over the land in Mindanao has discouraged foreign investors from coming in to develop these areas. At the same time, uncertainty over their ownership of the land provides little incentive for farmers to develop their land for the long-term.

Thus, there is a call to:

- Increase agricultural technology training for farmers.
- Include all farmlands in Mindanao in region-wide irrigation systems.

Related to this, there is also a call for national government to take over the implementation of irrigation projects previously conducted by LGUs.

- Rationalize agencies overseeing irrigation of agricultural lands. Two agencies have been identified: the Department of Agriculture (DA) and the National Irrigation Agency (NIA).
- Create a framework for clearer land ownership laws. As a necessary step, interface indigenous and Muslim modes of land ownership vis-à-vis western modes of land titling.

Lack of capital for Muslims from the banking sector limits local investments.

- The rules and regulations of commercial banks are perceived to be less favorable to Muslims. In some areas, these banks do not even operate or when they do, they only service depositors and do not extend loans.
- Islamic banks are seen as the best vehicle to help Muslims secure needed capital. However, no such bank currently operates in Mindanao.

The recommendations are to:

- Strengthen Islamic banking in the country by providing much needed capital to Islamic banks such as the Al-Amanah Islamic Investment Bank[1] .
- Relatedly, a different system should be developed to govern such banks, preferably one separate from the Bangko Sentral ng Pilipinas (BSP) system to give these banks room to develop into truly Islamic banks.

Bias and discrimination against Muslim Mindanao, in general, and Muslims, in particular, contribute to the slow rate of development of the region.

- The general perception among the business sector is that doing business in Mindanao, particularly in Muslim Mindanao, is risky because of the continued armed conflict in the area.
- Biased media reporting that tend to sensationalize aggravates the situation in Mindanao.

The recommended actions are to:

- Work with media to portray the situation in Mindanao more realistically.
- Encourage more local radio and television stations to operate in Muslim Mindanao. The government-owned PTV 4 should also increase its operations in these areas.
- Support affirmative action for Muslims to encourage greater participation in mainstream society.

On the whole, there was a strong recommendation for federalism in order to address the wide disparities in development between Muslim and non-Muslim areas.

IV. THE ROLE OF WOMEN IN MUSLIM SOCIETY

The following issues were identified:

- There is a need for statistics and indicators of women status in Mindanao.
- There is a need to provide focused educational intervention that will provide skills useful for sustainable livelihood.
- The women in Mindanao continue to be vulnerable due to the continued political strife in the region.
- The women continue to be marginalized, especially those in agriculture in terms of assets and land reform opportunities.
- Lack of women representation in the peace process and other agencies.

To address these issues, the recommendations included:

- Set-up an academic consortium that would initiate empirical studies on women in Mindanao.
- Train Muslim leaders and managers in LGUs and strategic agencies in sustaining economic activities especially for women and the youth.
- Specifically, provide formal and non-formal education and training for leaders and development managers including business and economic catalysts by tapping key institutions (e.g., the Development Management Program of the Asian Institute of Management).

- Ensure the sustainability of efforts and activities of Non-Govermental Offices in this area by strengthening these organizations.
- Create a technical sub-committee to provide support to the peace panel, particularly on the issue of women and children victims of the armed conflict
- Formulate an integrated rehabilitation plan/program for families affected by the Mindanao crisis.
- Inform, review and implement laws that will benefit women.
- Strictly implement the Local Government Code provision granting sectoral representation to women.
- Seriously follow-up on the 5% national budget allocation for gender and development programs. Relatedly, create clear guidelines on how this budgetary allocation should be spent.
- Empower women within the framework of their respective cultures. Development interventions designed for women should be sensitive to their respective cultures and history in order to be effective.
- Pursue discussions on federalism. A federalist structure could allow LGUs to be more responsive and sensitive to the needs of Muslim women to live according to the tenets of the Islamic faith.

V. THE STATUS AND IMPACT OF EDUCATION AND THE MADARIS

- Muslim students in Mindanao face two systems of education, which are often conflicting. The government-recognized schools teach them the skills that get them employed but do not provide instruction on Muslim religion and the Arabic language. Thus, Muslim students end up enrolling in a *Madrasah*, which is not recognized by the government.
- Apart from not being accredited by the government, the *Madaris* also operate with very limited funding.

The recommended measures include:

- Implement the Comprehensive Mindanao Education Program, which includes the *Madrasah* education as one of its flagship components. Many in the Muslim communities see the need to fast track the integration of the *Madaris* curriculum into the Department of Education (DepEd)-approved school curriculum.

- In the short-term, encourage schools, particularly elementary and secondary schools with a large number of Muslim students, to offer alternative modules on the Islamic religion.
- Accredit the *Madaris* so that graduates from these institutions (including those who studied abroad) can practice their profession/ find gainful employment in the country.
- Extend funding support to the *Madaris* to make teaching in these institutions a more viable career option for Muslims.
- Create a separate office in DepEd for an Undersecretary for the *Madaris* or for Mindanao to address the educational needs of the Muslim and indigenous communities in Mindanao.
- In the long run, federalism should be pursued. Such a structure would allow the Muslim areas in Mindanao to accord greater priority to the development of the *Madaris* in the country.

A common thread which appears in all the workshops has been the proposal to amend the Constitution to allow for the full implementation of the 1996 peace agreement and equitable representation of the Muslims of the Philippines. Implementation of genuine autonomy is viewed with skepticism, under the present system. Leaders ask how ARMM can be autonomous when its purse strings and politics are controlled by Manila. Although independence has been mentioned as a solution to the conflict in the South, federalism seems to be the mode of governance widely viewed as the most viable system to address the wide disparities between the Christian majority and the Muslim minority.

It is clear that the Muslim leaders who participated in the series of conferences and workshops are dissatisfied with the status quo. From the proposals, it is evident the leaders do not believe that central government has effectively provided for the implementation of the 1996 Peace Agreement under the present political system. Morever, there is cynicism about the future of the ARMM when past and present regional administrations have not been able to provide even the most basic of services.

The issues and recommendations presented by the participants of the project hopefully will serve as input to the ongoing discourse in search of solutions to the ethnic conflict in Mindanao. There can be no road to peace and reconciliation if the Muslim perspectives on the Mindanao Conflict are not considered by our national leaders.

Endnotes

* Synthesis of recommendations from March 23 Workshops and Validation Workshops conducted in Marawi City and Zamboanga City.

1 The Al-Amanah Islamic Investment Bank is in the final stage of privatization.

Appendix

Selected Speeches Delivered During the Conference "The Road to Peace and Reconciliation: Muslim Perspectives on the Mindanao Crisis" and List of Speakers and Participants

Appendix A
Welcome Remarks

ROBERTO F. DE OCAMPO
President, Asian Institute of Management

Senate President Aquilino Pimentel, USAID Director Patricia Buckles, Ms. Amina Rasul, distinguished participants, my colleagues in the Asian Institute of Management, ladies and gentlemen.

Mindanao, the southern Philippines island, has been, for some time, a victim of misconception. For one, the island's name has long conjured images of bloody battles between Mindanao Muslims and Christians. From the rise of Jolo in the early Seventies to the brutal battles between the military and the Moro forces in the late Seventies and early Eighties, to the resurgent confrontations in recent months, Mindanao has not ceased to embed itself in the nation's consciousness as a violent, violated land.

But behind the imagery told to us by the media, there is a side to the story not being properly told. While seemingly less controversial and less sensational, the story not visible to the public is more so tragic. It is a story that tells of the oppression, poverty, illiteracy and under-development that have plagued the southern island in the years of neglect by the central government. While the importance of Mindanao to the country has not been overlooked, the different perspectives to shed full light on the issues have been greatly ignored.

As the national government picks up the initiative to get the peace process back on track, one glaring realization to officials and people alike is that no holistic assessment of the crisis can be made without considering the points of views of those most affected.

This is the reason why we are gathered here today, to examine the different sides of the crisis in Mindanao. As we continue the quest for regional peace and prosperity, the founding tenets, which inspired the establishment of the Asian Institute of Management, we cannot afford to not look at the bigger picture—for its implications, while too distant from the safety and comfort of Metro Manila, will have a huge impact in the future of our country and our children.

On behalf of the Asian Institute of Management, W. SyCip Policy Center, Harvard Kennedy School of Government Alumni Association, UP Islamic Institute and the Foundation for Economic Freedom, I would like to welcome all of you to this momentous occasion as we trace the path to peace and reconciliation from a different perspective. It is my hope as we leave this place today that we would help to take away the misconceptions and bring with us instead a lasting impression of the peace and development in store for our nation.

Welcome to this first series, and we hope to see you all at the next conference on March 23. Thank you and good day.

Appendix B
Opening Remarks

PATRICIA K. BUCKLES
Director, USAID

Senate President Aquilino Pimentel, AIM President Roberto de Ocampo, Research Fellow Amina Rasul and President of the Kennedy School of Government Alumni Association Chato Calderon, welcome.

I am delighted to be here this morning representing the U.S. Agency for International Development and to have the opportunity to address such a distinguished group of scholars and public policy analysts. This conference provides an opportunity for us to hear the viewpoints of a number of Muslim leaders and scholars on a whole range of matters that indeed are crucial to peace and reconciliation in Mindanao. It is long overdue and I hope it is only the beginning of a process in which the views of Mindanao's Moslem community are regularly sought out and listened to when matters touching on peace and development in Mindanao are discussed.

All here are well aware that the conflict in Mindanao has been going on for a very long time now and the situation, both with respect to the conflict and with respect to the economic progress of the island, seems to become more complex as time passes. It is also apparent to all that the present situation is the result of a historical combination of cultural, economic, and political problems.

Culturally, research suggests that the conflict is driven by intense feelings of relative denigration of values among the Moslem minority in opposition to the Christian majority. In surveys, many Moslems express concerns of feeling like being second-class citizens in a society. Statistics show that Muslims in Mindanao are indeed generally less well off than their Christian counterparts.

This economic disparity between the two groups, as well as the disparity between Mindanao and the rest of the country, has fueled resentments by Muslims of Christians. These perceived realities are part of a broader sense among Mindanao residents that the island is comparatively neglected. Indeed, statistics bear out the fact that Mindanao's quality of life is way below the national average. Of the country's poorest 20 provinces, 16 are in Mindanao. All of the provinces belonging to the Autonomous Region in Muslim Mindanao (the ARMM) and the surrounding provinces are included in this unfortunate set. Mindanao's poverty rates are 50 percent higher than the national average. Moreover, an AIM study shows a majority of Moslems perceive the government, specifically the regional government of the ARMM, to not addressing the needs of the people. Above the layers of perceived cultural prejudices and economic inequities are perceptions of political inequality.

The studies suggest that many Muslims feel marginalized by democracy in which they are permanent minorities. They perceive Mindanao in general and themselves in particular as suffering from the tyranny of the majority. The establishment of the ARMM and decentralization under the Local Government Code have not met the expectations for local autonomy.

Another AIM study found that local development councils in the ARMM and elsewhere were not even convened, much less institutionalized, due to a lack of professional capacity as well as a lack of resources. The weak organizational realities of the ARMM have greatly impeded the efforts of the Southern Philippines Council for Peace and Development to institutionalize the 1996 Peace Agreement between the Government and the MNLF.

Given these perceptions, it is very important now, more than ever, that the views of all Mindanaoans on the situation of Mindanao be heard, including, most importantly, the views of the members of the Moslem community of Mindanao.

In this regard, USAID enthusiastically welcomed President Macapagal-Arroyo's comprehensive peaceful approach to resolving Mindanao's insurgency. The President has taken steps to re-establish the framework that led to the Philippine Government's 1996 Peace Agreement with the MNLF. She has also declared a suspension of military operations against the MILF and proposed a resumption of peace talks.

We are pleased to see a renewed emphasis on accelerating economic development efforts in Mindanao. The focus on addressing the root economic and social causes of this long-running conflict is well placed. As most of you are aware, since the early 1990's Mindanao has been a key focus of the U.S. and other bilateral and multi-lateral development aid in the Philippines. In addition to island-wide support for business and investment expansion activities, USAID responded to the 1996 Peace Agreement with several highly-effective programs that encouraged former combatants to take up peaceful pursuits such as farming and small businesses. With the MILF still fighting and the flow of displaced persons continuing, these programs remain equally vital today to safeguard and strengthen hard-won areas of stability.

Indeed in monitoring the programs, we have seen the progress that can be made in Mindanao when peace and stability reign. We have seen annual jobs and income growth in the Socsargen area more than triple in the last several years. We have seen thousands of micro-enterprises around the island become more productive and more profitable. We have seen hundreds, if not thousands, of new small businesses start up. We have also noted however that this occurs only where peace and stability actually does reign.

Unfortunately, this generally has not included those provinces that are home to the majority of the Moslem community in the island. As noted earlier, those provinces remain the poorest provinces not just in Mindanao, but in the entire country. That situation must change and we know that the situation can change.

I am pleased to note that the U.S. remains prepared to provide assistance to the government of the Philippines as it goes about the difficult process of securing place and reconciliation in Mindanao. Specifically, assistance we have provided to help integrate former MNLF combatants and to give them the skills that they need to make a living. This assurance can be provided to former MILF combatants as well once peace with this group is established. Second, we will gladly support initiatives that may help ensure that peace negotiations between the Philippine Government and the MILF reach a satisfactory conclusion, and also help ensure that both sides increase their capacity to manage their relationship on a continuing basis. Third, assistance needed to help government units and agencies in the ARMM areas effectively exercise the new authorities and responsibilities of the amended Organic Act for the ARMM can be forthcoming. And fourth, I will continue to assure that a major portion of the over-all USAID assistance to the Philippines remains focused on Mindanao with an appropriate share focused on the Moslem areas of Mindanao.

In conclusion, I would like to thank the AIM and SyCip Policy Center and my friend, Amina Rasul, for organizing this conference and for bringing together this distinguished group of thinkers and speakers. It is through meetings like this that, over time, perhaps, better mutual understanding on the part of different sectors of Philippine society can indeed be reached. With this perhaps, the road to peace and reconciliation can be shortened. Thank you again for inviting me to join you this morning. May this be a fruitful conference for all. Thank you and good day.

Appendix C
Keynote Speech

SENATOR AQUILINO PIMENTEL JR.

Thank you very much, Amina, for those kind words. With your introduction, how can I now refuse to endorse your mother for another term in the Senate? But kidding aside, I would like to say, thank you indeed. And as for those who think that I played a heroic role in the installation of the new government, I would like to disabuse their minds by saying that the only significant thing I did was to hold the microphone for Mrs. Macapagal-Arroyo when she took her oath. In any event, thank you, Amina, and let me greet President Bobby Ocampo and Pat Buckles of the USAID and Chato.

My dear friends, I have spoken on this topic innumerable times, so many times indeed that I decided not to put my thoughts into writing because if I did, I'd be repeating what I've said in many of the speeches that tackled this issue of peace and progress for Mindanao. And so I decided to speak extemporaneously. Some time later, my staff will be providing you with a sheet of statements that I have made on various issues that include this problem that we are facing in Mindanao.

So, let me begin by saying that I do not see the war in Mindanao as a war between Muslims and Christians, I see it as a war of bigots—the bigotry of the central government that insist on integrating and assimilating the Moslem people. And the bigotry of those outside the government who fear a more open democratic way of life for the peoples of Mindanao, including the Muslim people.

I will also tell you, my dear friends, that the solution to the problem faced by Mindanao today cannot be addressed by force of arms. We have tried that over the years, from the Spanish colonial era to the American Commonwealth period through our old government, up to this moment. Force has never worked to subjugate the Muslim peoples of Mindanao.

My own limited lifetime experience alone will show that what I say is true. For example, when I was still a young boy, when I was not going to school yet, I used to hear my uncle sing a song about Dimakaling. Dimakaling was branded a bandit by the American colonial government and he was operating in Sulu, trying to rouse his people against the government, principally for a better treatment of the Muslim people. The Commonwealth government sent troops to subdue Dimakaling. They killed a lot of people in the process including Dimakaling, and for a time there was quiet and peace in the province of Lanao, because Dimakaling was a native of Lanao.

Then when I was in high school, a Muslim-led uprising broke out in the island of Sulu. This time, it was led by Kamlon. The government called Kamlon a bandit, and sent troops to subdue him. They killed a lot of people. Finally, they captured Kamlon, put him in prison, and for a time, there was peace and quiet in the island of Sulu.

When I was a young professional, I remember that when I turned on the television set, there was the fourth infantry division bombarding the stronghold of Ugtog-matalam of Cotabato. Ugtog-matalam led a Mindanao independence movement for the peoples of Mindanao, particularly the Moslem peoples of Central Mindanao. Again, the solution of government was to pour more troops and finally it quelled the Ugtog-matalam uprising. Before long, another Muslim rebel rose up again in Sulu and led the fight against the government by organizing the Moro National Liberation Front (MNLF). That rebel was Professor Nur Misuari.

The fight against the government lasted roughly 24 years, uprooting roughly about 200,000 people from their residence in Central and Southern Mindanao, forcing many to evacuate to Sabah. As a matter of fact, many of our native Jolowanos and Maguindanaoans and people from Lanao still reside in Sabah today.

The solution of government, of course, was to fight back. It took a long time before they decided to try the ways of peace and got the MNLF to sign a peace agreement with the government of then President Fidel V. Ramos in Jakarta in 1996. The peace agreement was signed and even before the ink dried out completely, we had another outbreak of Moslem hostilities in Central Mindanao, this time under the AEGIS of the MILF, led by Chairman Salamat Hashim. The government fought Salamat Hashim, and lots of lives were lost. The state of hostilities still exist between the government forces and the forces of the MILF.

What I'm trying to say, ladies and gentlemen, is that, the solution to the so-called Muslim problem in the South must be holistic, it cannot be based on tribal considerations or sectoral approaches because, as you see in my own lifetime, I was witness to a series of Moslem uprisings, the first being that of Dimakaling in Lanao. After Dimakaling was subdued, Kamlon of Sulu led a rebellion that also took a lot of lives. After Kamlon was pacified, Ugtog-matalam of Cotabato broke out in rebellion against the government. When Ugtog-matalam was suppressed, Nur Misuari of Sulu took up the cudgels for the Moslem people. And after Nur Misuari returned to society, Hashim Salamat of Cotabato went back to Central Mindanao to take up arms against the government. What I'm trying to say now to the government is this: negotiate with Hashim Salamat so that you can offer some concrete solutions to install a lasting peace in Mindanao. But do not get bogged down by considerations of whether or not the camps that were overrun by the government should now be given back to the MILF or whether or not the peace negotiations should be held here or abroad. I think these are superficial matters.

What is important for the government today, in the light of the examples that I have given, is to offer something that will put an end to the recurrence of violence initiated by Moslem rebels from one tribe to another. I have in mind a comprehensive peace solution in the form of a federal system of government. That, my dear friends, I believe is the only legal, feasible, constitutional solution to the problem faced by the government vis-à-vis the Moslem rebels exemplified by the MILF as of this very hour.

Now, very briefly, let me run through the proposal to adopt the federal system for the Philippines, not just for, let's say, the *Bangsamoro*. In that respect, I would like to see four federal states in Luzon: the federal state of Northern Luzon, Central Luzon, Southern Tagalog Region and the Bicolanos. Metro Manila can be created as a special administrative federal capital along the lines of Washington D.C. or, if you want, Kuala Lumpur of Malaysia or even Canberra in Australia. And the Visayas can have three federal states—Eastern Visayas, Central Visayas and a Federal State for Western Visayas. For Mindanao, we can also have three—Federal State of

Northern Mindanao, Federal State of Northeast Mindanao and Federal State for the *Bangsamoro*.

These are rough ideas I know but the proposal can be refined so as to bring about the kind of federal states we envision. Why is it important that the whole republic be federalized? The reason is that by federalizing the republic, we will more or less ensure an equitable opportunity for the economic development of the various federal states that will no longer be dependent on imperial Manila for the things they need. I'd like to cite to you an example of this talk about "Imperial Manila" is not just rhetoric because shortly before we adjourned our session in the Senate, we found out that about P40 billion has been set aside for unnamed programs under the auspices of the Department of Public Works and Highways (DPWH). About 70 percent of the billions of pesos set aside for unnamed project, were to be allocated for Metro Manila and other places in Luzon and the 30 percent would be divided for the rest of the country. And so I think you will understand why the people of Mindanao are always griping against being treated as second-, third- or even fifth- class citizens of this republic. That is why we believe that the federalization of the republic is very important not just to address the Muslim unrest in Mindanao but to address the economic complaints of the rest of the country vis-à-vis the central government in Manila. Now, as far as the Moslem people are concerned, the federalization of the *Bangsamoro* will enable them to pursue their own cultural aspiration, as a people, so that they will no longer always feel as if they are being killed slowly by the Christianization of the Muslim areas in Mindanao.

Therefore, one specific advantage of the federalization of the Bangsamoro is to give an opportunity for the Muslim people to pursue their own cultural and economic development and, along this line, institute what many Muslims feel is very essential to their being, and that is the application of the Islamic legal system called the *Shariah*.

In connection with this *shariah* let me just say that I do not propose that the shariah that is being applied in Saudi Arabia, for example, be applied to the *Bangsamoro* Federal State. I think that it is possible, having talked to Islamic legislators from Indonesia and Malaysia that our shariah may be modified according to advances in modern systems of penology. If we were to apply the *shariah* that it is being applied in Saudi Arabia, for example, I understand if you are caught stealing, they can cut your hand off. And if you are a rapist, something else is cut off. That cannot be done in this country for the single reason that we have a Constitution that forbids cruel and unusual punishment. I think that we should follow a set-up where shariah may be modified as it is being done in Malaysia and in other more advanced Islamic countries. Therefore, in my opinion, shariah should apply to the confines of the *Bangsamoro* Federal State among Filipino Muslims. If, let us say, the litigation involves Muslim against Muslim, then *shariah* will be made to apply. But if the litigation involves Muslim against Christian or Muslim against *Lumad* or Christian against *Lumad* residing within the *Bangsamoro* Federal State, the national law will apply.

So, my dear friends, these are some of the thoughts I'd like to share with you. I am thoroughly convinced that there is no other solution to the problem that we face cyclically in Mindanao: the uprising of Muslim rebels fighting a just cause for the betterment of the lives of their own peoples. In closing, I'd like to say that living in a predominantly Christian country, I do not see why Islam, which is a religion of peace, should compete against Christianity, which is a religion of love. After all, both Christians and Muslims alike believe that they have common ancestors, a Biblical father who is called Ibrahim in the Holy *Qur'an* and Abraham in the Holy Bible. With that, my dear friends, I'd like to say thank you in your kindness for listening to me.

Appendix D
Closing Remarks

SECRETARY EDUARDO R. ERMITA
Presidential Adviser on The Peace Process

Before anything else, allow me to congratulate the Asian Institute of Management, Washington Sycip Policy Center, for the many achievements of your prestigious institution. I would also like to acknowledge the center's vital mission, which is to foster a public-policy environment that emphasizes the primacy in economic, social, and technological progress, and in building a truly humane society. For this mission echoes the four core beliefs that underscore our present program of government: the fight against poverty; good governance; the new politics of genuine reform; and leadership by example.

I am glad that in this meeting, we have a distinguished array of leaders from private business, government, the academe, the diplomatic corps, and mass media.

It also gives me particular pleasure to be here today, for the first in a series of conferences on Mindanao, specially, "The Road to Peace and Reconciliation: Muslim Perspectives on the Mindanao Crisis." This is a strong signal that the priorities of industry and the priorities of this administration are indeed, one and in tune.

From the very start of Gloria Macapagal-Arroyo's presidency, she chose the way of peace on her first working day at Malacañang. She briefed senior officers of the Armed Forces of the Philippines and the Philippine National Police on her plan to reconstruct the peace process. She specifically referred to peace in Mindanao. For although the violence and kidnappings in southern Philippines were physically removed from the rest of the archipelago, the conflict had severely affected the nation. I need not enumerate the losses our country suffered in terms of death, destruction of property and dislocation of communities, as well as the erosion of both local and foreign investor confidence.

Suffice it to say that to rebuild the economy, President Arroyo knew she had to begin with peace in Mindanao. And she vowed to attain this with the tripartite actions of negotiation, rehabilitation and development working hand in hand to reinforce each other.

With an urgency born out of need, the framework for the comprehensive peace process was therefore immediately set forth in the President's second and third executive orders, which were recently issued.

Executive Order No. 2 created an inter-agency committee for relief, rehabilitation and the development of areas affected by armed conflict in Mindanao, or in short, Interact-Mindanao. Chaired by the Presidential Adviser on the Peace Process, the committee is composed of eighteen department secretaries and other government and elected officials. It is tasked with coordinating, prioritizing, synchronizing and monitoring all government efforts for relief and development in Mindanao. These include, among others, dealing with evacuee situations, peace education and advocacy, as well as coordinating with the international donor community.

Executive Order No. 3 defines the policy and administrative structure for the government's comprehensive peace efforts. Six paths to peace are laid out:

First, the pursuit of social, economic and political reforms, aimed at addressing the root causes of internal armed conflicts and social unrest.

Second, consensus-building and empowerment for peace. This involves continuing consultations to build consensus for a peace agenda, ensuring full people's participation.

Third, peaceful, negotiated settlement with the different rebel groups, through face-to-face negotiations and the effective implementation of peace agreements.

Fourth, programs for reconciliation, re-integration into mainstream society and rehabilitation. This component safeguards the legal status and security of rebel returnees, and provides for the economic, social and psychological needs of former rebels, demobilized combatants, and civilian victims of armed conflict.

Fifth, addressing concerns arising from continued armed hostilities. This deals with the strict implementation of laws and policy guidelines to protect non-combatants and their communities.

And sixth, building and nurturing a climate conducive to peace.

Executive Order No. 3 places the president at the helm of the comprehensive peace process, with our office in charge of its management and supervision. It also creates government peace negotiating panels, with corresponding panels of advisers assigned to each.

The past administration adopted the policy of "all-out war" against the Muslim separatists, the communist insurgency and the Abu Sayyaf terrorist group. And while our soldiers valiantly gained ground during their military operations, it took more than four months of bloodshed, displaced families, appalling property damage and a drained treasury, before it became painfully apparent that the armed offensive did not win us the peace we have sought.

"All-out peace" is what we are brokering today. This avenue gave the Filipino people a victory five years ago, when a peace agreement was successfully concluded with the Moro National Liberation Front. It took all of 47 months to negotiate the settlement with the MNLF, and I can tell you that being the vice-chair at the time, it was worth all the time, energies and sacrifices we put into it.

The leading principle set by the President is that all peace negotiations shall be in accordance with the Philippine Constitution, the rule of law, and the principles of the sovereignty and territorial integrity of the Republic of the Philippines.

President Arroyo has likewise called for a principled and peaceful resolution of the armed conflict, with neither blame nor surrender, but with dignity for all concerned.

Pursuant to these, each government panel is instructed to develop its discussion agenda, hammer out a workable timetable, and finally, in the actual deliberations, seek the middle ground between the rebel group concerned and the Philippine government.

The government peace negotiating panel for the southern Philippines autonomous group, chaired by Secretary Jesus Dureza, is highly qualified for its role. It is composed of three Muslims and two Christians, divided into two women and three gentlemen. Each one has had extensive contacts with the Muslims communities; each one possesses high credibility with the rebel, civilian and military sectors in their respective areas of concern. From day 1, they have been back-channeling and working towards confidence building, which is crucial for the talks to move forward.

Trust on both sides is essential. Differences in positions can be bridged with openness and understanding.

Which is why a conference such as this one is an enormous contribution to the peace process. As public policy-makers, you can help provide direction to our negotiating panels. The Muslim perspective on the Mindanao crisis that has been shared today is information that is vital to the success of our peace and development initiatives in the south.

With the help of a private enterprise such as the AIM Washington Sycip Policy Center, and the participation of leaders such as those in this esteemed audience, I am therefore confident that we will achieve our objectives in the comprehensive peace progress. As President Gloria Macapagal-Arroyo said in her inaugural address, "let us build an edifice of peace, progress and economic stability."

It is my hope that we can always be together in responding to this mandate.

Thank you again for this honor and privilege.

Appendix E
Government Response

SECRETARY RENATO S. DE VILLA
Former Executive Secretary

First of all I would like to commend the Asian Institute of Management—W. Sycip Policy Center and its partner institutions for organizing a series of conferences on the Mindanao crisis that for the first time highlights the perspectives of the Muslims and Mindanaons.

It is a singular honor for me to be able to present the government's response to these conferences that is aptly titled "The Road to Peace and Reconciliation." My personal journey, so to speak, in this "road to peace and reconciliation" dates back to when I was a constabulary battalion commander in Zamboanga del Norte in 1975. Back then, there was no road to peace as we were in the midst of an intense armed conflict with the Moro National Liberation Front. My direct participation began in the 1986 GRP-NDF peace talks. This was followed by the series of conferences that were held between the Cabinet Cluster E, where I represented the Armed Forces as its Chief of Staff, and multi-sectoral peace advocates during the last year of President Aquino's term. Most of all, I remember well the historic National Unification Commission, where we were able to hold the widest range of consultations in 71 provinces throughout the country and with the broadest sectors of society that resulted in the adoption of principles and paths to peace that remain valid and ageless.

Indeed, the challenge to any government in articulating its peace agenda is to ensure that the diverse voices of the people are heard—not just the resonant sounds of the majority but the feeble voices of the minority. We therefore welcome initiatives such as these that give voice to the aspirations and dreams of our brothers and sisters in Mindanao.

As I look through your recommendations, I am reminded of one enduring truth about peace building: that every initiative to secure peace must involve a conscious and deliberate effort to address the very roots of conflict.

In the NUC consultations, the root causes most commonly identified were poverty and economic inequity, systematic political inequity, injustice, malgovernance, and exploitation of indigenous cultural communities. It did not find a religious or tribal aspect to the conflict, as some are wont to attribute the conflict in Mindanao. These root causes were identified eight years ago. Unfortunately, some of these continue to haunt us to this very day.

Five years ago we successfully brokered peace with our Muslim brothers from the Moro National Liberation Front (MNLF). Central to the success of the peace negotiations in 1996 was the commitment government displayed to exert every effort to understand and respond to the legitimate grievances and sentiments of our Muslim brothers and sisters.

The peace agreement between the GRP and the MNLF established in Mindanao a Special Zone of Peace and Development (SZOPAD). This is administered by the Southern Philippines Council for Peace and Development (SPCPD) which coordinates and monitors all development efforts in the 14 provinces and 10 cities. Jess Dureza is Presidential Assistant for Southern Mindanao and chairman-designate of the government peace panel for talks with the Moro Islamic Liberation Front.

The second executive order signed by President Gloria Macapagal Arroyo, Executive Order No. 2, created an inter-agency committee, called *Interact-Mindanao*, tasked specifically to coordinate, prioritize, synchronize and monitor government's relief and rehabilitation efforts in the areas affected by the armed conflict in Mindanao. We want speedy, deceisive action, tight and effective coordination, and focus on immediate crucial steps towards the social and physical rebuilding of these affected communities and relief for the thousands of evacuees. With Secretary Ermita, Presidential Adviser Paul Dominguez, and Secretaries Corazon Soliman (Social Welfare and Development) and Teresita Deles (lead convenor, National Anti-Poverty Commission) among the lead agencies of Interact-Mindanao, the President made sure that the objectives will be met.

She followed this with a declaration of unilateral suspension of offensive military operations (SOMO) against the MILF, but still ensuring the civilian population that the armed forces and police remain vigilant in protecting the public's welfare and safety.

The President's third executive order, Executive Order No. 3, issued shortly thereafter, lays out the NUC's original principles and "six paths to peace" that embody government's holistic approach and comprehensive efforts to achieve a just and lasting peace in the country. It also brought back the various peace bodies under the aegis of the Presidential Adviser on the Peace Process, and created the government peace negotiating panels.

The President considers herself as a Mindanaoan. Vice-President Teofisto Guingona was picked because, among others, he is a Mindanaoan. I assure you that Mindanao will always be in her mind and attention.

I would like to congratulate the participants in these conferences. Your recommendations are valuable inputs to the peace process. They can help set the direction of peace initiatives in Mindanao in much the same way that NUC's public consultations helped define the principles that guides the government's comprehensive peace process.

Through this, government has continuously explored, and will continuously explore avenues in which to involve the different sectors in the process. Let us continue these dialogues. Let us continue to enhance an environment for the peaceful resolution of our problems in Mindanao. And let us not forget that peacebuilding, as in EDSA People Power II which involved the broadest sector of society in a peaceful and constitutional undertaking to remove a corrupt and discredited administration, will be a collective undertaking of all sectors of society.

Appendix F

List of Conference Speakers and Participants

March 15 Conference

Asian Institute of Management Conference Center

Welcome Remarks:

Mr. Roberto F. De Ocampo
President, Asian Institute of Management

Opening Remarks:

Ms. Patricia K. Buckles
Director, USAID

Keynote Speech:

Senator Aquilino Q. Pimentel,, Jr.

Presentations:

History of the Conflict

Dr. Samuel K. Tan
Director, Mindanao Studies Program (UP-CIDS)

Dr. Parouk S. Hussin
Presidential Adviser on Muslim Affairs

Reactors :

Mr. Alex Magno
Exec. Dir., Foundation for Economic Freedom

Dr. Asiri Abubakar,
UP Asian Center

Dr. Abdulla Madale
CHED & DOF Consultant for Muslim Affairs

Regional Security and the Mindanao Conflict

Prof. Julkipli Wadi
UP, Institute of Islamic Studies

Reactors:

Dr. Abraham Sakili
UP College of Arts and Letters

Mr. Rigoberto Tiglao
SVP & Editor in Chief, Inq7

Prof. Mariano Lopez
Assoc. Dean, AIM

Muslims in the Philippines or Filipino Muslims?
Former Sen. Santanina T. Rasul

Government Negotiations and Modes of Conflict Resolution
Ms. Alma R. Evangelista
Executive Director, OPAPP

Reactors:

Mr. Ibrahim Iribani
Consultant, National Defense College of the Philippine

Ms. Mirriam Ferrer
Exec. Director, UP 3rd World Studies Center

Prof. Romulo Neri
Head, Cong. Planning & Budget Office

Col. Vic Corpuz
Chief, Intelligence Service Armed Forces of the Phil.

Assessment of Government Negotiations and Modes of Conflict Resolutions
Amb. Alunan Glang,
Adviser, MILF Peace Panel

Closing Remarks:

Hon. Eduardo R. Ermita
Presidential Adviser on the Peace Process

March 23 Workshops at the AIM

Welcome Remarks:

Dr. Federico M. Macaranas
Executive Director, AIM-W. Scycip Policy Cntr.

Highlights of the First Conference

Ms. Amina Rasul
Research Fellow, AIM-WSPC

Presentations: The Islamic State

Mr. Michael O. Mastura
Former Congressman, Maguindanao

Com. Nasser A. Marohomsalic
Commission on Human Rights

Impact of Religion and Culture:

Justice Saaduddin Alauya
Jurisconsult, Islamic Law

Role of Women in Muslim Society:

Dr. Carmen Abubakar
Dean, U.P. Institute of Islamic Studies

Business Development and Poverty in Muslim Areas

Mr. Ibrahim Mamao
Former Director
Al-Amanah Islamic Investment Bank

Status and Impact of Education and the Madaris

Dr. Camar A. Umpa
President, Mindanao State University

Prof. Salipada Tamano
Dean, King Faisal Center for Islamic/Arabic and Asian Studies

Closing Remarks:

Hon. Renato De Villa
Former Exec. Secretary

Mr. David Chiel
Country Representative, Ford Foundation

Participants in Conferences and Workshops

NAME	DESIGNATION/COMPANY
Abdulla, Primo	MURID
Abella, Gerardo	Division Chief, DTI
Abellana, Esperanza	Project Officer, UNICEF
Abidin, Dennison	Chief, CAD-OMA IX
Abubakar, Michael	M. Abubakar Consolidated Eng'g
Abubakar, Carmen	Dean, Int. of Islamic Studies
Abubakar, Onnong	M. AbubakarConsolidated Eng'g
Agben, Marriz	MindAnao Business Council
Aguam, Melanie	Accountant, MSU
Aguila, Marilou	VP-Internal Affairs, NREA
Ahmad, Faris	2nd Sec., Embassy of Malaysia
Aida Sarangani Mama	Mindanao State University (MSU)
Alba, Abet	Reporter, The Yominia Shimbua
Albuna, Almyn	Reporter, RPN 9
Alcantara, Ronnie	Insular Investment & Trust Corp.
Aleja, Habiba	NCIP IX
Ali, Malambut	President, MCCI
Ali, Noraida	U.P. Institute of Islamic Studies

NAME	DESIGNATION/COMPANY
Alinea, Lowella	R.A., BPI-H.O.
Almagro, Joel	VP, Malayan Ins. Co., Inc.
Alonto, Datu Haj Ansari	Federation of Muslim Organization
Alvia, Eric	Manager, Pinkerton Consulting
Ambiong, Datu Amerol	MPOCC
Ambutong, Abdulgari	SPDA
Amerodin M. Guro	Mindanao State University
Amsid, Jay Innocent	ABFRI
Ancheta, Angelina	President, Ancamp Corp.
Andigo, Lilia	UA & P
Anonas, Barbara	Commissioner, NCRFW
Añonuevo, Tos Q.	Prog. Coordinator , FES
Apolencia, Rogelia	UA & P
Aquende Henry	Vice Chairman/BOD, AAAIM
Aro, Ernesto	Dept. of Labor & Employment
Arroyo, Francis	Project Director, ABRFI
Asmulao, Wadja	UP-UBIS
Asuncion, Jessie	Women's BusinessCouncil
Aterejos, Randolph	PNA-OPS
Atienza, Paul	Reporter, Today
Azfad, Hasan	Planning, DSWD IX
Balindong, Eskak	MSU - Office of the Pres.
Bandaying, Amilpasa	OMA IX-A
Bangcola, Alex	Consultant, SPDA
Batuampar, Dayang G.	Mindanao State University
Baviera, Aileen	Assoc. Prof., Univ. of the Phil.
Bayani, Isa	SPDA
Benitez, Rene	Amalgamated Investment Corp.
Benizano, Noemi	Phil, Senate
Bernardo, Romy	Vice Chairman, FEF
Bicencio, Byron	Cong. Planning and Budget Officer
Bontogon, Candido	MIKA
Bubun, Nirza	CEDP
Buckley, John	Australian Embassy

NAME	DESIGNATION/COMPANY
Buena, Felipe	Security Officer, RCBC
Buskan, Lacsaman M.	AVP-OVPAP, MSU
Bustamante, Ma. Rita	Prog. Officer, EU
Cabatingan, Edgar	MSU - Office of the Pres.
Cabili, Leni	Prop. Coleman
Caharodin A. Cali	Vice-Chancellor, OVCAA
Calderon, Rosario	USAID
Cali, Ibrahim U	MSU
Cali, Noraida U.	Student, MA, IIS UP
Calimlim, Joan	BEA-JOYCE Photoshop
Calvo, Angel	Chair, PAZ
Camlian, Bahari	OMA
Camlian, Abdullah	
Candao, Datu Yusoph	PGO, Maguindanao
Candido, Ritchie	Community Org., ABRFI
Cañeda, Teng	PR, GEM-USAID
Caparas, George	Assoc. Editor, Diplomatic Post
Carumba, Annabelle	Community Org., ABRFI
Carpizo, Farouk	Al-Amanah Islamic Investment Bank of the Phils.
Castro, Ma. Victoria	National Security Council
Castro, Pia	Reporter, IBC13
Cetkin, Judith	U.S. Embassy
Chan, John	Manager, Itochu Corporation
Chow, Christopher	Makati Business Club
Clastez, Cynthia	Usec, DBM
Climaco, Nonette	Makati Business Club
Co, Mary Ann	Hanns Seidel Foundation
Coelho, Pedro	Embassy of Portugal
Cortez, Miguel M.	Photographer, Business World
Cruz, Ma. Christina	Manager, BPI Head Office
Cruz, Manolo	Chief of Staff, PIA
Cuyugan , Cristina	GEM, Comm. Team Leader
Datu, Imam Tan	

NAME	DESIGNATION/COMPANY
De Jesus, Manuel	Integral Chemical Corporation
De Leon, Alma	Wise Securities
De Leon, Benjamin	Poc-Attlantic Holdings I
De Quilla, Janeth	Office in Charge, Asset, Inc.
Derico, Dr. Cosain	Mindanao State University
Deriquito, Sr., Rodolfo	Ofc. of the Presidential. Asst. for Muslim Affairs
Detoyato, Nerissa	Acct., MSU-M10
Diesta, Alexander	Research/Publication, UA&P
Dimagiba, Eve	OIC, Museum Pambata
Dimapunong, Delilah	Budget Officer III, MSU-M10
Dinggi, Desdimona	UP-ACABIYYAH, UPIIS
Dipay, Marah	Pres. Lanao, GAD Adv., MSU
Domingo, Patricia	PAC, AUSAID
Esmail, Yvonne	Progr Staff, Kalimundan Inc.
Fabre, Raymund	C. Virata & Associates, Inc.
Failani, Kadil	UP-II, II-UP Diliman
Feibel, Charles	Chief of Party, GEM-USAID
Fernando, David	MERALCO
Ferrer, Jerick	Student, UA & P
Ferrer, Teodoro	General Manager, Mirmac, Inc.
Ferron, Miriam	The World Studies Center
Flores, Laura	Teacher-III, UA&P
Follente, Cecilia	Int'l Com., Red Cross
Fontanilla, Crisanta	Prof., CEU
Forbes, John	Pres., Eastern Voyager Corp.
Frehner, Willibold	Konrad Adenauer Foundation
Gabijan, Crecencio	Professor, UST
Gallat, Bruce	Canadian Gov't Ottawa
Gatarin, Grace	Asst Proj. Off., DAP/PTF 20/20
Geronimo, Hernani	Lapanday Foods Corporation
Goling, Aminah	Asian Muslim Action Network
Gollara, Allyssa	The Marco Polo Davao
Gordove, Donna	PO, DAP/PTF/20/20

NAME	DESIGNATION/COMPANY
Griggs, Tom	Financial Times Elec. Pub.
Groult, Philippe	French Embassy
Gu, Edward	Consul, Rep of Sengal
Guerero, Daniel	Investigative Journalist
Guichard, Alec	Int'l Committee of the Red Cross
Guro, Ellen Arisha	Director, MSU - PIO
Harkess, Linn	Attache, European Commission
Hayhurst, Justin	3rd Sec. Australian Embassy
Hidalgo, Aurora	Publication Manager, UA&P
Hidalgo, Aurora	Publication Manager, UA&P
Hsu, Patrick	Bean Central Roastery, Inc.
Hundegger, Debra	
Hussin, Dr. Parouk	Pres. Adviser on Muslim Affairs
Ibad, Dr. Ahmed	
Ibrahim D. Mangondato	Prof. IV, CED, MSU
Jagoe, Neil	2nd Secretary, British Embassy
Jailani, Kadi	U.P. Institute of Islamic Studies
Janalan, Jamil	Lawyer
Jara-Puyod, Maricar	Reporer, Manila Standard
Jimenez, Lyneth	Autoveyor Phils. Corp.
Jose, Susan	Division Chief, RDCS
Jovellanos, Jose	Eng'g & Dev't Corp. of the Phils.
Kohora, Tiroko	UNICEF
Kruse, Jeremy	1st Secretary, Australian Embassy
Kuile, Maurits ter	2nd Secretary, Royal Netherlands
Laborte, Liwanag	PSRS-DAR Embassy
Lacquian, Jose	Netherlands Embassy
Lacsina, Evelyn P.	Philippine National Red Cross
Laidan, Zenaida Hadji-Raof	DOST-Region XII
Lapuz, Jose David	UNESCO
Larot, Gloria	Commissioner, NCRFW
Larsen, Dan	Political Officer, US Embassy
Lawi, Abdul Malik	Proj. Dir., Murid Center
Layador, Rowena	Institute for Strategic Dev't Studies, Inc.

NAME	DESIGNATION/COMPANY
Lim-Yuson, Nina	Museo Pambata Fnd., Inc.
Lininding, Derieza	ARCSO, Youth President
Liporada, Cesar	United Nations Development Programme
Loberiano, Ramon	University of Asia & the Pacific
Luo, Znenid Wang	Spokesperson, Chinese Embassy
Lusica, Domiciano	Vice President, TCGI Engineers
Macabalang, Dr. Bacani	Director, UESC, MSU
Macabundo, Farmidah	SWO-III, LGU-Marawi
Macapanton, Sultan Abbas	
Madale, Dr. Abdullah	Al Mauaf University
Magtajas, Pablo P.	Conference CDO
Mama, Somirado	Office on Muslim Affairs
Mamba, Mabel P.	Chairperson and CEO, NYC
Mamung, Lilla	FES
Manansala, Rossana	Executive,Assistant, Asset, Inc.
Mangahas, Rose	Institute for Labor Studies-DOLE
Mañgalindan, Mia	Manager, SWS
Mangondato, Al-Farouk	Clerk II, MSU-Off. of the Pres.
Mangondato, Aminah	Asst. Dir., MSU-M10
Mansilla, Francis	SZOPAD Social Fund
Marahomsalic, Nasser	Commissioner, CHR
Marohombsak, Haron	Protocol Officer, MSU
Maulion, Alain	Consultant, DFA
Maunting, Sittienor	PDO-III, MSU-M10
Mendiola, Caesar	Board of Investments
Mendoza, Antonio P.	PSO V, OP PMS
Mikarram, Nagdir	SPDA
Mikhailov, L.	2nd Secretary, Russian Embassy
Militante, Clarissa	Program Officer, PDRC
Milvar, Belen	NCIP IX
Mindalano, Abdulcarim	CAO - II, Community Relations
Mirandilla, Mary Grace	Phil-China Dev't Resource Center
Misalucha, Charmaine	De La Salle University
Mitmug, Ayesah D.	Acting Chief Cashier, MSU

NAME	DESIGNATION/COMPANY
Mitra, Dr. Minu	University of Selmi
Mogatu, Manny	Reporter, Asahi Saimbu
Mohammad, Sitti Rahma	Foreign Exchange Dealers Association of the Philippines
Mondejar, Irene	Teacher II, UA&P
Montalbo, Gil	Director, DBM
Monteyfel, Galina	2nd Secretary, Russian Embassy
Munir, Sanihu	Journalist, Republic of Indonesia
Musip, Buawag	MSU
Naman, Norina	Student, MMCD UP
Nani, Dr. Tatiaz	
Narciso, Aurora	Eco. III, DAR
Nasser, Andam	Office of the President
Nonhaya, Mohamad	NORKIE, MSU
Nuevaespaña, Alexis	Phil. Senate
Ofreneo, Ana Elzy	Commission on Human Rights
Omar L. Khalid	Office of the Pres. Mgmt. Staff
Omboy, Tirso	Agri-Ext Tech., ABRFI
Ondrik, Richard	Chief Officer, ADB-PhCo
Ong, Angel	Jose Cojuangco & Sons Org.
Oplas, Bienvenido	Think Park, Inc.
Ortiz, Allan	Eco. Intelligence Unit Phils., Inc.
Orullo, Jr. Norberto	Executive Director, UE-FRASI
Oviedo, Shella	NSC Analyst, NSC
Pallorina, Samuel	Operations Ctr., Nat'l Peace &
Pangan, Angela	President, NORFIL Foundation, Inc
Pangandaman, Annalyn	AC II, MSU-Manila Info. Office
Pascual, Danilo	YEMEY, PTE LTD
Perez, Adora	AUSAID
Pineda, Ma. Christina	Sr. Program Officer, CIDA
Piniera, Cathy	FES
Pivetta, Gildo	European Commission
Pompona Pinky	Hadji Ali Bangsamoro Women
Potestas, Ihdissa	The Marco Polo Davao

NAME	DESIGNATION/COMPANY
Preclaro, Ramfrel	National Youth Commission
Prior, Chris	Project Adviser, CEP
Pula, Norma	U.P. Institute of Islamic Studies
Puntakan, Babyjane	IIS, UP-IIS
Quiamco, Jelly	Balay Staff, Balay, Inc.
Quiroz, Raymond	Budget Manager, PNOC-EDC
Ramos, Minombao	Faculty, MSU
Rebollos, Grace	PAZ-WMSU
Revilla, Teresita	Assistant Division Chief, DTI
Reyes, Jason	Proj. Officer III, ABRFI
Reyes, Rizal Raul	Correspondent, Business Today
Reyes, Susan	Officer-in-Charge, MMCD UP
Reyes, Victor	Reporter, Malaya
Reynoso, Remedios	Dev. Chief, PSRS-DAR
Rezk, Ahmed	Amb., Embassy of Egypt
Ricalde, Godelia	Unit Head, Ateneo CSPPA
Rodriguez, Jr., Alejandro	Legal Counsel, Pacific Tall Ships
Rosales, Flor	Reporter, DZRH
Sacerdoti, Guy	Consultant, Medley Advisors
Safid, Dr. An	Dir., De La Salle University
Sahibil, Nuraim	U.P. Institute of Islamic Studies
Salasain, Abdusalim	SPDA
Salman, Emma	Area, Head, GEM-USAID
Sampao, Datu Farouk	Muslim Fed. Mov. of the Phil.
Sanchez, Ali	Lakas NUCD-UMDP
Sangid, Baibonn	National Youth Commission
Sanihin, Salim	Legal Officer, OMA IX
Santella, Mel	National Youth Commission
Santillan, Tinso	CEO, Alto Power Corporation
Santos, Lily	Australian Embassy
Santos Jr., Soliman	Lawyer
Sarangani, Datumanong A.	Office of the Exec. VP
Setiyawan, Edi	Central Bank of Indonesia
Silva, Esteban	Filipino Pipe & Foundry Corp.

NAME	DESIGNATION/COMPANY
Sinsuat, Datu Olav	Int'l Committee of the Red Cross
Sryvkov, A.	Press Attache, Russian Embassy
Sto. Domingo, Larry	Student, UP
Subido, Renne	Federation of Muslim for GMA
Sucgang, Armando	GEM-USAID-Central Mindanao
Suhaili, Muktar	Texas Instrument
Suñga, Ricky	Policy Researcher, DAR
Suyat, Anecita	Department of Finance
Tabao, Salma	OMA, Zamboanga City
Tabayoyong, Estrella	Department of Agrarian Reform
Tabiliran, Gildo	Texas Instrument
Tabuñar, Gabby	Bu. Chief Manila, CBS News
Tamano, Marline	Exec. Dir., CWSDR
Tamano, Salipada	Mindanao State University
Tan, Carlos	GEM Program
Tavakkoli, Mohammad Ali	3rd Counsellor, Iranian Embassy
Tayenglo, Linda	Chapter President, NREA
Thompson, Scott	Professor
Tiglao, Remy	SB Capital Investment Corp.
Tikmasan, Hurma	Pres. Cabaliram Foundation
Tillah, Mirsharif	UA&P
Torres, Josefino	Director IV, DOLE
Traub, Rudolf	Res. Rep. FES
Trillana, Rey	Prof., UAP
Tritt, Gavin	The Asia Foundation
Ubarra, Cecilia	Research Fellow
Uman, Narcisa	Canadian Embassy
Umpa, Camar A.	President, MSU
Umpa, Normina	MSU-Manila Info. Office
Usman, Marjaman	OMA, Zamboanga City
Usman, Norina	MMCD, U.P.
Usodan, Samina	MSU-Manila Info. Office
Viray, Narcisa	Canadian Embassy

NAME	DESIGNATION/COMPANY
Wali, Sali	
Wang, Lou	Spokesperson, Chinese Embassy
Yam, Alex	Petron Corporation
Yanvaria, Stella	DBP
Young, Suzanne	GEM Program
Yousefi, Gholamreza	Ambassador, Embassy of Iran

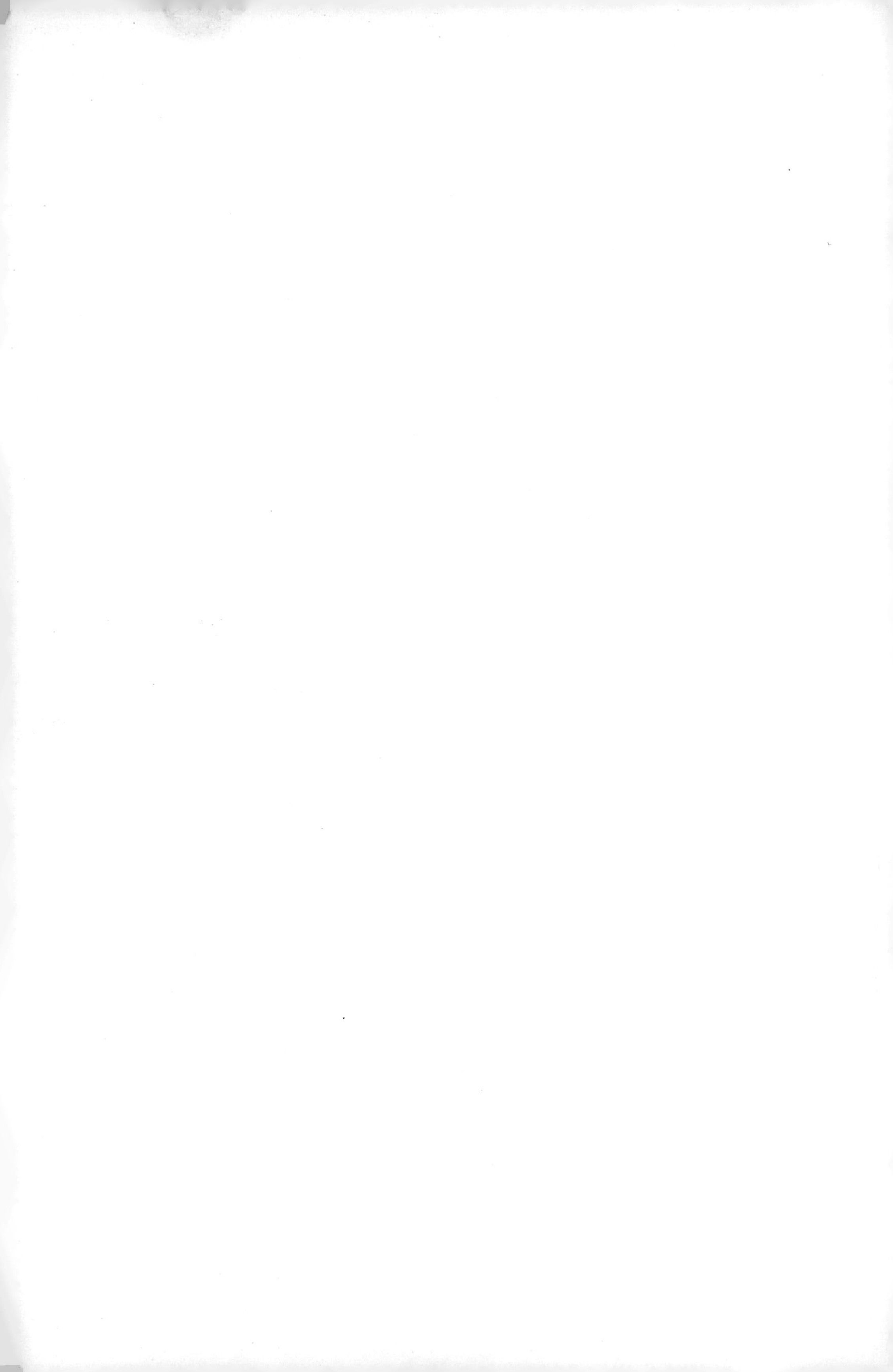